Tyttenhanger

Excavation and Survey
in the Parish of Ridge, Hertfordshire,
undertaken by Archaeological Services and
Consultancy Ltd

Jonathan R. Hunn

With contributions by

Chris Turner, James Rackham, John Giorgi,
Martin Lightfoot, Pippa Bradley, Lucy Whittingham,
Nicholas Doggett and Andy Richmond

BAR British Series 381
2004

Published in 2016 by
BAR Publishing, Oxford

BAR British Series 381

Tyttenhanger

ISBN 978 1 84171 678 7

BAR Publishing is the trading name of British Archaeological Reports (Oxford) Ltd.
British Archaeological Reports was first incorporated in 1974 to publish the BAR
Series, International and British. In 1992 Hadrian Books Ltd became part of the BAR
group. This volume was originally published by Archaeopress in conjunction with
British Archaeological Reports (Oxford) Ltd / Hadrian Books Ltd, the Series principal
publisher, in 2004. This present volume is published by BAR Publishing, 2016.

Printed in England

BAR

PUBLISHING

BAR titles are available from:

BAR Publishing
122 Banbury Rd, Oxford, OX2 7BP, UK
EMAIL   info@barpublishing.com
PHONE   +44 (0)1865 310431
FAX   +44 (0)1865 316916
www.barpublishing.com

CONTENTS

PART 1

TYTTENHANGER 9

List of Figures

PART 2

THE MESOLITHIC SITE 93
by Martin Lightfoot

PART 3

PART 4

FOREWORD

This volume is a result of a combination of a series of separate fieldwork projects undertaken in the late 1990s and early 2000s. The principal impetus behind this work was due to the dynamics of gravel extraction undertaken by Lafarge Aggregates Ltd (previously known as Redlands Aggregates). They were behind three of the four projects reported in this volume and funded this publication.

All four projects are linked by their location within a narrow 'strip parish' called Ridge that stretches from the river Colne in the north to Arkley in the south (now in Greater London) a distance of 10. 1 km (6.3 miles). It had an average width of about 1 km, though it varies between 2.45 km in the north to as little as 0.75 km in the middle. In addition to this area there were four detached portions, the largest of which lay about 1.4 km to the west (Fig. 1). The largest portion was also linear in character and had a maximum length of 4.7 km and an average width of about 0.5 km which varied between 150 m in the north and up to 700m in the middle. The main portion of the parish amounted to 1286 ha (3177.7 acres), while the detached portion was 176.7 ha (436.8 acres).

Three of the four projects (Part 1-3) were located in the north of the parish while the fourth (Part 4) was located in the south of the parish towards Arkley. Of the four projects, one was classified as an 'enhanced watching brief' (Part 1), one was an 'evaluation/mitigation' (Part 2), one was a formal excavation (Part 3) and one was a landscape assessment of a small estate held by Hertfordshire County Council (Part 4). Each of these disparate projects is of interest in their own right. However, by combining them in this volume it is hoped that their value will be enhanced and that they will contribute towards a better understanding of the evolution of the local landscape.

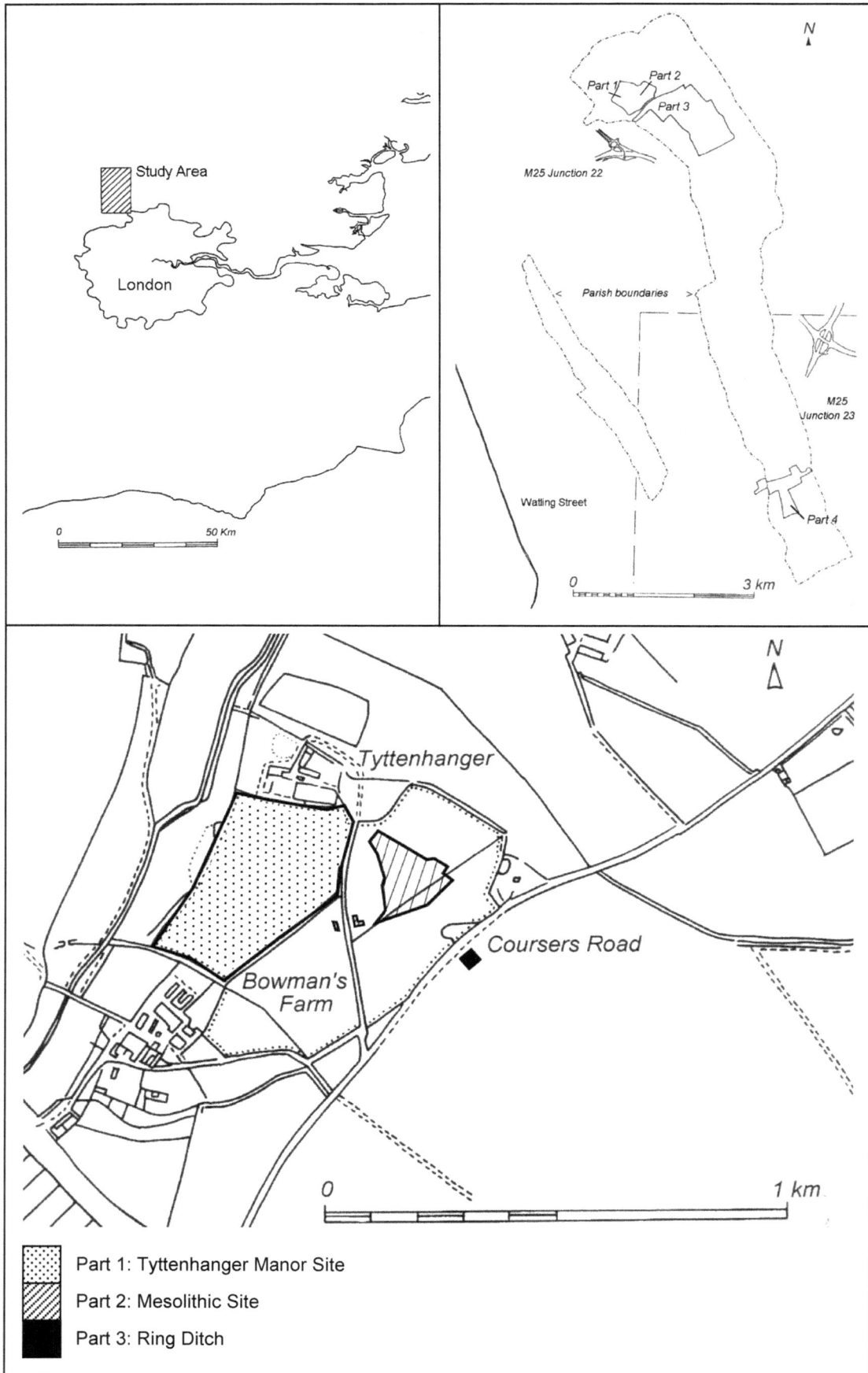

Fig. 1: Location of the study area and individual projects within the parish of Ridge

PART 1

TYTTENHANGER MANOR

SUMMARY

In late 1999 and late 2002, ASC Ltd carried out a programme of archaeological mitigation on a gravel quarry located about 1 km to the north of Junction 22 of the M25 at Tyttenhanger near St Albans, Hertfordshire. The project revealed a sequence of land-use change and alignments associated with agrarian activity, tile production, garden features, buildings and brick enclosure walls belonging to the manor house and later mansion of Tyttenhanger. An early medieval field system and two corn dryers were located in the southern half of the site. To the south of the present house, two late manorial enclosures were discovered. The first enclosure comprised an inner courtyard whose entrance was flanked by the foundations of projecting gatehouses or towers. Within the second enclosure was evidence for domestic buildings, stables and kilns. Further to the south were several hollows, resulting from the extraction of raw materials for the manufacture of tiles. In the early post-medieval period the production of tile appears to have ceased on the site, and was replaced by a formal garden and tree avenues. In addition to the gardens, a range of post-medieval agricultural and domestic outbuildings were erected at the northern end of the site, in front of the 17th-century mansion. All the buildings were later dismantled and buried in the later part of 18th century, when the grounds were emparked and an avenue of trees planted. The site remained in this state, some as pasture and some in arable use, until the present day.

ACKNOWLEDGEMENTS

I would like to thank those individuals and organisations who have assisted in undertaking this project. Firstly, I would like to thank *Lafarge Aggregates* for funding the work, in particular Stuart Wykes, Mike Pendock and Andrew Richmond of Phoenix Consulting who commissioned the project on their behalf, as archaeological consultant. Thanks are also due to staff at the County Archaeology Office who were responsible for the curatorial aspects of the project, namely Stewart Bryant, Tony Hurley, Alex Hunt and Jonathan Smith. I am also grateful to the earthmoving contractors and their staff, Keith Johnston and Trevor Martin, and to the quarry managers, Tony Clark, Rick Lewis and Tom Coleman. The fieldwork was led by the author and Chris Turner, assisted by Nigel Wilson (supervisor), Justin Neal (illustrator), Mark Roberts and Nigel Sunderland (staff), Kate Jackson, Nicki Hegdi and Kate Bell (volunteers), John Rowsell (JCB driver), and metal detectorists, Chris Ribbans and Roger Paul. I wish to thank Chris Turner in particular for writing much of the first draft of the text for the original report and preparing the site plans. I also wish to thank the specialists, James Rackham, John Giorgi, Nicholas Doggett, Lucy Whittingham and Andrew Richmond; and the staff at the Hertfordshire Archives and Local Studies Library. Thanks are due to Oliver Kent, David Dawson and Pat Ryan for their helpful observations on the tile kiln and aspects of production. Thanks are also due to Jack Bonnington who together with Lafarge Aggregates, was instrumental in commissioning John Price to secure and conserve a late medieval tile kiln. I also wish to thank J.T Smith for his comments on the excavations in the northern area of the site in 2002. Finally my thanks to Bob Zeepvat for editing the text and Claire Griffiths for assembling the volume.

INTRODUCTION

The original report on which this publication is based has been prepared on behalf of *Lafarge Aggregates Ltd*, as part of a programme of archaeological mitigation work carried out on land south of Tyttenhanger House, St Albans, Hertfordshire. It describes the results of a programme of archaeological investigation that was implemented ahead of the extraction of gravel from the site. This programme was based on the results of previous phases of archaeological work, including a geophysical survey, evaluation trenches and a desk-based assessment carried out by *Tempvs Reparatvm* in 1996. The report sets out the nature and extent of the archaeological deposits encountered within the site limits, supplemented, where possible, with historical sources.

The site is located on the south-east side of the Colne valley, centred approximately 0.8km north-west of London Colney at NGR TL 191 044. The land slopes gently upwards to the north-east, ranging in elevation from 69m to 73.5m OD across the extraction area. The site is bounded to the west by the Colne, to the east by the access road to the house, to the south by Bowmansgreen Farm, and to the north by the present Tyttenhanger house. This same house graces the front cover of J.T. Smith's study of English houses from 1200-1800 (Smith 1993). The extraction area encompasses approximately seven hectares over two fields, designated 'A' and 'B' (Fig. 2). Field 'A' was open grassland, with a few mature trees. Field 'B' was partly arable and partly pasture.

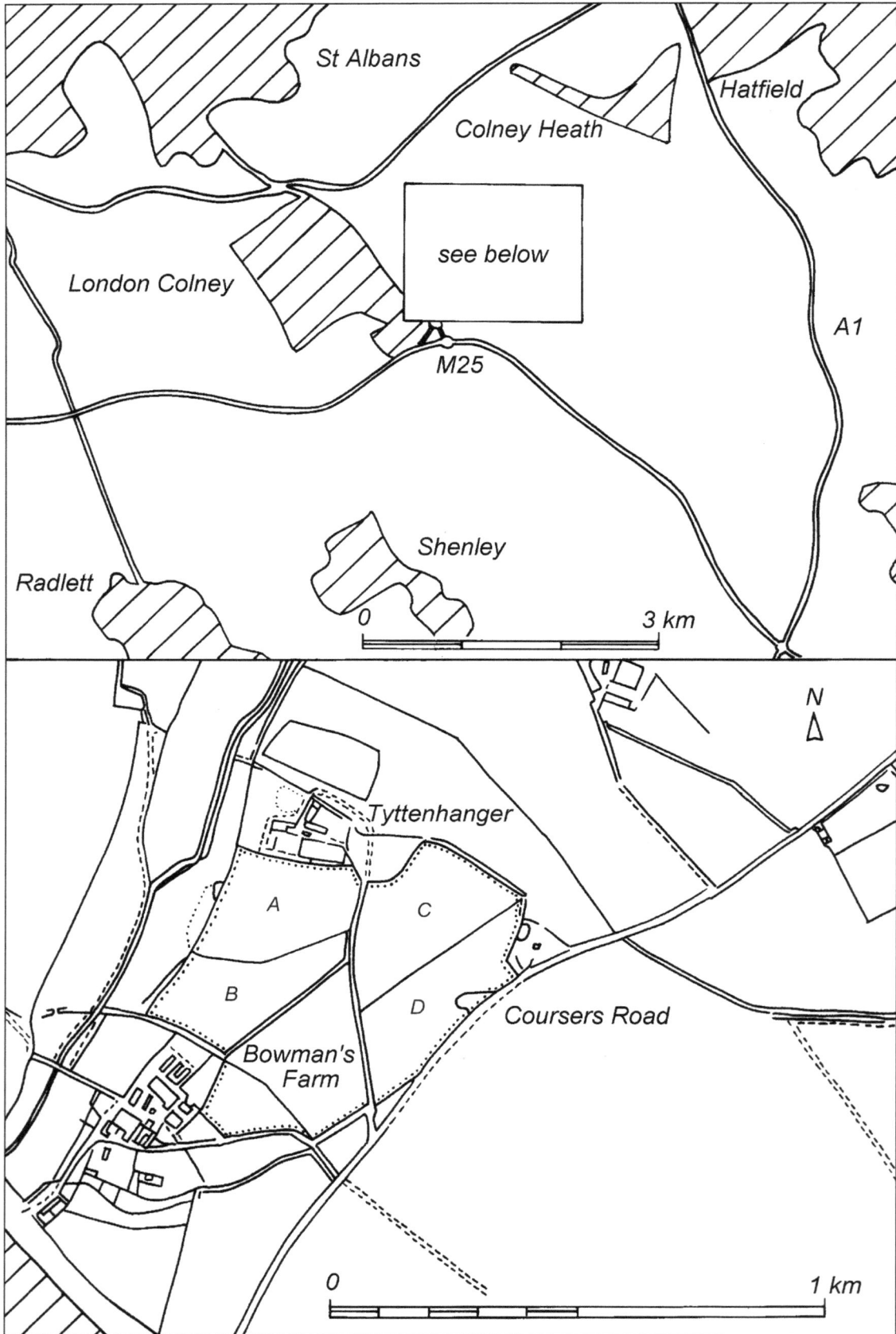

Fig. 2: Location of Tyttenhanger in relation to the modern landscape

Two areas of Field 'A' were environmentally sensitive: a badger den on the western margins of the field, and bats in one of the trees at the northern limits. In addition, a large tree at TL 1917 0453 was also protected. These areas were carefully avoided by the archaeological works and the extraction operation.

The geology of the site consists of underlying chalk bedrock at a depth of 8-14m, which is overlain by deposits of gravel, sand, brickearth and clay. Brickearth was observed across Field 'B', and in the north-west corner of Field 'A'. The soils across the site were derived from periglacial brickearth deposits, with some isolated patches of glacial tills. The topsoil was approximately 0.3m deep: below it was a silty gravel subsoil a further 0.3m deep. The subsoil in Field 'A' contained a high degree of late medieval/post medieval brick and tile debris.

The mitigation programme was divided into three stages, namely:
- an enhanced watching brief on an area at the north end of Field A, on the opposite side of the lane to Tyttenhanger house (0.6 hectares);
- excavation of an area in Field A, to the south of the enhanced watching brief (0.96 hectares);
- an intermittent watching brief during topsoil stripping on the remainder of Field A and on Field B (5.0 hectares).

ARCHAEOLOGICAL & HISTORICAL BACKGROUND

PREVIOUS ARCHAEOLOGICAL WORK
Prior to the programme of archaeological work described in this report, an evaluation of the site was undertaken by *Tempvs Reparatvm* in 1995/96. This comprised the following stages:

Desk-based Assessment
This 'base-line study' suggested that remains associated with predecessors of the present Tyttenhanger house may survive in the vicinity, possibly dating from the medieval period.

Fieldwalking
A programme of fieldwalking across the site, based on a 10 × 10m grid, provided inconclusive evidence of buried archaeological remains. Flints, sherds of medieval and post-medieval pottery and fragments of tile were recovered. The distribution patterns of these artefacts were interpreted as 'background noise' (Percival & Richmond 1996, 8).

Geophysics
Ten areas were subjected to geophysical survey, involving magnetic susceptibility, magnetometric scanning and detailed magnetometer survey. This highlighted a large disturbed rubble area in Field 'A', a possible kiln and a number of services crossing the site. (*ibid.*, 8-9).

Test Pits
A series of test pits was excavated to investigate the potential for the survival of Palaeolithic horizons in the brickearth deposits in the southern half of the site. No artefacts or archaeological deposits were observed in this phase (*ibid.*, 9).

Trenching
Thirty-four trenches were excavated, eighteen of them within the confines of the present site (Fig. 3). These trenches were positioned to clarify the results of the geophysical survey, and to characterise the nature and extent of any buried archaeological deposits. The results of the trenching suggested that Field 'B' was devoid of archaeological remains, and there was limited surviving medieval features in Field 'A'. The evaluation did identify a series of post-medieval remains, mainly relating to garden and agricultural features, within the bounds of a large concentration of rubble in the western half of Field 'A'. This was also observed in the geophysical survey (*ibid.*, 17-18).

HISTORY
The site of the archaeological investigations described in this report lies immediately to the south of Tyttenhanger house (Fig. 4). Until the 1995/96 evaluations, nothing was known about this area. To the north of the extraction zone is the original site of the manor house, which is believed to be an early 14th-century foundation, if not earlier, constructed by Abbot Richard of St Albans Abbey (Page 1908, 387). That house was demolished around the mid-14th century, and the materials were sold off (*ibid.*). The manor remained in the hands of the abbey, and in the late 14th century Abbot John de la Moot rebuilt the house, completing it in 1411. In the 1430s a deer park was created adjoining the manor (Koughnet 1895, 13), extending into the parish of St Peters to the north. Tenants were also moved from the meadows near the house, and this area was also enclosed by a hedge and ditch (*ibid.*). The abbey owned the manor until the Dissolution, and the second house survived until well into the 17th century. It was partly demolished in 1620, the process being completed in 1654 (Smith 1996, 148). No description of the old manor or its exact location survives (see *Discussion*). Although the cellars are believed to pre-date the present house, no other contemporary building survives above ground. The partially surviving earthworks to the west and north of the house have never been studied. Apart from the 19th-century kitchen garden, the terrace and a few 'ancient' trees, little remained of Tyttenhanger's former garden layout. The site was not included in the Register of Historical Gardens maintained by English Heritage.

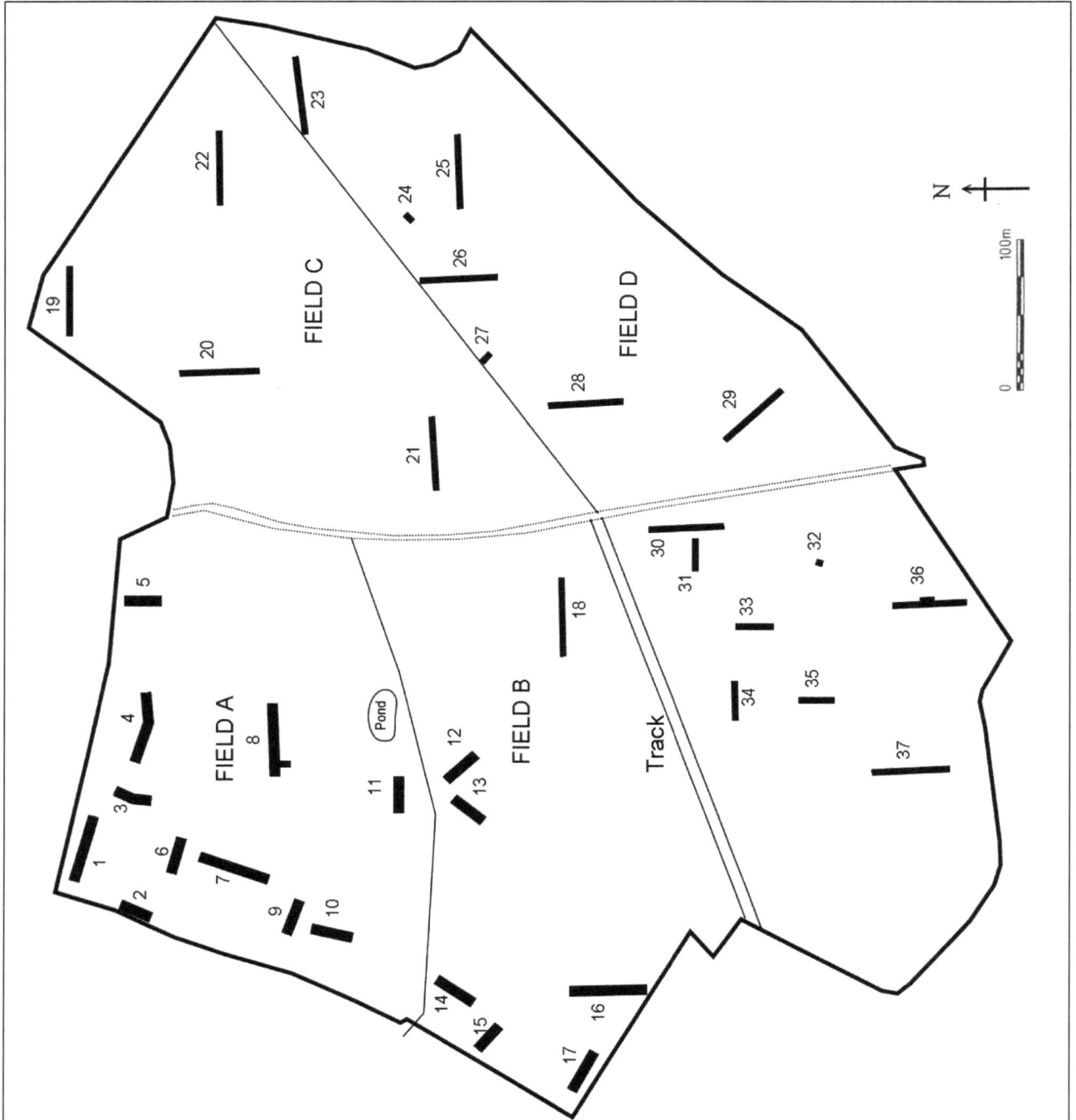

Fig. 3: Location plan of evaluation trenches

METHODOLOGY

The archaeological works were carried out according to a specification prepared by Phoenix Consulting (Richmond and Percival 1997), and a project design compiled by Bob Zeepvat of ASC, and approved by the County Archaeology Office. Detailed sampling strategies were agreed with the County Archaeology Office during fieldwork. As originally defined, the project comprised three stages:

STAGE 1. ENHANCED WATCHING BRIEF

The northern limits of Field 'A' were stripped in order to create a bund to stockpile topsoil and subsoil removed from the site, and to shield the house from the gravel pit. Archaeological features within this area were subject to a higher degree of recording than those in a normal watching brief, but deposits were not excavated, as they were to be preserved beneath the bund (*ibid.*). The bund area measured approximately 40m in width and 240m in length. A photographic record was maintained of identified features and their wider context.

STAGE 2.1. 1999 EXCAVATION

The excavation area was defined by the results of the geophysical survey and the evaluation. It extended from the edge of the northern bund in front of the present house, southwards into Field 'A'. The excavation area measured 40m in width and 150m in length. Following the removal of overburden, features in this area were identified, cleaned, surveyed, and sampled in accordance with the agreed strategy. Dating evidence, in the form of artefacts or radio-carbon samples, was recovered from identified contexts where possible. A photographic record was maintained of excavated features and their wider context, as for the enhanced watching brief.

STAGE 2.2. WATCHING BRIEF

An intermittent watching brief was carried out on the stripping of Field 'B', and the land beyond the excavation area and the northern bund. This area covered approximately 5 hectares. Features encountered within the bounds of the watching brief area were cleaned, and recorded using an EDM. Where possible, samples of the brickwork or dateable artefacts were also recovered. An unexpected corn dryer was discovered in Field 'B' and excavated with the agreement of the local authority and the archaeological consultant for *Lafarge Aggregate*, but none of the other features in this area were excavated. A photographic record was taken of identified features and their wider context. The removal of topsoil and overburden from the site for all three stages was carried out by a Komatsu 30-tonne, 360° excavator, fitted with a toothless ditching bucket. During Stages A and B, machining was carried out under continuous archaeological supervision. Spoil was moved to bunds at the edge of the site by 30-tonne dumper trucks. Temporary roadways were established for the vehicles to get to the spoil heaps, to stop the exposed underlying deposits being churned up or disturbed.

STAGE 3 2002 BUND EXCAVATION

In the autumn of 2002 the northern bund of the site that lay adjacent to the garden of Tyttenhanger House was re-examined prior to gravel extraction (Fig. 4). This consisted of an examination of several features which had been exposed but not excavated in 1999. These were a tile built L-shaped feature [1534], a possible garderobe [1532] and several other ill-defined spreads of rubble. The results of this work have been integrated into this report.

Because of the great extent of the site, archaeological features and structures were spatially recorded using an EDM, and tied in to the OS National Grid. Detailed planning of features (eg. tile kilns) was carried out using planning frames, tied into the overall plans by EDM. Levels were taken in relation to a quarry survey point (Station 2), located at TL 19209 04450 on the access road to the house. The elevation of this point was 73.05m OD. In addition to the works specified in the brief, circumstances permitted the following additional investigations to be carried out:

METAL DETECTOR SURVEY

While the site was stripped of its overburden, C. Ribbans and R. Paul carried out an unsupervised metal detector survey over Field 'A'. The nature and location of the finds from this survey are recorded in the finds section of this report.

HISTORICAL RESEARCH

As a supplement to the earlier 'base-line study' undertaken by *Tempvs Reparatvm* in 1995, a more detailed documentary research programme was carried out during the course of the project. This permitted an enhanced understanding of the site, and helped to place it in its wider landscape setting.

EARTHWORKS SURVEY

A rapid earthwork survey around the immediate vicinity of the present house was undertaken using an EDM. From this it was possible to identify the presence of a former moat and fishponds in the house. Hitherto, neither of these features had been recorded in the Hertfordshire Sites & Monuments Register.

POST EXCAVATION

The post excavation procedures followed the approach outlined in the project design. Artefacts recovered during fieldwork were cleaned, identified and assessed. Environmental samples and the pottery and animal bone assemblages were sent to appropriate specialists for examination. The archaeological records were checked and the information collated. Groups of related contexts were identified and interpreted. The results constitute this report.

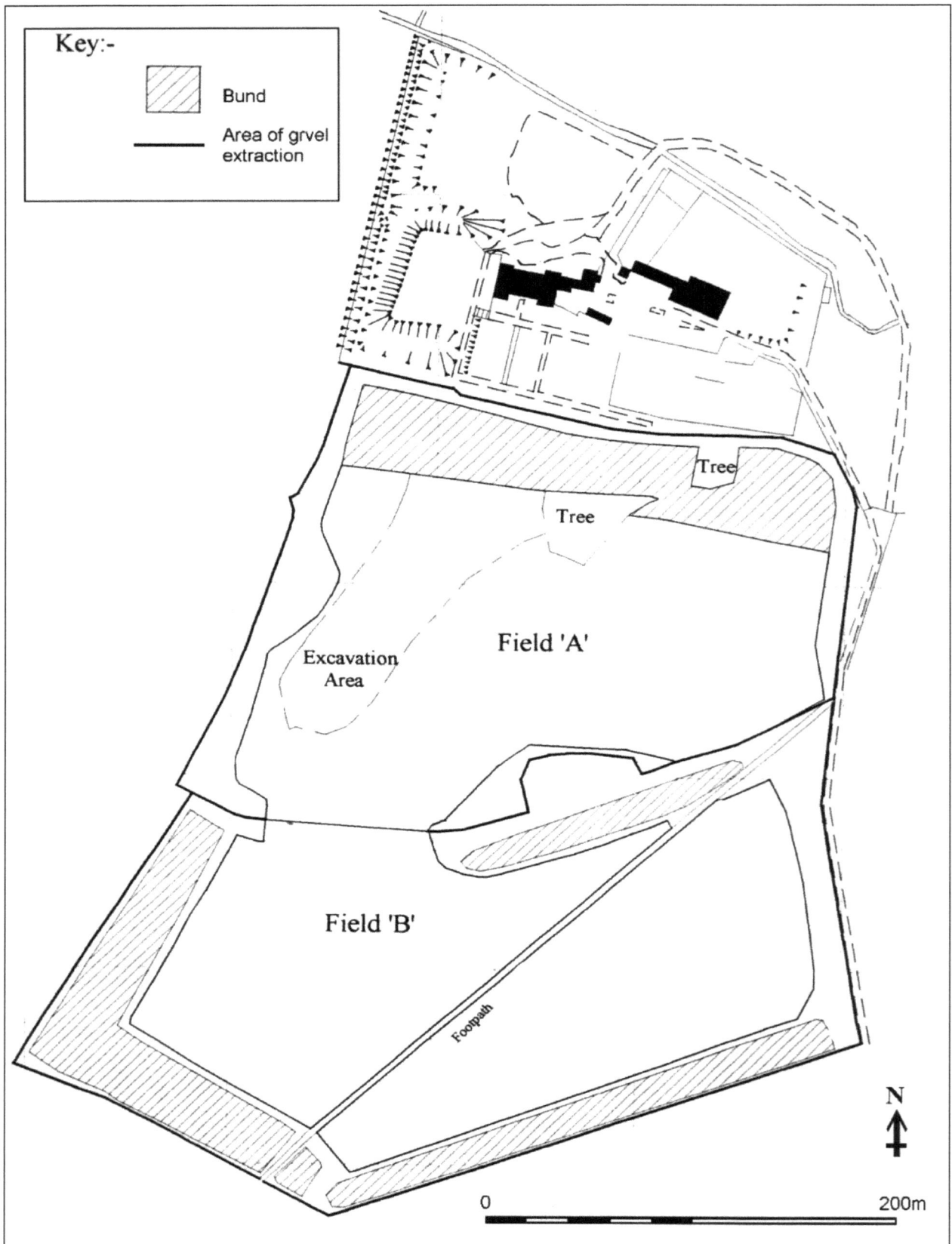

Fig. 4: Location of excavation area in relation to extraction zones 'A' & 'B'

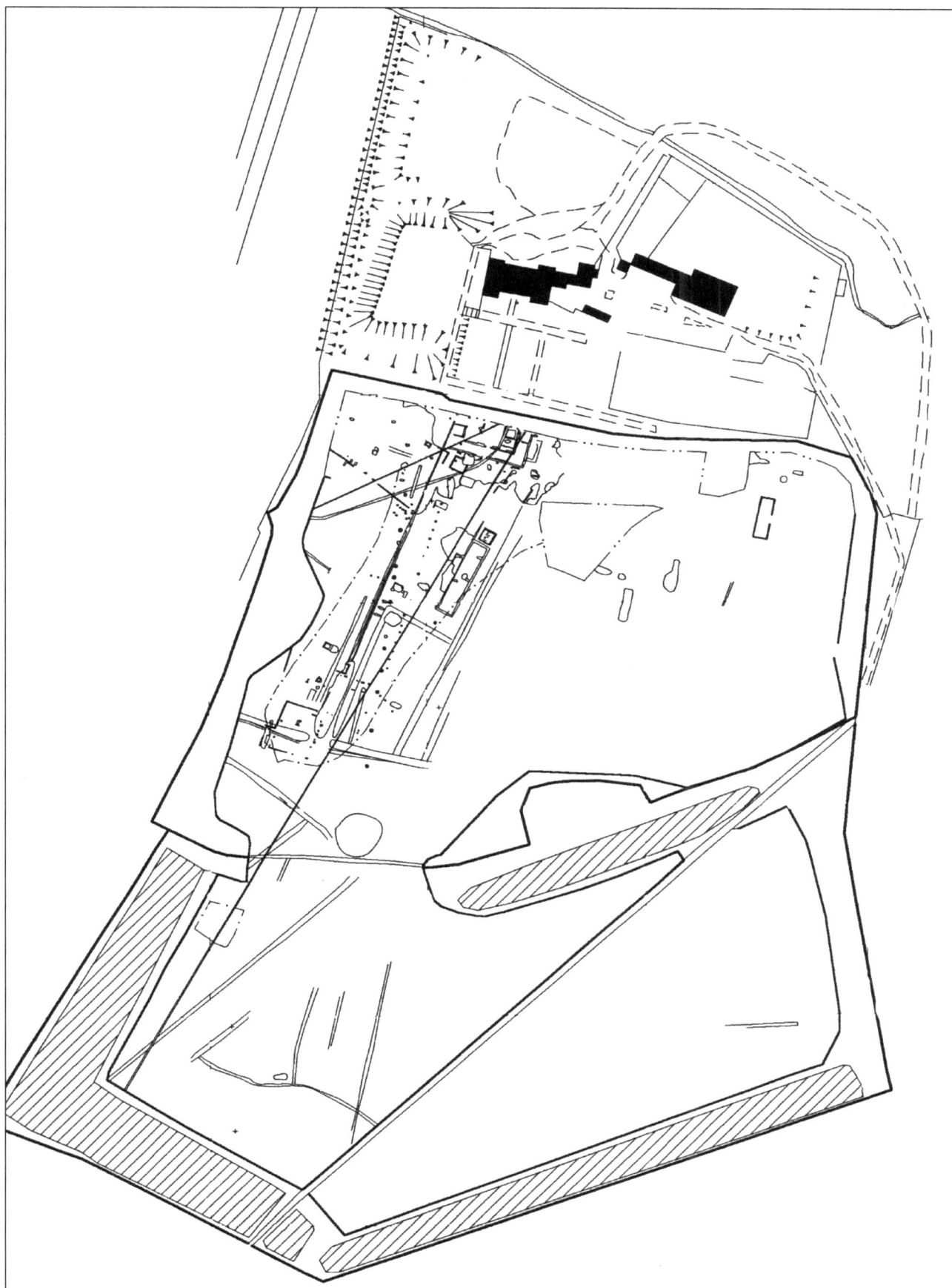

Fig. 5: Overall plan of archaeology in relation to the moated manor site

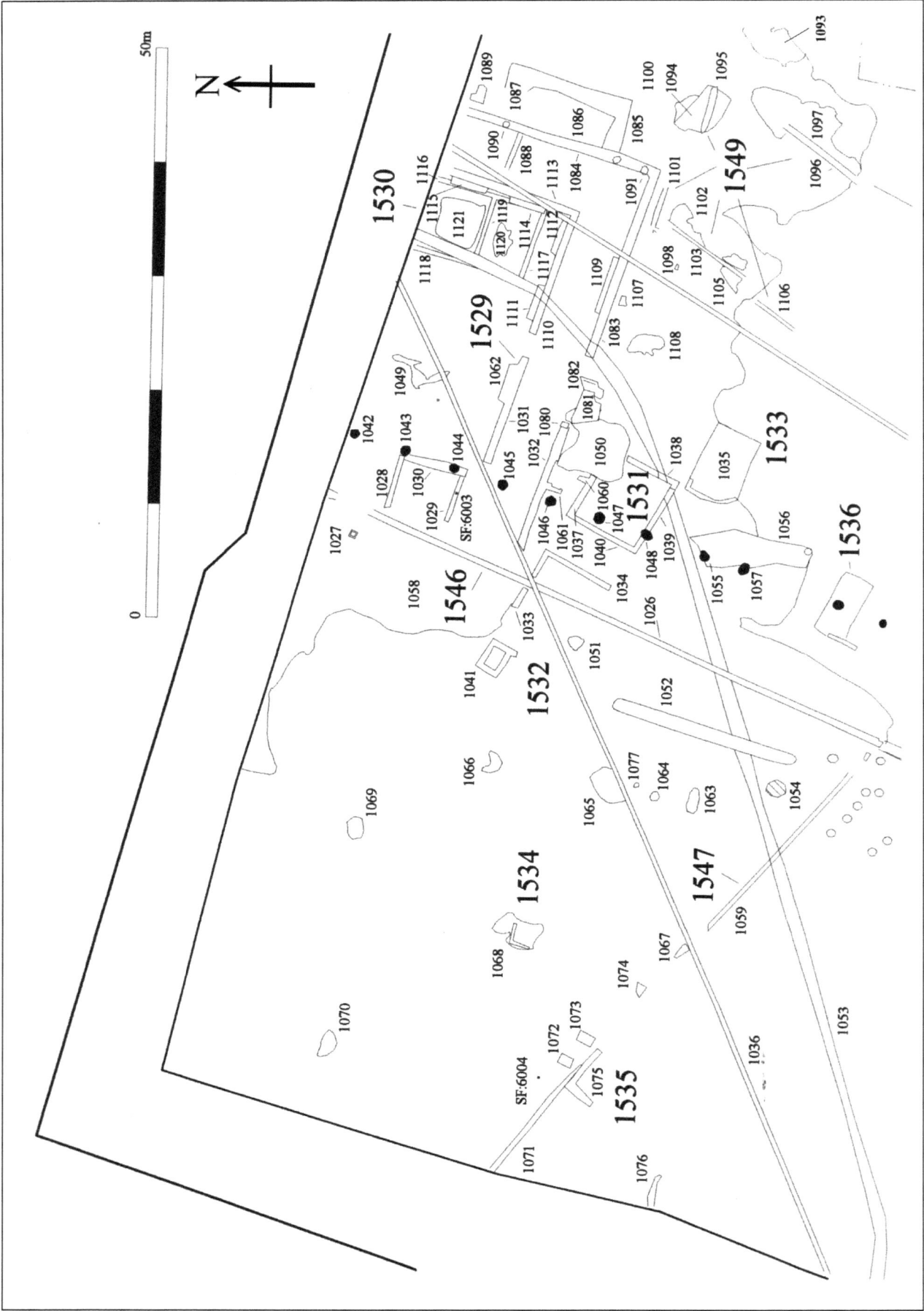

Fig. 6: Overall plan: structures at the north end of Field A

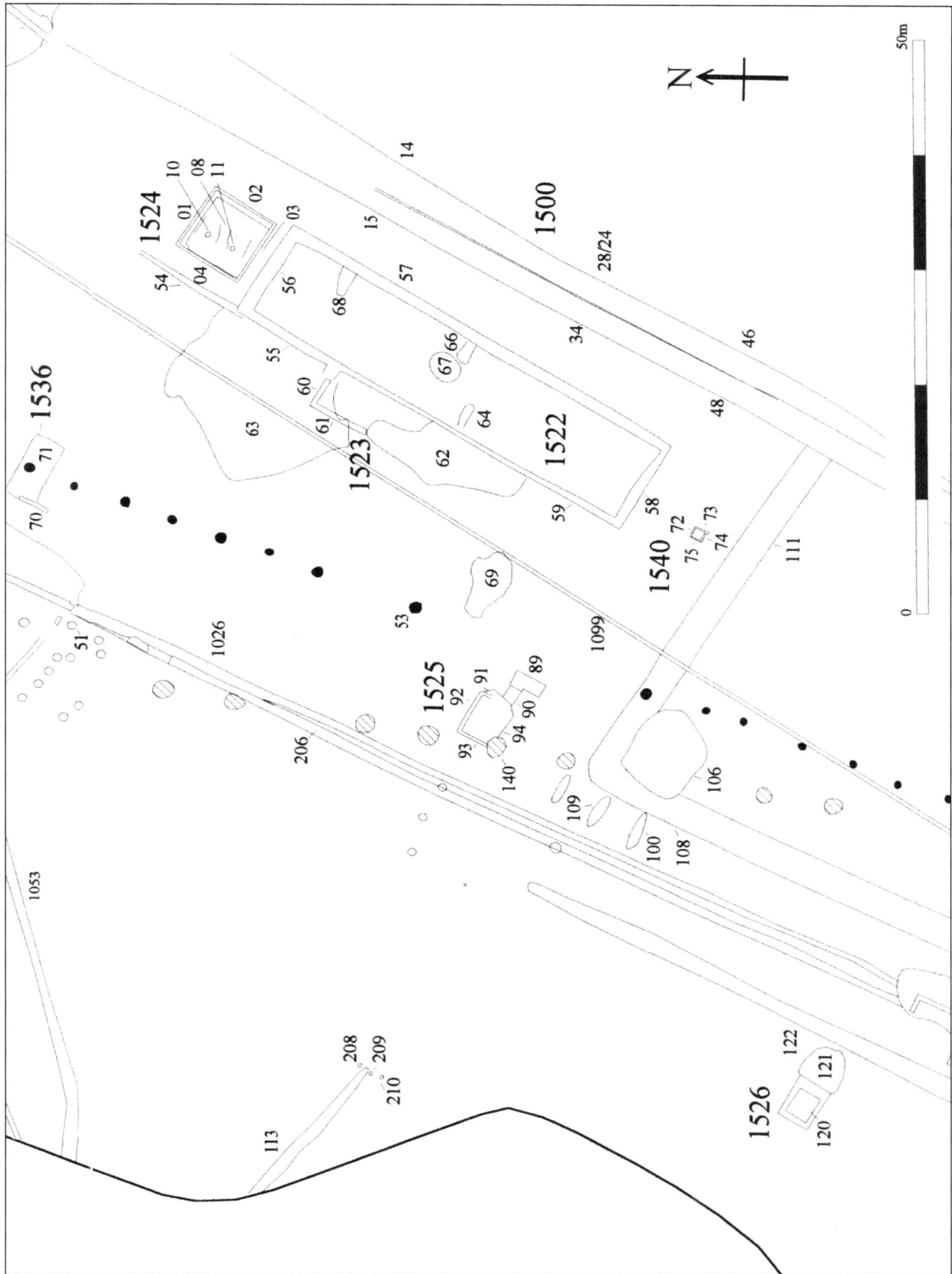

Fig. 7: Overall plan: centre of field 'A'

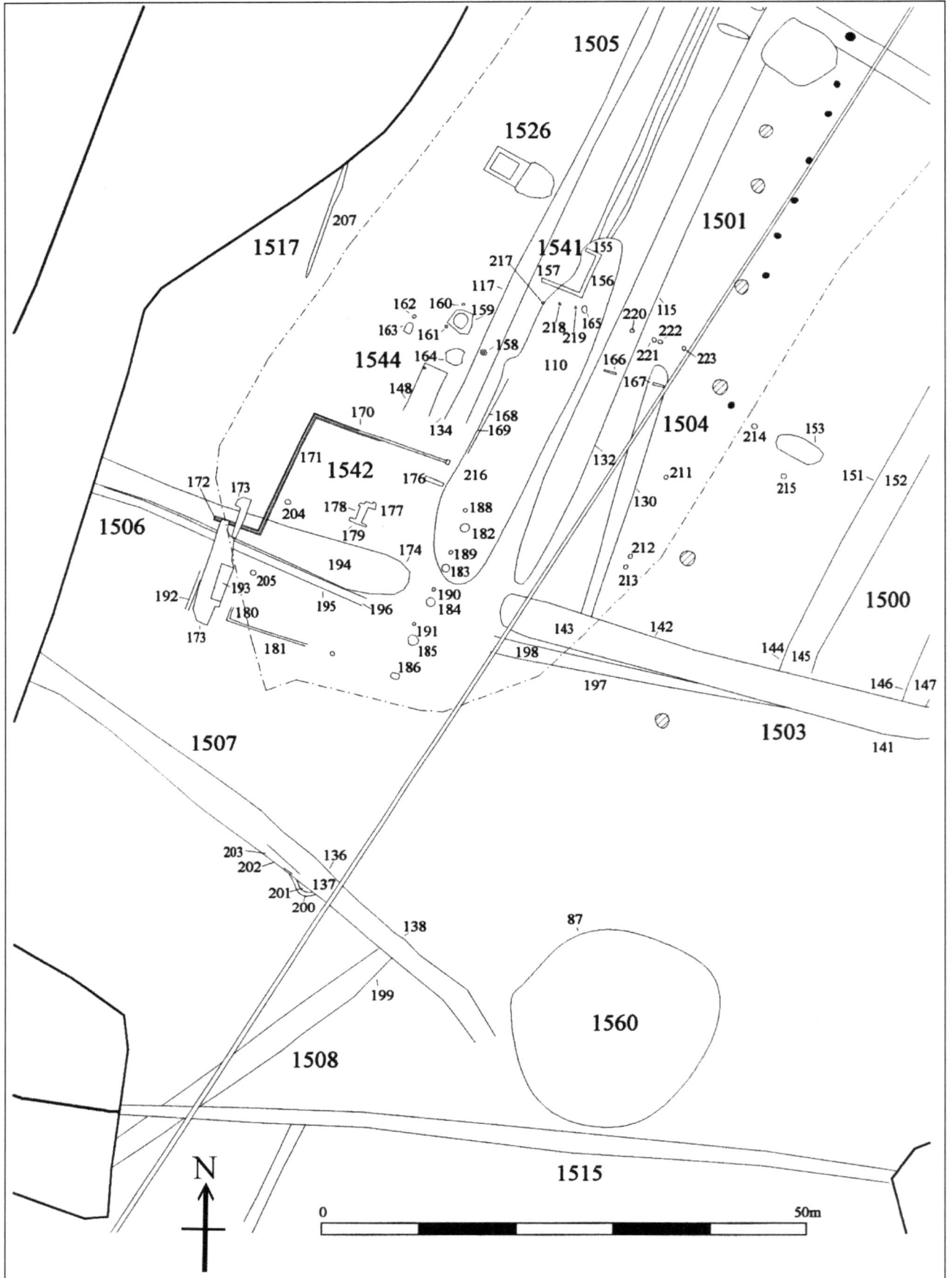

Fig. 8: Overall plan: southern edge of field 'A'

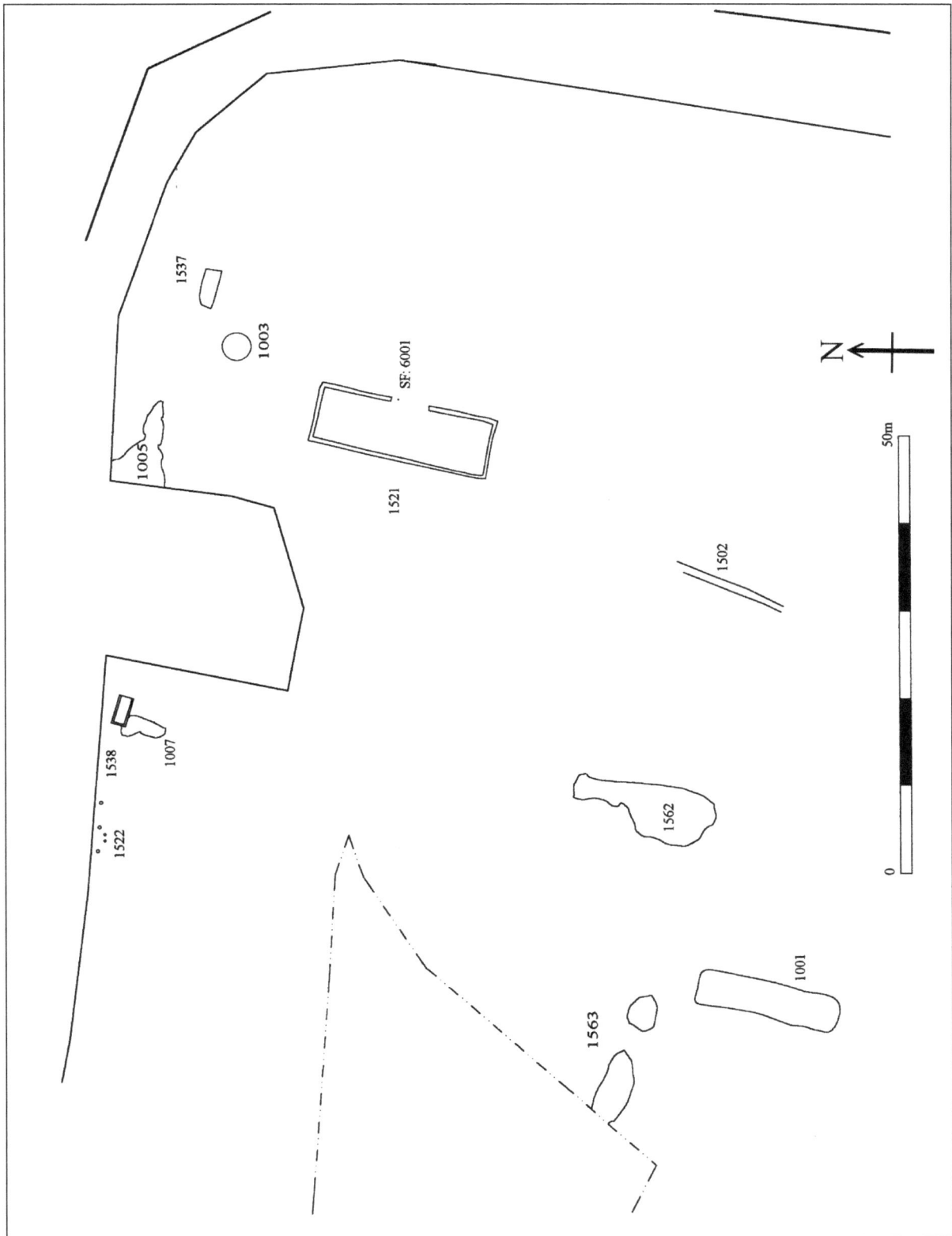

Fig:.9: Overall plan: north east corner of field 'A'

1537

1003

1005

SF: 6001

1521

1502

1538

1007

1522

1562

1563

1001

N

0 50m

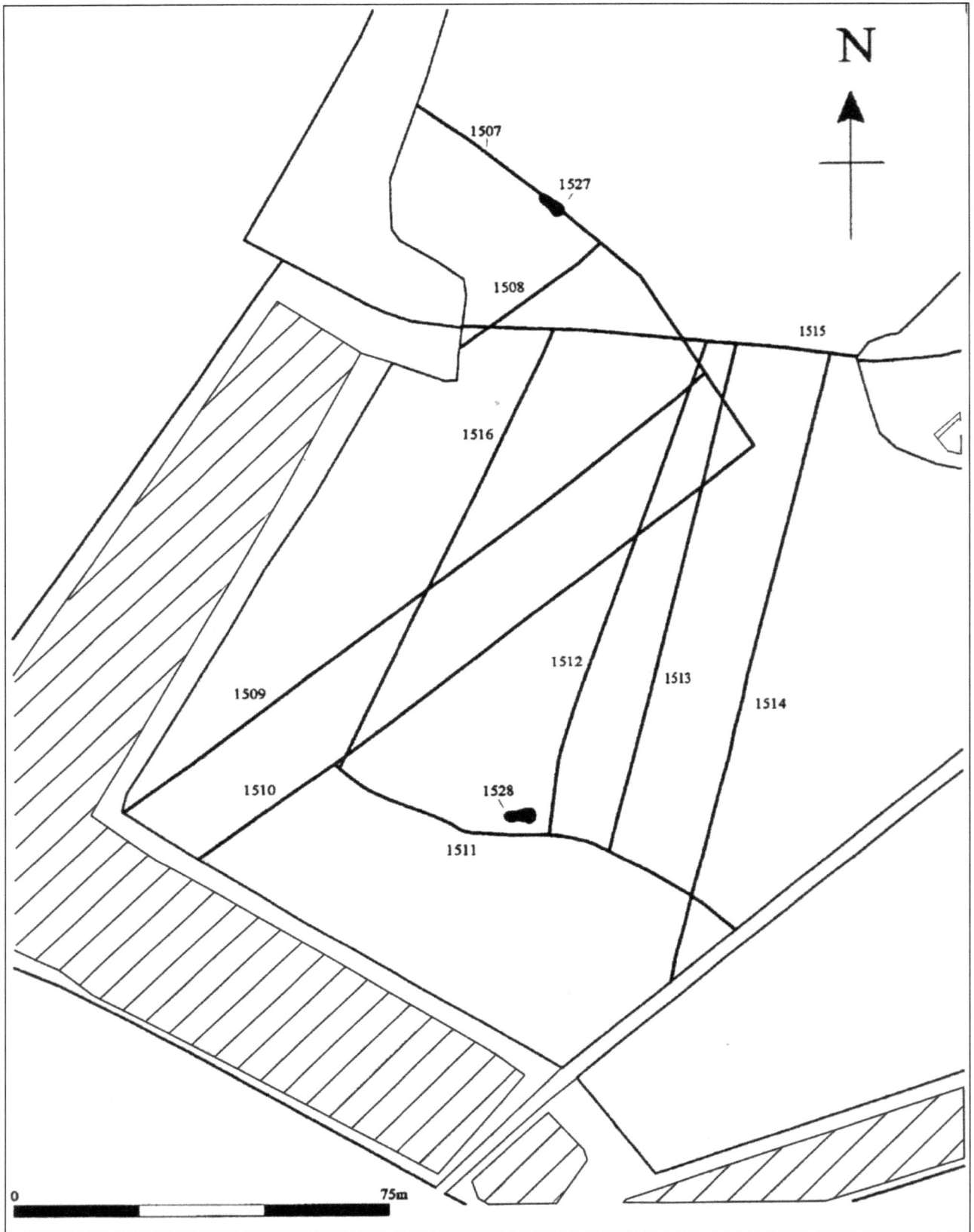

Fig. 10: Field divisions in field B and the SW corner of field A

EXCAVATION RESULTS
By J.R. Hunn & C. Turner

CHRONOLOGY

As most of the archaeological activity on the site occurs within a relatively short span of time, several problems arise with the dating of the archaeological information. In particular, the continuation of building traditions and the common practice of re-using materials hinder the precise dating of many of the archaeological features in the late medieval and post-medieval periods. For the purpose of this report, the following chronological framework has been employed to overcome some of these difficulties:

Period 1: Prehistoric

Period 2: Post- Norman Conquest

Phase 1: Early medieval (1066-1399)
Phase 2: Late medieval (1400-1499)
Phase 3: Late medieval/early Tudor (1500-1539)
Phase 4: Early post-medieval (1540-1620)
Phase 5: Later post-medieval (1620-1775)
Phase 6: Modern (1900-present day)

PERIOD 1: PREHISTORIC

No prehistoric features were observed during fieldwork. Six flint tools were recovered from the natural gravels: Material of this period recovered during fieldwork is listed in Appendix 1.1. The adjacent Mesolithic site which lay to the south - west will be described separately in Part 4.

PERIOD 2: POST-NORMAN CONQUEST

PHASE 1:EARLY MEDIEVAL (1066 - 1399)

Field Systems 1511-1514 & 1516 (Fig. 10)
Five ditches [1511], [1512], [1513], [1514], [1516], formed a system of small rectangular fields in Field 'B' (Fig. 10), dated to the medieval period. The field system consisted of a curved ditch [1511] aligned broadly east-west, forming the southern extent of the field system, and four north-south ditches which appear to respect the east-west field boundary between Fields 'A' and 'B'. However, one of the north-south ditches [1514] truncates [1511], suggesting that the field system extends southwards towards Bowmansgreen Farm.

The relationship of the north-south ditches to the field boundary between Fields 'A' and 'B' indicated that the present-day ditch alignment has obscured an earlier boundary ditch relating to this medieval field system. This system of ditches encloses three rectangular fields. The area of the largest, bordered by Ditches [1516] and [1512], measured approximately 3240m^2 (0.8 acre). To

the east of this was the smallest of the fields, measuring 1320m^2 (0.32 acre). This field was equivalent to a typical medieval furlong of around a third of an acre (Wood 1968, 111). The third field, bounded by ditches [1513] and [1514], measured 2050m^2 (0.5 acre). Some striations, interpreted as plough marks, were observed which appeared to share the same north-south orientation as the fields.

The dating of this field system is problematic, as only the curved ditch [1511] contained datable fragments of pottery. They indicated that this ditch silted up between the 10th and 12th centuries. However, a medieval corn dryer [1528] was located in the south-eastern corner of one of the fields, where Ditches [1511] and [1512] met. Flint building material and mortar from the corn dryer were observed within the fill of Ditch [1511]. Furthermore, a dump of burnt material, thought to be from the flue of the corn dryer, was observed within the fill of Ditch [1512]. This suggests that the decline of the ditches was contemporary with the destruction of the corn dryer, which is dated to the late-13th century. This field system was cut by a later series of ditches on a different north-east to south-west alignment formed by Ditches [1507], [1508], [1509] and [1510]. This later field system appears to relate to Bowmansgreen Farm (Fig. 10).

Corn Dryers 1527 & 1528 (Figs 11 & 12)
Two similar features, [1527] and [1528] were identified as corn drying kilns. Corn dryer [1528] was located in the south-eastern corner of a medieval field system in Field 'B', at TL 19035 04270 (Fig. 10). The dryer consisted of a narrow rectangular flue, 0.70m in width and 2.85m in length, with a central flue, leading to a sub-circular domed chamber (Fig. 11: Plate 1). The dryer was constructed with large sub-angular flints, loosely mortared together, and had a compact gravel floor surface within the eastern stoke-pit chamber. Roman brick had been used in its construction, particularly in the flue lining. The structure was aligned broadly east-west, with the flue facing westwards, and measured 6.25m long by 3m wide and 1.22m deep (from ground surface) overall. The flue walls survived to a height of about 0.3m, approximately 7 courses of brick. It is likely that the flue walls would have carried a brick barrel vault, above which would have been a tiled floor of some sort. Alternatively, the floor of the drying chamber could have been constructed of wooden planks, but such an arrangement would have been prone to catch fire. Along the length of the flue and into the stoke pit chamber ran a duct with steep sides and a flat base, measuring 0.25m wide, 0.35m deep, and 3.0m in length. The fills of the duct contained clear evidence of burning. Charred seeds were observed in an environmental sample which was taken from a burnt deposit at the neck of the flue: the seed assemblage is described in Appendix 1.9. A radiocarbon reading obtained from the charred grain taken from the fill of the flue provided a date of between 1295 and 1445 (2 sigma).

Plan of Kiln 1528

A) East Facing Section Acrss Maltin Kiln

N   S

e

c,full feature profile

section A

section B

Artificial Edge

0   2m

0   1m

Full Feature Profile of Kiln 1528

E   W

0   1m

B) West Facing Section

N   S

0   1m

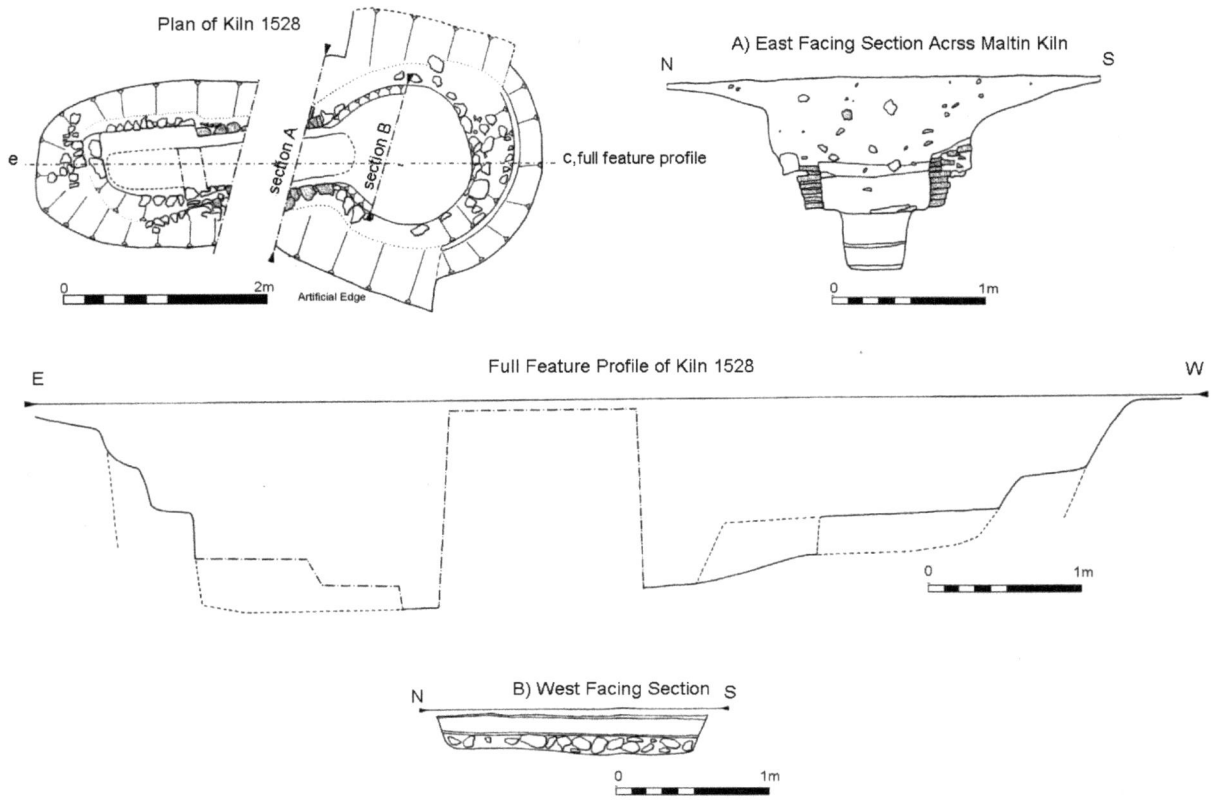

Fig. 11: Plan of corn dryer 1528

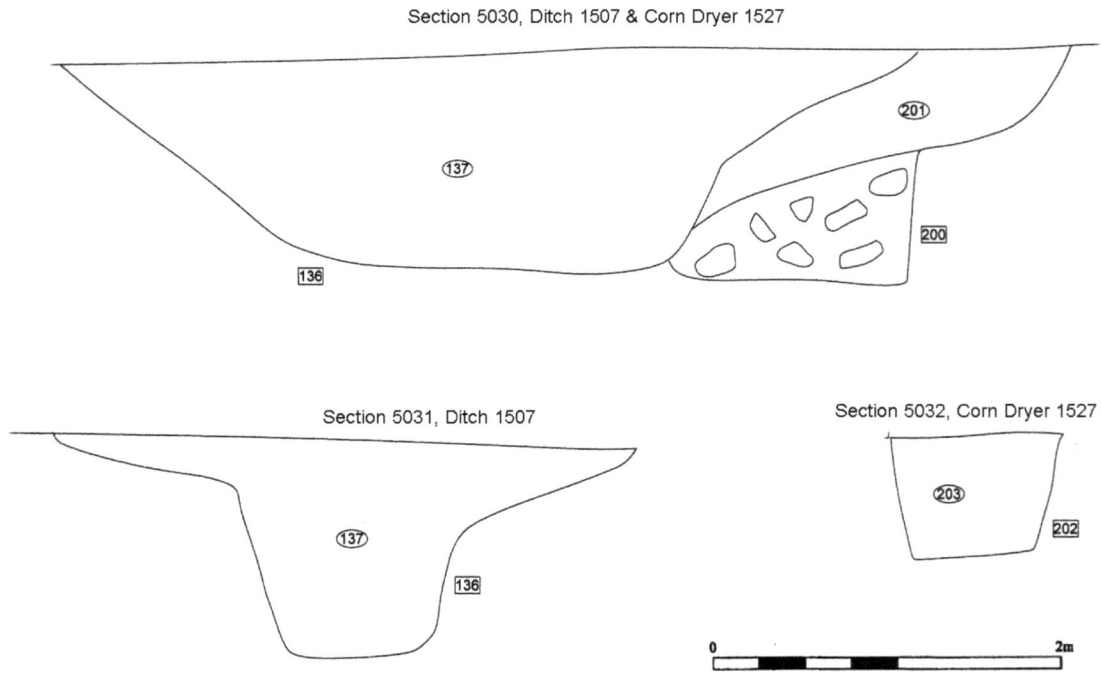

Section 5030, Ditch 1507 & Corn Dryer 1527

201

137

200

136

Section 5031, Ditch 1507

Section 5032, Corn Dryer 1527

137

203

202

136

0   2m

Fig. 12: Sections of Ditch 1527 & Ditch 1507

Another corn dryer [1527] was located in the south western corner of Field 'A' at TL 19035 04400 (Figs. 10 & 12, section 5030). This corn dryer had been heavily truncated by Ditch [1507], which left only a small fraction of southern wall and the base of the flue intact. The construction of this feature was identical to that of [1528], comprising large, poorly mortared flints and re-used Roman brick. This dryer was aligned north-west to south-east, with its flue facing westwards. Its overall length was approximately 7.0m, its width 3.0m and its depth 1.0m. Fragments of pottery recovered from deposits in its flue were dated to the mid 12th-14th centuries.

PHASE 2 LATE MEDIEVAL (1400 -1499)

Outer court (Fig. 14)

During the later part of the medieval period, a system of ditches was dug enclosing a rectangular area, approximately 4 acres in size, in the north-west corner of Field 'A' (Fig. 14). The southern half of this area was sub-divided into two small rectangular enclosures, linked by a joint entrance leading to a larger area to the north, which covered 64 per cent of the entire enclosure. There was no cartographic evidence for this complex of ditches, which appeared to relate to the medieval manor. Structures relating to the manorial estate and tile production were associated with the northern and south-western parts of this complex. However, the south-eastern area was distinctly different, containing no evidence of industrial processes or associated structures. It appears this enclosure fell into disuse sometime between the end of the 16th century and early 17th century.

The southern boundary of the whole enclosure was defined by Ditches [1506] and [1503]. These ditches were orientated ENE-WSW and two phases of construction were recognised in both. The earliest comprised a small ditch, which was replaced and partially removed by a very substantial ditch on a similar alignment. These ditches probably represent the southern boundary of the outer court of the manor. Between these two ditches, an entrance was clearly visible. It measured 10m in width, and led to a narrow strip of land of the same width, bordered on either side by ditches. This strip of land has been interpreted as an entrance corridor, leading to the larger enclosure to the north (Figs. 14 & 8). On the west side of the entrance were two parallel ditches, comprising Group [1506] (Fig. 8). The smaller ditch [195] had concave sides stepping down to a square base, and measured 0.92m wide by 0.85m deep. Sherds of pottery of 17th-century date were recovered from it. This small ditch was superseded by Ditch [174], which ran parallel to, and north of, Ditch [195]. These two ditches were only 0.30m apart for most their length, but appeared to merge together as they approached the western limit of the site. The 'V'-shaped profile of this ditch measured 4.0m wide by 1.7m deep (Fig. 15, section 5029), and it

was traced for a distance of some 34m. The fills of this substantial ditch contained no archaeological finds. Both boundaries were truncated by the later north-south ditch group [1517] and Building [1542]. In addition, the drain associated with that building ran into Ditch [174], and its outflow had clearly given the fill of that feature a 'washed-out' appearance.

The two boundaries on the east side of the entrance way [1503] mirrored the ditches comprising Group [1506]. The smaller ditch [197] had concave sides, stepping down to a square base. It measured 1.10m wide by 0.85m deep and was traced for approximately 30m, to where it was fully truncated by the larger Ditch [142] to the north. No dating evidence was recovered from [197]. The larger 'V'-shaped ditch was similar in size to Ditch [174], measuring 3.6m in width and 1.2m in depth, and was traced for 50m. Within the southern baulk of Field 'A', this same feature was observed. It appears to run across the entire field and beyond the current access road to the house, along the eastern limit of Field 'A' (Fig. 8). Two ditches, [1500] and [1502], butt onto this boundary. The relationship of Ditch [1504] and Ditch [1503] is unknown, but the former probably cuts across the latter. Although no datable artefacts were recovered from [1503] it does not appear on the 18th-century estate plans. This feature was originally thought to represent a possible boundary of the deer park established in the early 15th century. However, its primary function was probably as the principle boundary of the outer enclosure of the medieval manor.

Section 5015, Ditch 1504

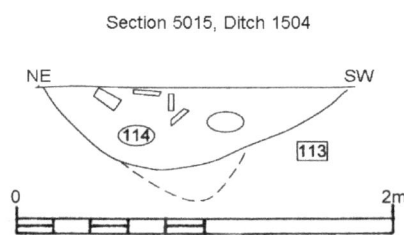

Fig 13: Section of Ditch 1504

The eastern limit of this complex of ditches was defined by Ditch [1502] (Fig. 14). This 'U'-shaped ditch measured 3m wide by 0.80m deep, and was orientated NE-SW, broadly parallel with Ditch [1500], and butted onto Ditch [1503]. Due to the leached nature of its fill and its high content of redeposited gravel, this ditch could only be clearly traced for 50m. There was no evidence that this ditch turned before it reached the northern limit of the site, where the area was highly disturbed and still covered by large spreads of post-medieval building debris. No datable evidence was recovered from this feature. There was a significant 'fall-of' in the number and antiquity of archaeological features to the east of this ditch, though this impression was doubtless exaggerated by the nature of overburden stripping and position of the haul road in this area.

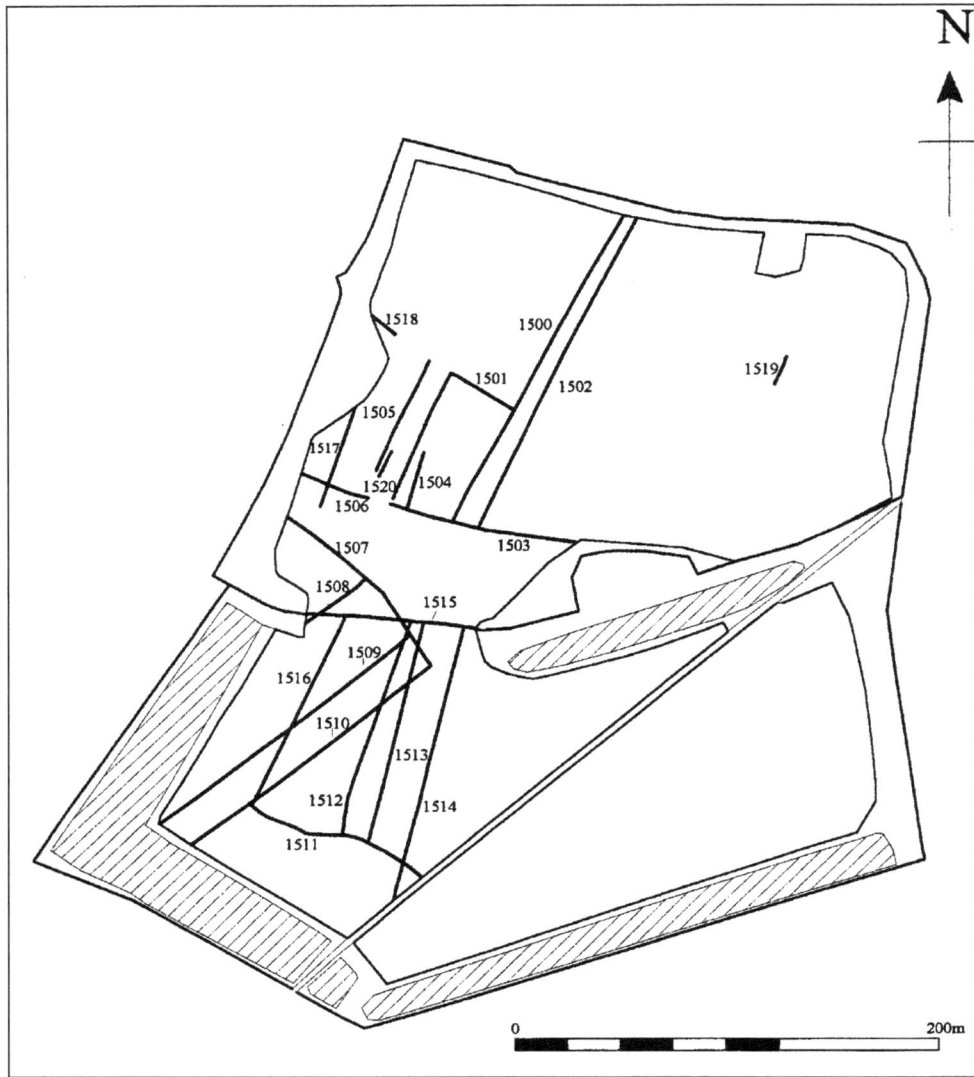

Fig 14: Plan of boundary ditches

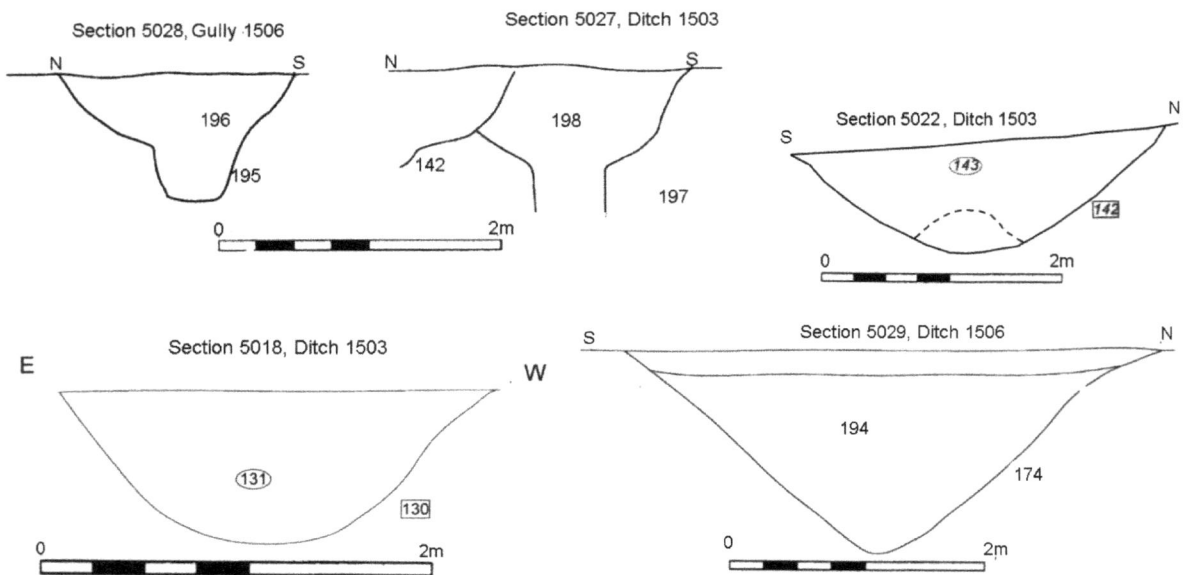

Fig 15: Ditches [1503] & [1506]

Ditch 1500 (Figs 14 & 16)

This ditch comprised several phases of inter-cutting linear features aligned NNE-SSW, some with evidence of repeated re-cuts, showing this feature had been kept open for some time. This ditch was located approximately 10m west of Ditch [1502], and butted onto Ditch [1503] to the south. The northern extent of this feature was difficult to define, although its constituent cuts appeared to be diverging slightly some 50m from the northern limit of the site. This feature was traced for 130m.

This sequence of ditches appears to have originated in the 13th/14th century as two small parallel ditches, less than 0.5m wide, which were subsequently recut, increasing the width and depth of the feature to 1.2m wide × 0.75m respectively. Over time, the boundary was defined by a series of smaller re-cuts. The western element of these recuts may be associated with a robbed-out wall, part of Structure [1549], forming the eastern limits to a compound around some buildings associated with tile production. Finally, most of these recut boundaries were superseded by a single large ditch, 3.6m wide by 0.6m deep (below reduced level), which removed the evidence of earlier phases. This boundary, and probably the whole enclosure complex, fell out of use by the start of the 17th century.

Ditch 1501 (Figs 14 & 17)

This ditch defined the northern and western limits of the south-eastern area of the enclosure (Fig. 8). This ditch also formed the eastern side of the entrance corridor where it runs parallel to Ditch [1505]. The latter butts onto Ditch [1500], and runs westwards for 35m on a north-west to south-east alignment, the same orientation as Ditch [1518] to the west. At TL 19082 04496 the ditch turns 90° to the south-west and was traced for a distance of 70m, terminating 1.2m from Ditch [1503]. This broad 'U'-shaped ditch was 3m wide and 1m deep. Its silty fill contained concentrations of redeposited gravel, but no dating evidence. Unlike the first two areas, the enclosure delineated by this ditch and [1500] does not contain any evidence of tile production. Ditch [1501] is cut by some of the tree-pits associated with Avenue [1558], a garden feature [1559] and a post-built structure [1543] (Fig. 30).

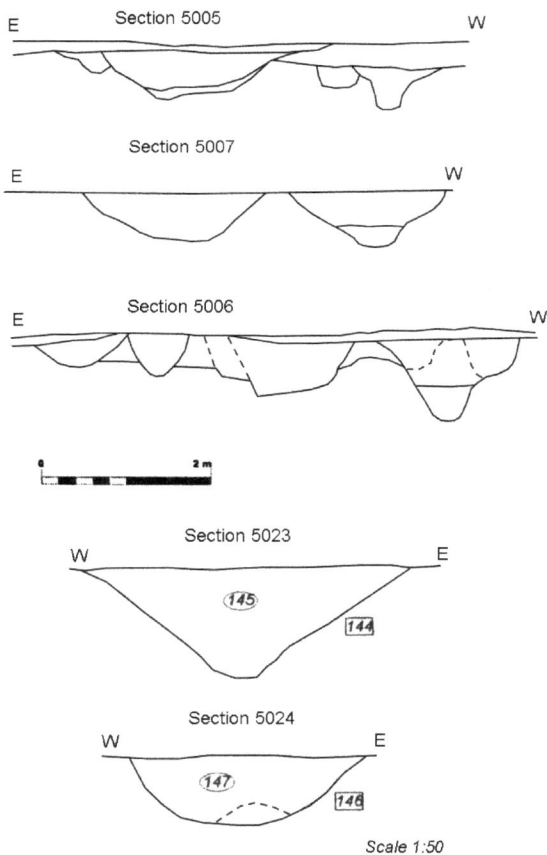

Fig 16: Sections of Ditch [1500]

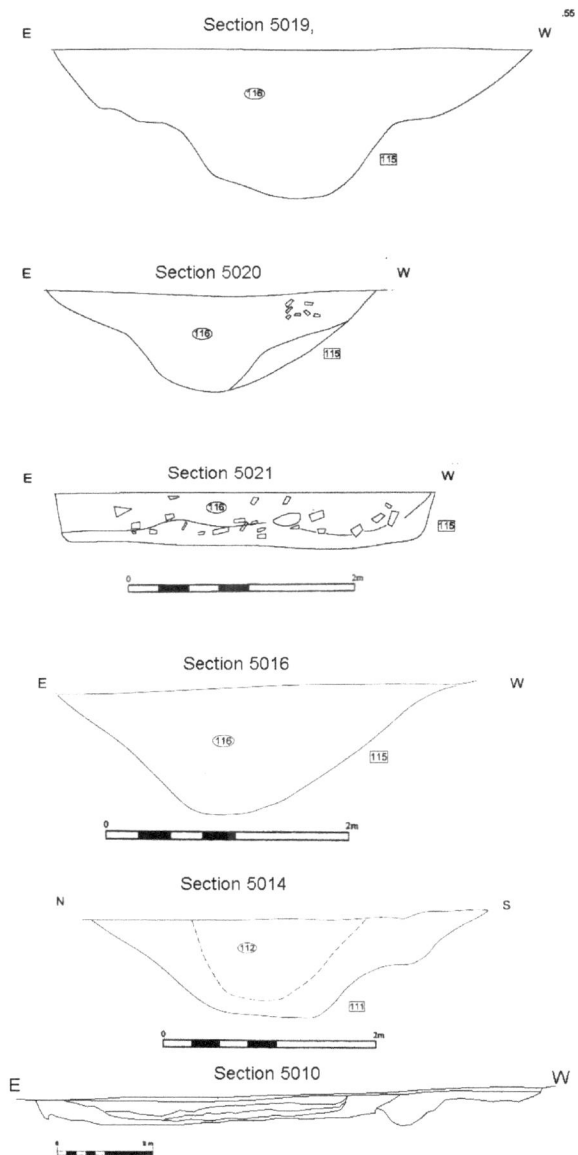

Fig 17: Sections of Ditch [1501]

Ditch 1505 (Figs 14 & 18)

This ditch ran parallel to [1501], forming the western extent of the entrance corridor (Fig. 8). It also marked the eastern boundary to a small rectangular enclosure containing a tile kiln [1526]. Ditch [1505] was orientated NNE-SSW, and measured over 56m in length. It terminated at its north end, but it's southern end was obscured by the collapse debris of Building [1542]. It is believed to have terminated just short of Ditch [1506], just as Ditch [1501] terminates short of Ditch [1503]. This 'U'-shaped ditch was 3.0m wide and 0.8m deep. No archaeological finds were recovered from this feature, though it was cut by a post hole belonging to Structure [1544], suggesting that it predates the late 17th century.

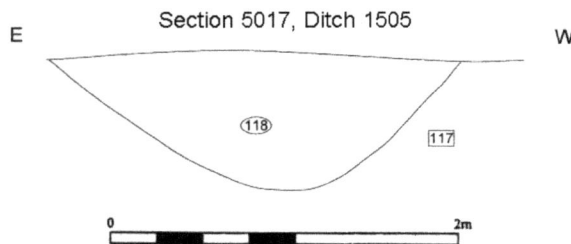

Fig 18: Sections of Ditch [1505]

Ditch 1518 (Fig. 14)

Ditch [1518] was a small shallow linear feature on the western limits of the site (Fig. 30). It was orientated north-west to south-east, a similar alignment to the northern part of Ditch [1501]. Ditch [1518] was traced for 15m, terminating at a possible north-south fence line [1550]. Its section was 'U'-shaped, and it was 1.2m wide and 0.25m deep. No dating evidence was recovered from this feature. This ditch represents an internal subdivision of the enclosure complex, defining the southern limits of the large enclosed area to the west of the entrance corridor.

Field System (Fig. 14)

Ditches [1511] to [1514] and [1516] were later superseded by a new ditched field system, established on a north-east to south-west alignment and located in the south-west corner of Field 'A' and on the western side of Field 'B' (Fig. 14). The northern limit of this field system was defined by Ditch [1507]. This feature followed a north-west to south-east alignment, had stepped sides and a square base, and measured 1.5m wide by 0.90m deep. It was traced for 60m, and may have continued for a further 40m to join the northern end of Ditch [1510]. Ditch [1507] truncated Corn Dryer [1527], leaving only a small section of the structure remaining. Sherds of 12th to 13th-century pottery recovered from the ditch are thought to be residual, originating from the corn dryer and not relating to the silting up of the ditch.

From Ditch [1507], three parallel ditches ran south-westwards, bounding two narrow strips of land (Fig. 14). These may relate to Bowmansgreen Farm to the south of the site, but this is by no means certain. All three ditches had leached fills with a high content of redeposited brickearth, making them almost indistinguishable from the natural subsoil in this region of the site. The westernmost ditch [1508] was 2.5 m wide and was traced for 38m. The middle ditch [1509] was also 2.5m wide and was traced for 150m across Field 'B'. Only a short section of the eastern ditch [1510] in this group was identified, extending for 38m and measuring 2m in width. The latter ditch truncated medieval Ditch [1511]. The exact date of this field system is unknown, but it clearly post-dates the corn dryers, which must have gone out of use after 15th century according to the C14 date. If Ditch [1507] does respect Hollow [1560], turning southwards to avoid it (below), then the date of this field system is likely to fall between the 14th and 16th centuries.

Structures (Figs 6,7,8 & 30)

There were several structures identified within the northern limits of Field 'A' belonging to this phase (Fig. 6). The walls of all three features were constructed with large irregular flints bonded by mortar, and were aligned WNW-ESE. Building [1531] appears to have pre-dated the inner courtyard since it was cut by the western gate house [1210].

Building 1522 (Figs 7 & 30)

[1522] was a large rectangular building orientated NNE-SSW, located at TL 19115 04510 (Fig. 7). It was constructed of mortared brick, tile and flint, and had overall dimensions of 37.4m × 9.0m (Plate 6). Its east wall [57], 0.8m wide, was the most substantial, composed mainly of tile (each *c*.250 × 170mm) and brick (varying between 230/235 × 115/119 × 60mm). The building appeared to have been sub-divided into three unequal bays (Fig. 7). There was no evidence for any surviving floor surfaces, and there appeared to be a pit or depression in the centre of the building [67]. Whether or not this was a contemporary feature was not established. The building was similarly oriented to Ditches [1500] and [1501].

Building 1523 (Fig. 13)

[1523] adjoined [1522] immediately to the north west and was sealed by a large semi-circular dump of tile debris, calcified stones and evidence of burning [62], measuring 15m in diameter and 0.25m in depth. The structure measured 13m x 4m. It had a substantial brick wall on its northern, eastern, and southern sides, with a thinner, more ephemeral wall forming its western side. The eastern wall [57] consisted of an irregular bonded brick sub-structure 0.80m in width, upon which was set a wall of large mortared flints, faced on both sides by bonded bricks. In contrast, the western wall [59] was only about 0.4m in width, consisting mainly of poorly mortared tiles in a dark silty matrix. From this difference in structure it appears either that the western side of the building remained open, or that it was made up of wooden panels, rather than a substantial flint and brick wall. The north and south sides of [1523] had been extensively robbed out. However, both were more substantial than the west wall, measuring between 0.8 – 1.0m in width and constructed of brick in a high density of lime mortar. Internally, this structure had three internal divisions. These short walls [64, 66 & 68] were located on both sides of the building, separated the floor space into a series of bays. None of these internal divisions spanned the full width of the building. It is unknown if these walls represent partitions or supports for shelves or racking. Another feature located within the building was a large sub-circular pit [67]. This feature was positioned almost in the centre of the building and measured 2.3m in diameter. The pit contained fragments of tile and calcified flints, indicative of burning. The precise function of this feature was not clear, but it may represent a storage pit, possibly for water brought up from the river to the west or storing clay or other raw materials.

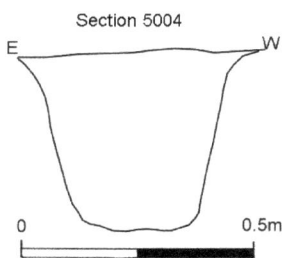

Fig. 19: Section of post-hole in [1524], Feature 10

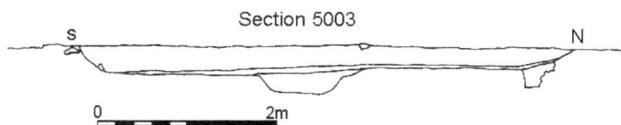

Fig. 20: Section of Building [1524], feature 1

Building 1524 (Figs 19, 20 & 30)
[1524] consisted of a square structure 6m × 6m and lay 1m to the north of building 1522 (Plate 9). This building was located at TL 19126 04530, and was aligned NNE-SSW (Fig. 7). The walls measured 0.38m in width, with a further brick plinth or off-set on the inside of the wall, possibly to support a suspended floor. The three courses of mortared brick were supported by a foundation layer of large flints and dark sandy silt which sat upon a thin layer of redeposited chalk and silt. Below the rubble infill of this building was evidence of two sub-circular postholes [10 & 11] and a narrow gully [08] running east-west across the feature. Both of these features appear to be contemporary with this structure. The inside of this building was filled with collapsed debris consisting of tile and brick fragments with a high concentration of lime mortar. The location and alignment of this building suggest that it was associated with the large barn or stable to the south.

Building & Garderobe 1531 (Figs 6,21,22, 30)
This was a rectangular masonry building Fig. 30 (formerly divided into building 1531 and garderobe 1532), located at NGR TL 11908-04586. It had an external measurement of 20m by 7m. Its walls were constructed of mortared flint and tile, and were 0.50m wide. The building was divided into three, possibly four rooms (3m x 6m, 5m x 6m, 3m x 6m and 6m x 6m. There

was no evidence for any surviving internal floor surfaces, nor any sign of a hearth or chimney foundation. In the north west corner of the building was located a garderobe, (previously [1532] divided into [1217] and [1041]) that probably served a first floor room. It consisted of a masonry lined pit 2.76m x 2.1m and 2.7m deep. Its walls were 0.44m wide and were composed of mainly flint with irregular courses of tile (215 x 170 x 14mm) and bonded by a hard yellowish brown mortar. There were occasional small blocks of clunch included and the lower foundations were made of weak red, unfrogged bricks (225 x 105 50mm), (Figs 6 and 18; Plates 3). The walls were slightly battered down and on the north side was an arched recess. The arch was built of tile and was centrally positioned. The recess measured 1.9m in height and was about *0.5m* wide. It penetrated through the width of the wall and had been extended a further 0.6m into the adjoining natural sand. The brick foundations lay directly on what looked like natural gravel. Within the pit itself the gravel had a black organic appearance and smell. However, due to a persistent rise in the level of the ground water it was difficult to investigate this deposit any further. From the very lowest fill (building rubble) came four pieces of well preserved timber. One of these was a carefully sawn plank (0.7m x 0.28m x 0.1m), which must have belonged to some sort of structure. Two further pieces of timber had been shaped into posts or stakes (1.03m x 0.08m and 0.69m x 0.05m). The fourth timber was probably a fragment of a plank (0.9m x 0.05m). See Fig. 43. The feature is believed to be a garderobe and was probably associated with a medieval rectangular building to its east [1531]. The fill yielded fragments of a Raeren drinking jug (1480-1600) but no dating was obtained from the structure itself.

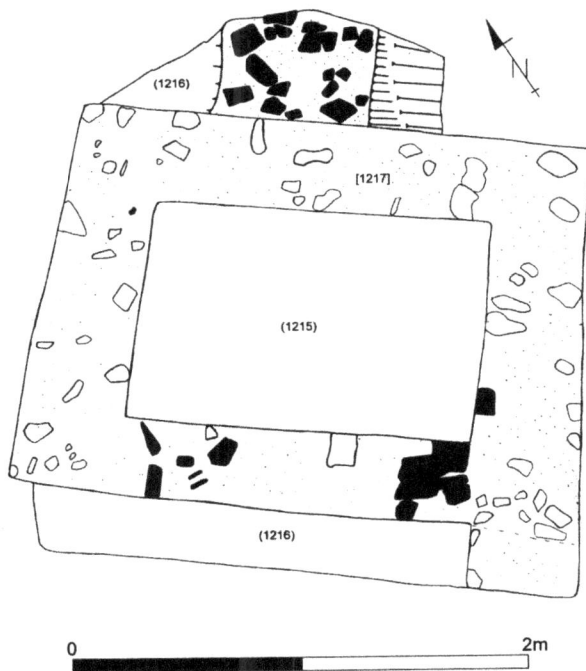

Fig. 21: Plan of garderobe (part of [1531], formerly [1532])

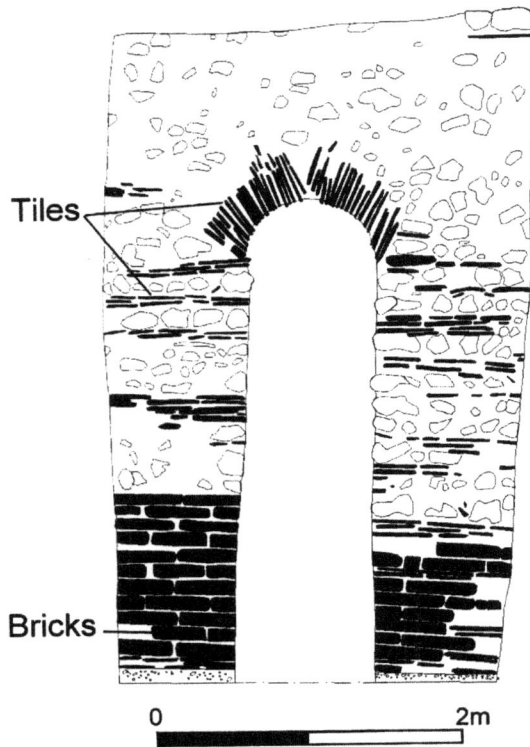

Fig. 22: South facing elevation of garderobe (part of 1531, formerly 1532)

Ancillary buildings and structures

Tile production

The production of tiles requires a readily available source of clay and sand (or brickearth), a water supply, a source of wood for fuel and a well-drained working area (Dury 1981, 135). Field 'A' at Tyttenhanger fits all these requirements adequately. Although no cartographic evidence exists for tile manufacturing structures in this area, the recent investigations have revealed a number of features associated with this activity in Field 'A', to the south of the present house. These structures are confined within the ditched enclosure described above (Fig. 14).

Tile Kiln 1526 (Figs 7, 23, 24, 25)

[1526] was located at TL 19054 04475, and was oriented WNW-ESE (Figs 24 & 25). This well-preserved tile kiln consisted of a semicircular flue pit on the eastern side of a rectangular parallel flue kiln (Plates 19-21). No evidence remained for a structure over the kiln. The flue pit [121] measured 3.0m in length, 3.6m in width and 0.84m in depth. The sides of the pit were vertical on the northern and southern sides, and the eastern side gradually sloped up to the surface. The loose dark silty fill of the flue contained a small amount of charcoal. The rectangular kiln [120] was constructed entirely from tiles, and measured 3.80m long, 3.00m wide and 0.85m deep (Figs 24 & 25). Within the structure were eight piers aligned north-south, built of tile wasters, and each pierced by two parallel arches. The piers were set at 0.15m intervals, and

consisted of a single line of tiles measuring 0.18m in width. The north, west and south walls were approximately 0.40m wide and the eastern wall, the one pierced by the stoke-hole, measured 0.95m in width. The tiles (215 x 160-170 x 15mm) appear to have been bonded with a sandy clay and there was no sign that any mortar had been used in the construction. The eastern wall above the northern flue arch had partially collapsed, but the rest of the structure appeared to be intact. Resting on the tile piers were 13 rows of tiles stacked 'on-edge', on the same alignment as the piers (Oliver Kent pers comm). Between seven of the rows were packed tiles, placed edge to edge on a north-south alignment, wedging the whole layer tightly together. Many of the complete tiles had two circular nail holes, around 20mm in diameter, at one edge, spaced approximately 60mm apart. The individual tiles measured between 240-250mm in length and 180mm in width. Some of the tiles appeared considerably shorter, measuring 180-190mm in length. The area available for stacking tiles in the kiln measured 4.95m^2, equating to approximately 330 tiles to a stacked layer. The height of the kiln, and therefore the number levels that could be stacked, is unknown. The flues on the eastern side were filled with sandy silt and tile debris, but the interior of kiln itself contained only loose tiles. The southern half of the remaining 'tile load' was removed in order to view the internal arrangement of the flue system. This tile kiln may have been constructed to serve the rebuilding of the house at Tyttenhanger in the late 14th and early 15th centuries.

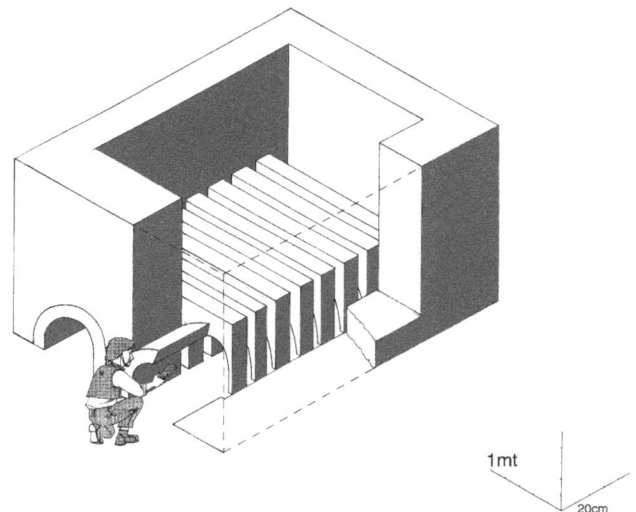

Fig. 23: Reconstruction of kiln [1526]

Kiln 1525 (Figs 7 & 26)

[1525] was a possible kiln located at TL 19085 04505 (Fig. 7). This structure was also oriented WNW-ESE. The kiln comprised three elements: a brick base for a chimney stack [89] positioned on the east side, a single flue [90] and a robbed out rectangular kiln structure [91]. The chimney base [89] measured 2.80m in length and 1.50m in width, and was constructed from lime-mortared bricks with tiles, laid 'on-edge', along the eastern side. Two courses of brick survived. The bricks in the centre

Tittenhanger Kiln 1526

Stoke Pit

North

0   2mt

Fig 24 Plan of Kiln [1526]

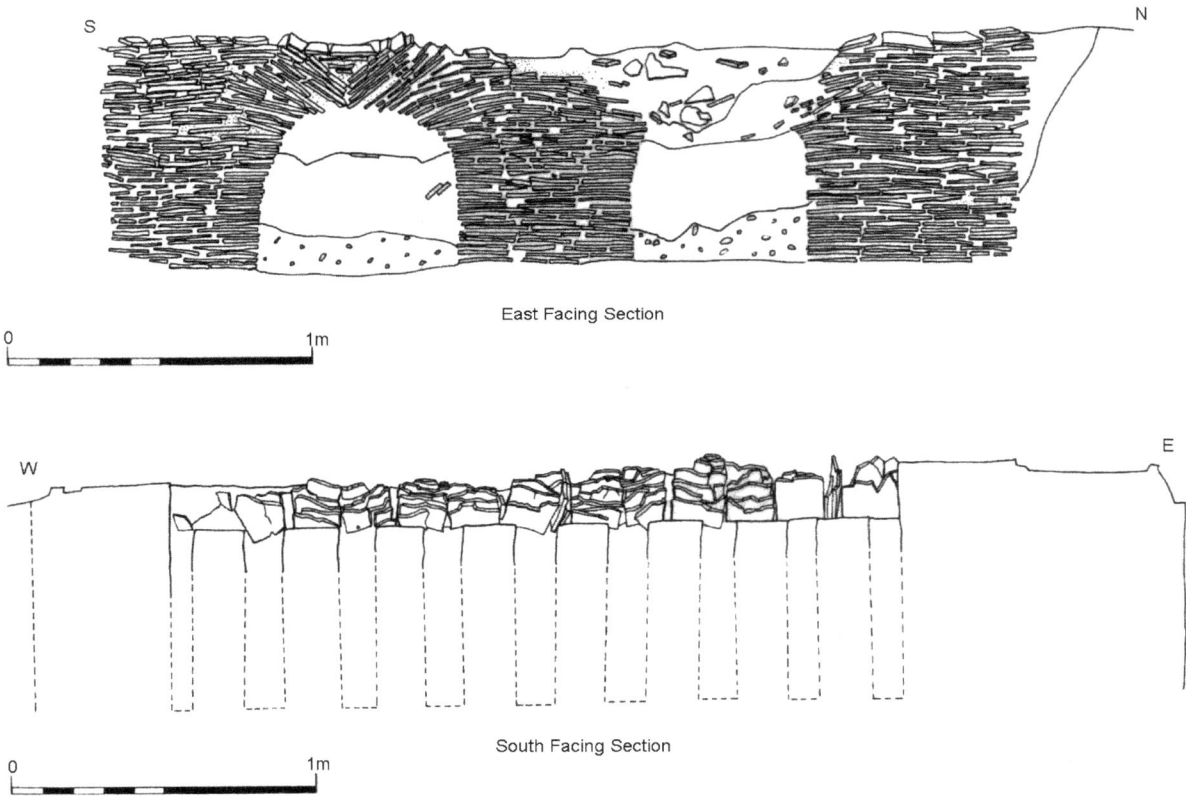

S   N

East Facing Section

0   1m

W   E

South Facing Section

0   1m

Fig. 25: Elevation of kiln [1526]

of the structure displayed clear signs of burning. A single 'U'-section flue ran from the middle of the eastern side of the kiln to the north-west corner of the chimney stack. The flue [90] measured 1.1m wide, 2.0m long and 1.3m deep. It was filled with a leached silty deposit containing large quantities of tile fragments and broken bricks.

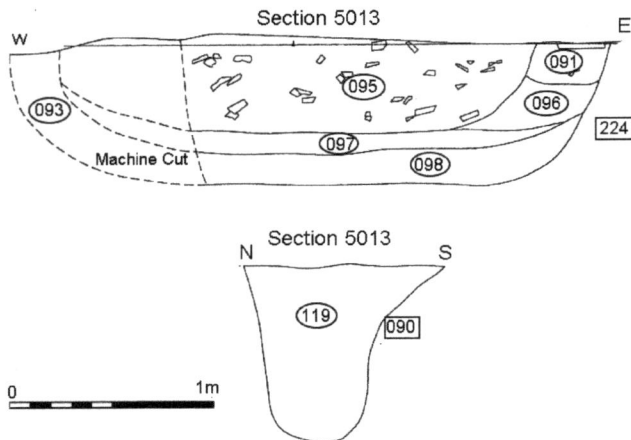

Fig. 26: Sections of Kiln [1525]

The rectangular pit [91] had been largely robbed out, leaving no trace of the internal structure. However, the outline of its walls did survive to a limited degree, measuring 4.0m in length and 3.5m in width. The structure appeared to sit on a foundation of compressed mortar, overlain with a deposit of collapsed material [95], 0.85m deep, containing a large amount of fragmented tile and brick. A floor tile with an incised representation of a stag (Appendix 1.4 Fig. 44) was recovered from this layer. Individual tiles recovered from this deposit were larger than those from Kiln [1526], measuring 290 × 172mm.

This structure, with its large chimney stack and single large flue, was relatively poorly constructed compared to Kiln [1526]. It was also located closer to the workshops (15m as opposed to 50m). Its construction could indicate that Kiln [1526] was not sufficient to meet the demand for tiles at this time. Alternatively, it might have been constructed as part of a consolidation of tile production on this site, along with the workshops. Its poor survival cannot be entirely attributed to its relatively poor construction: it appears to have been robbed out after tile production ceased on site, and one of the tree-pits of Avenue [1557] was later cut through the south-west corner of this kiln.

Enclosure walls 1549 (Fig. 6)
To the north of Building 1522 were a number of sections of wall, enclosing an area of approximately 600m² [1549], possibly some sort of compound. The centre of this compound was located at TL 19135 04540 in Field 'A' (Figs 6 & 30). The south-eastern wall [1096] was on a similar alignment to Ditch [1500]. The complex nature, orientation and location of Ditch [1500] suggests that one

or more of the 're-cuts' associated with this ditch may in fact be the robbed out footings for this wall. The walls forming the north-east side of this compound [1095, 1101] are not in exact alignment, suggesting that some outbuildings may have been constructed against the wall. However, no remains of any such structures were observed.

The sections of wall forming [1549] were mostly 0.4m in width, and were constructed from large irregular flints bonded with a loose lime mortar. Most of the northern end of the compound was covered with a spread of post-medieval debris, which obscured the full extent of these walls. However, the southern end of the east wall was found to butt onto the north-west corner of Building [1522]. These features were similar in construction to the existing walls to the east of the present house, with a foundation layer of flints overlaid by brick courses. These walls appear to have gone out of use some time in the late 16th century.

Extraction Hollow 1560 (Figs 8, 27 & 39)
A large sub-circular pit [1560] measuring 20.0m in diameter and 1.3m in depth was located at the southern end of Field 'A' at TL 19070 04385 (Figs 8 and 39). This feature had been dug through the gravel subsoil and into the underlying natural clays and sandy pockets, both of which are essential raw materials for tile production. The primary fill of this pit consisted of a series of deliberate deposits, tipped in from the northern edge. Several of these contexts contained a high degree of broken tile, possibly wasters. After the feature had been about half-filled in this way, it was left to silt up naturally, with the occasional addition of further dumped material. It is possible that excavation of this pit ceased during the 16th/17th century, before the establishment of the gardens south of the house.

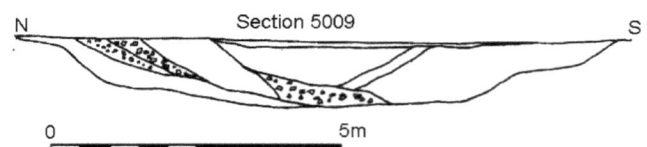

Fig. 27: Section of Extraction Hollow [1560]

On the southern boundary of Field 'A', about 100m to the east of [1560] is a large oval depression extreme SW corner of Fig. 8. It measured at least 60m long, 25m wide and over 5m deep. The feature had been planted with trees, and was partly backfilled with a variety of household rubbish. On modern Ordnance Survey plans of the estate this hollow is marked as a pond. However, its shape, size and location indicate that its primary purpose was most probably an extraction pit for use in tile production. As the feature is located where the natural subsoil changes from gravel to brickearth, it is likely that this feature was the principal source for the raw materials used to construct some of the archaeological structural remains observed immediately south of the house.

PHASE 3: LATE MEDIEVAL / EARLY TUDOR (1500-1539)

Inner courtyard 1592

[1529] was located at the northern edge of Field 'A', at TL 19120 04575 (Fig. 6 & 28) and was the largest single structure observed on the site. The southern edge of the inner courtyard lay approximately 80m from the centre of the existing Tyttenhanger House. It was on a similar alignment to the present house, and to earlier 16th-century features to the south. The south-facing rectangular structure measured 35 × 5m, with two north-south 'wings', each measuring 18 × 12m (Plate 4). The east wing continued northwards beyond the edge of the site, but the west wing stopped short of it. These substantial walls were 0.7m wide, constructed from lime-mortared bricks set in an irregular bond pattern. Individual bricks measured 230 × 120 × 60mm: two courses of bricks survived. The main east-west walls belonging to this structure were each pierced by a 2.0m gap, forming an entrance (Fig. 28; Plate 16). On the north side of these walls were three rectangular flint buttresses (Plate 4). Two similar buttresses, each 3.2 × 0.66m, were observed on the west side of the east wing. These were constructed of mortared flint, butted to the wall. As the walls against which they butted were relatively substantial and well built they suggest that they may have carried up to at least to a two storey height.

Three robbed-out walls butted onto the east wing. Their robber trenches were poorly defined, containing a high degree of lime mortar, but little building debris. The walls forming this enclosure were 1.35m wide, and encompassed an area 5.0 × 2.5m. Inside, there was no evidence of a floor surface or any internal features. This enclosure could represent an additional room butted onto the main structure. Internal divisions were observed in both the east and west wings. These internal walls, all 0.4m wide, were comprised of flint and broken brick, bonded in an irregular pattern. Alongside the east wall of the east wing a row of three pits or post holes was observed. These features were similar to the tree-pits forming Avenue [1558], which traversed the west 'wing' of this structure. Although these pits could have marked the east side of that avenue, the row did not appear to continue beyond the structure, through the large spread of post medieval material which covered an area approximately 70 × 30m. The ground within the confines of these walls was darker in colour and more silty in texture than the surrounding spread of debris.

Entrance (1208 & 1210)

In the course of investigating what was thought to be a back-filled extraction pit, a square rubble filled feature was located. This turned out to be one of a pair of heavily robbed out 'gate towers' that flanked the former entrance to the inner courtyard of Tyttenhanger manor. Each of these will be described separately below.

Eastern gate tower 1208

Despite the thorough robbing of this structure it was possible to reconstruct its foundation plan. The building had an overall measurement of 4.5m north-south by 4.2m east-west and was set some 3.4m from the entrance to the west (Fig. 28). The lowest brick was set 1.25m below the existing gravel surface. Part of the westernmost foundation survived *in situ* [1205]. This consisted of an English bonded wall comprising brick, floor and roof tiles (Plates 11-15). The bricks were a weak red colour, unfrogged and measured 230 x 120 x 55mm. The south part of the wall was 0.36m wide while its northern end which was 0.46m wide butted onto [1083]. Elsewhere the wall had been completely robbed out and it was clear from what was left behind that the robbers were interested only in bricks. On the north eastern side of the structure, the wall had originally abutted onto a massive masonry footing [1207]. This consisted of mainly flint, broken bricks, tile and occasional clunch and measured 1.33m wide by 2.8m long. At least 0.9m remained *in situ*; its original depth below ground level would have been of the order of c. 1.5m (Plate 15). This foundation did not project beyond the gate tower footings, so presumably access was gained from within the interior of the courtyard as one might expect. The western buttress [1209] was of similar dimensions though its depth was shallower at 0.4m below the gravel surface (the original depth would have been c.1m). Projecting from this massive foundation the gate tower or 'house' would have had an internal area of 2.7m x 3.4m. From the centre of this building a dark, burnt, ashy layer was mechanically removed [1204]. This contained bones belonging to small animals and fowls, oyster shells, mussels and an assemblage of pottery (Plate 24). Whittingham suggests that the assemblage could belong to the early part of the 16th century (Appendix 1.3).

Western gate tower 1210

This western gate tower which post dated [1531] was even more heavily robbed than the eastern gate tower [1208] (Plate 17). It lay 3.1m to the west from the entrance and 9.2 distant from the eastern gate tower. It was butted by two massive foundations [1221 & 1223] at its northern end but there was no sign of the clunch wall [1083]. Apart from a few fragments of tile and a single brick its plan could only be discerned by tracing the extent of a mortary spread. This gave an overall dimension of about 4.3 x 4.5m or internally 3.5m x 2.5m. The robbed out foundation was at least 1m below the existing gravel level, which suggests it was about 1.5m below the original ground surface. At the base of the 'gate tower' an irregular hearth like deposit was also mechanically removed [1213]. This was similar to hearth [1204] though it contained fragments of flat window glass. When the back-fill from the robbed wall trench [1214] was manually excavated several moulded brick fragments were recovered (Plate 22). The pottery is believed to belong to the early 16th century (Appendix 1.3). The principal courtyard structure [1529] cut across Building [1530].

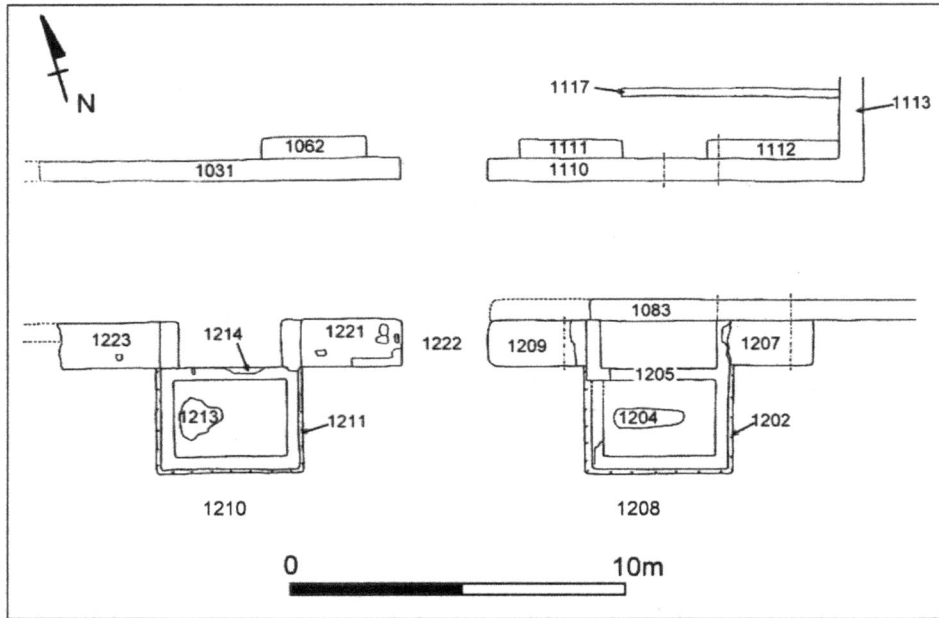

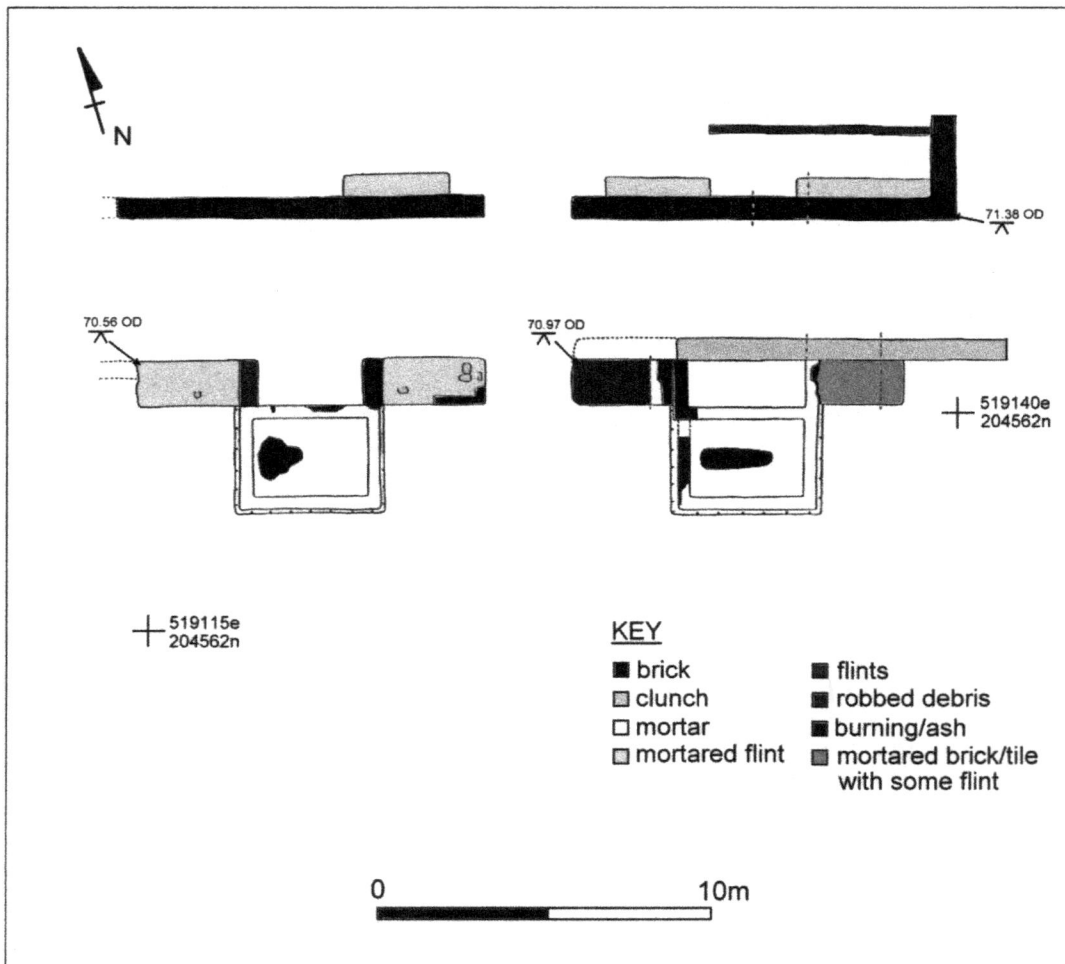

Fig. 28: Detail of composition of the entrance to inner courtyard [1208] & [1210]

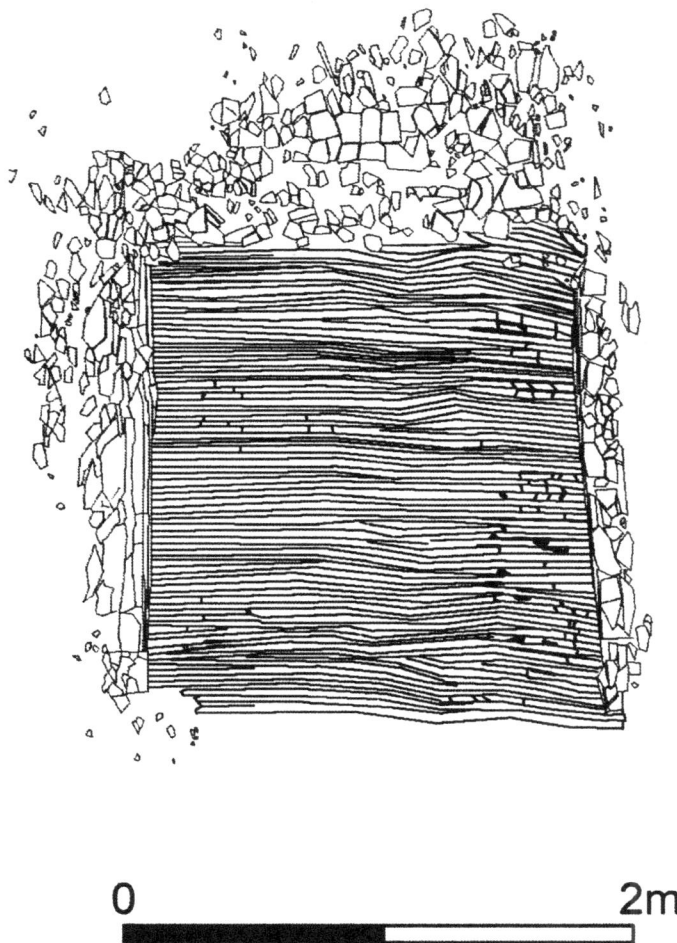

Fig. 29: Plan of hearth or kiln base [1534]

However, its western side had been truncated by Wall [1546], and the pits forming Avenue [1558] also cut across it. The inner courtyard complex was probably destroyed when Sir Henry Blount partly demolished the old manor in 1620 (Smith 1992, 148), completing the demolition and building the present house in the second half of the 17th century (Koughnet 1895, 51).

Building 1530 (Figs 6 & 30)
[1530] was located at TL 19135 04579 (Fig. 6). It was rectangular in plan, measured 10m long by 6m wide, and was sub-divided by an east-west internal wall. Its walls were 0.3m in width and were constructed of flint. Inside the building was collapse debris and the patchy remains of a chalk/mortar floor surface. The structure continued northwards, beyond the site limits.

PHASE 4: EARLY POST-MEDIEVAL (1540-1620)

Hearth or Kiln Base 1534 (Figs 6, 29, 30)
[1534] was located towards the western side of the site at NGR TL 19075-04772 (Figs 6 and 29). It consisted of a rectangular tile built structure with an overall measurement of 2.4m x 2m and aligned approximately north south (Plate 1). The floor of the feature comprised a layer of tipped tiles laid at a sloping angle of about 20° from north to south and bonded with a sandy mortar. The tiles were on average 290 x 180 x 10mm and had a pair of holes for fixing them with nails to the roof laths. The tile floor was 2m wide and consisted of 68 rows with between 10 and 11 tiles per row. The tile walls were built directly on the tipped tile floor, 0.21m wide thereby creating an area no more than 1.62m wide. Only two of three courses of tile wall survived so it is impossible to estimate how high the original walls would have been. At its northern end there was what appeared to be a wider tile wall which rose in a series of shallow steps. This was no more than 0.6m wide but it was too badly preserved to enable a reconstruction to be made with any degree of certainty. At the north east corner of this feature was an isolated area of iron slag (0.5m dia) and between 2.3m and 2.9m from the edge of the tile floor were several more isolated areas of iron slag. This feature was sealed by a layer of greyish brown clay containing pottery that gave a spot date of between 1480-1600.

PHASE 5 LATER POST-MEDIEVAL (1620-1775)

This phase of the site saw the demolition of the old late medieval courtyard building [1529] and its replacement with the present day house. The ancillary buildings to the south were also demolished and the ground turned into a formal garden containing small brick built structures, gravel walks and avenues. The ancillary buildings were replaced by stables and outhouses to the east of the 17th century house; while some 200m to the south a home farm (Homestall) developed.

Ditches (Fig 14)

In Field 'A' two ditches followed a slightly different alignment to the late medieval enclosure complex. They appeared to represent the east and west boundaries of an area containing a later set of agricultural buildings, positioned over the southern boundaries of the enclosure complex. These two ditches probably date to the late 17th to early 18th centuries.

Ditch 1504 (Figs 8, 13 &14)

Ditch [1504] was roughly parallel with and to the east of Ditch [1501] at TL 19066 04440 (Fig. 8). It ran northwards from Ditch [1503], terminating in a butt-end after 27m. Its relationship with [1503] was unclear, though it is presumed to be later in origin than [1503]. Ditch [1504] had a 'U'-shaped section, 1.7m wide by 0.65m deep, and probably represented the eastern limit of the farmstead area. It was later superseded by a fence line [1551], positioned approximately one metre to the east. A length of east-west wall [166-7], part of a possible building [1543] was found to be reinforced where it crosses the ditch (Fig. 8).

Gully 1517 (Figs 8 & 14)

To the west of Building [1542] was a narrow gully [1517], orientated NNE-SSW (Fig. 8). It was traced for 50m and ran parallel to Ditch [1504]. This gully was only 0.30m wide by 0.10m deep and cut across Ditch [1506]. Although no direct dating evidence was recovered from this feature, it defines the western limit of the 17th/18th-century farmstead [1542].

Ditch 1519 (Figs 8 & 14)

Ditch [1519] was located on the west side of Field 'A', at TL 19235 94504 (Fig. 14). It was orientated NNE-SSW, and measured 0.86m wide. As its fill was similar to the natural subsoil, it could only be traced for some 15m. No archaeological finds were recovered from this feature. This ditch is not shown on maps of the estate. However, its orientation was similar to Wall [1546], suggesting a date of 17th to early 18th century.

Walls (Fig 31)

Wall 1546 (Figs 7, 8, 30 & 31)

One of the most substantial walls on the site was [1546]. It was orientated NNE-SSW, and ran 130m from the northern limits of the site through the excavation area, in the middle of the earlier ditch enclosure (Fig. 30), terminating at Building [1541]. It also continued northwards towards the house, beyond the area of investigation. About one metre south of the north edge of the site, there was a 3m-wide gap in Wall 1546, possibly a gateway (Fig. 31). Structurally this wall had two phases, on slightly different alignments. The earlier wall [206] can only be observed running slightly to the west of the later wall [1026] (Fig. 7) some 52m south of the north boundary of the site, where the courses of the two phases begin to diverge (Plate 4). Little remained of the earlier wall, which was represented by a 'robber' trench, approximately 0.40-0.55m in width, with some collapsed brick and mortar deposits in its backfill. This feature was almost imperceptible towards the southern end of the wall, measuring less than 0.05m in depth. It cut through one of the tree holes for any early avenue and was therefore constructed after [1557]. The later, more substantial wall, was also extensively robbed out for most of its length (Fig. 31), surviving only to the north of the point where Wall [1547] butts onto it. North of this point, the wall stood to at least three courses high, and was 0.55 to 0.60m wide. It was well-bonded with lime mortar and constructed with alternate header to header and stretcher to stretcher courses (English bond). Evidence was observed of three small brick buttress on the west side of the wall. This phase of the wall represents the eastern boundary of a small enclosure formed with Wall [1547].

Wall 1546 cut Structure [1532] and truncated the west corner of Structure [1529]. In turn, it was cut by service trenches [1565] and [1566]. No direct dating evidence was recovered from this wall, but its composition and its stratigraphic relationship with other structures suggests that the length south of Wall [1547] was probably robbed-out in the late 17th century, when the present house was constructed. The northern part of the wall remained beyond this date, form part of an enclosure in the north-west corner of the field. It is harder to determine the date of the earlier phase of this wall. It seems unlikely that there was a wall in this position during the main phase of tile production, in the late medieval/ post-medieval period. Therefore, this earlier phase of the wall may have been part of the formal gardens in the 17th century.

Wall 1547 (Figs 7, 30 & 31)

Wall [1547] butts onto the [1546] to form the southern boundary to a trapezoid enclosure in the north-western corner of Field 'A' (Fig. 31). This enclosure covers an

Present Tyttenhanger House

N

1539

1530

1529

1532

1534

1535

1548

1547

1531

1533

1549

1536

1524

1546

1518

1523

1525

1505

1522

1526

1540

1501

1501

1541

1543

1500

1517

1544

1520

1502

1506

1545

1504

1542

1503

0   75m

Fig. 30: Building and ditch groups

35

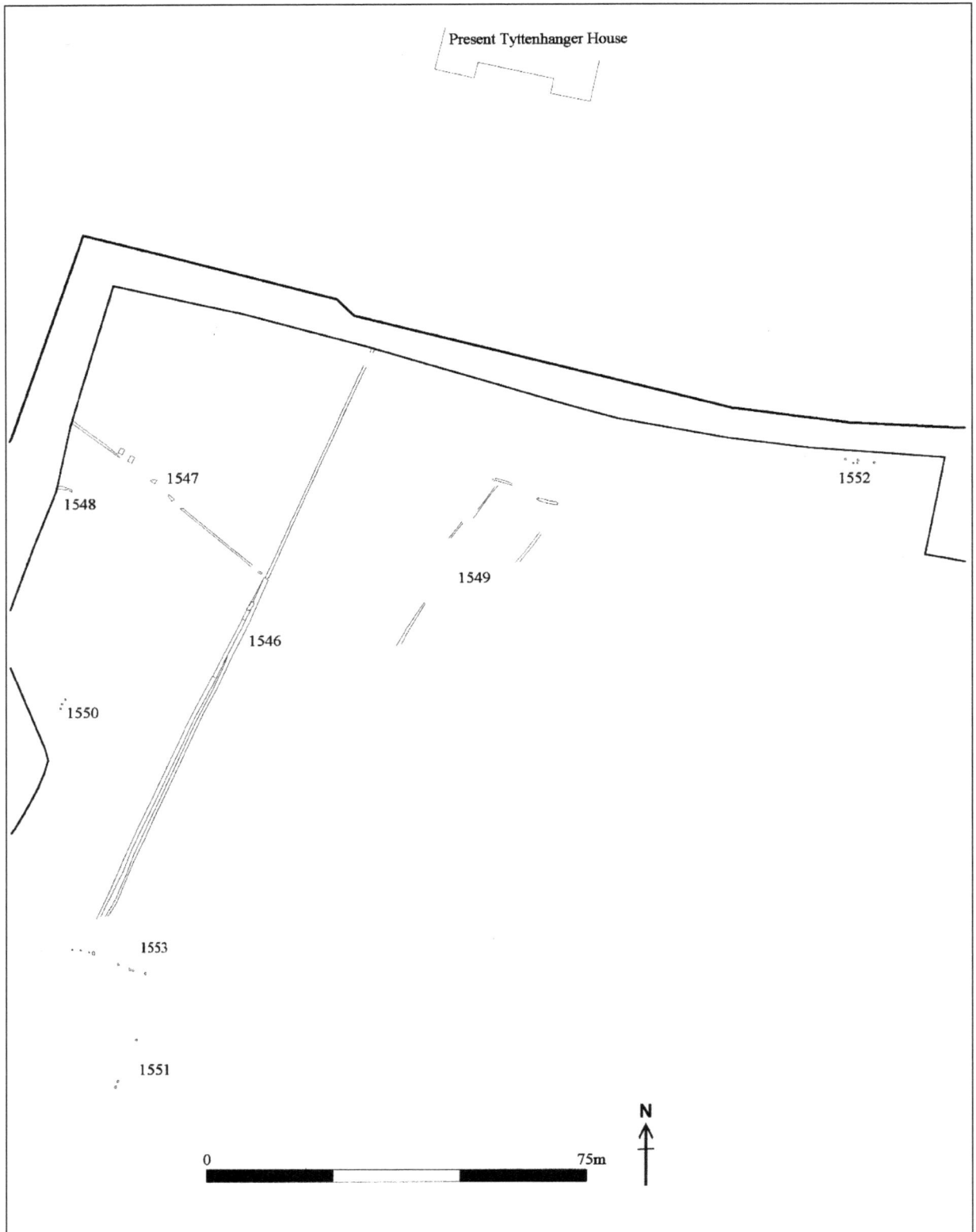

Fig. 31: Wall and fence groups

area of one acre, and is shown on the late 18th-century estate plan. [1547] measured 0.44m wide, was orientated north-west to south-east, and was traced for 50m. It was less substantially constructed than Wall [1546], and had fragmented along its length. Its structure consisted of reddish bricks measuring 210 × 110 × 80mm, laid as two rows of stretcher to stretcher, bonded with lime mortar. Two courses survived intact. Some fragments of tile were also observed within the matrix of this wall. The poor quality of this wall suggests it was probably not as tall as the more substantial Wall [1546].

Brick Platforms 1072 & 1073 (Fig. 6)

Two rectangular brick platforms [1072] and [1073] immediately to the north of this wall may represent buttresses, garden ornamentation or the position of steps. They each measured 1.5m in length and 1.0m in width, and were constructed from reddish bricks, 230 ×110 × 50mm, set in lime mortar. The bonding pattern appeared to be slightly irregular, and only two courses remained in situ. Within the limits of this enclosure was a large flower bed [1554], a possible small rectangular garden structure [1534], a garden brick base [1539], the western half of Structure [1532],and disturbed natural brickearth. These features suggest the enclosure was part of a discrete garden complex that may have survived after the gardens to the south of the house had been emparked.

Wall 1548 (Fig 31)

A short length of east-west wall [1548] was observed on the west side of the site, south of wall [1547], at TL 19052 04560 (Fig. 31). This structure was 4.0m long and 0.50m wide. Only one or two courses of poorly mortared bricks survived, and no clear bonding pattern was observed. The alignment of this wall was the same as the present house, and it does not appear to relate to the other walls and structures in this field. Interpretation of this feature is difficult, as such a short length was exposed. However, it appears to relate to a large rectangular spread of debris, which was encountered in an evaluation trench 10m to the west of this section of wall. The features in the evaluation trench were dated to the late 18th/19th century and appear to relate to the pump house 30m to the south-west (Percival & Richmond 1996, 13).

Fence lines

The post-holes left by fence lines are often difficult to trace across areas with a high concentration of similar structural features. Dating can also be a problem, as artefacts are rarely found in these small features, unless they have been used as packing for the post. However, four potential fence lines in Field 'A' have been tentatively identified.

Post hole alignment 1550 (Fig. 31)

A north-south line of three post holes [1550] was located at the eastern terminus of Ditch [1518] at TL 19055 04515 (Fig. 31). The post holes were each 0.2m in diameter, regularly spaced at 0.8m intervals. This fence line was traced for only 3.0m. These features were not associated with any other structural remains, and probably formed some sort of internal division of the enclosure complex in Field 'A'.

Post hole alignments 1551 & 1553 (Fig. 31)

A similar post hole alignment [1551] was located at TL 19068 04435, to the east of Ditch [1504]. The post holes were 0.25-0.30m in diameter. This alignment was traced for 11m, and was orientated at right angles to yet another post-hole alignment [1553] to the north. Although no direct dating evidence was recovered from these features, their alignment and location suggest that they are associated with the later agricultural buildings to the west, and not to the ditched enclosure complex. It is probable that this fence line was established to redefine the eastern extent of the group of agricultural buildings, after Building [1543] was constructed over Ditch [1504]. Associated with [1551] was a WNW-ESE alignment of eight post holes [1553], centred at TL 19064 04460, and traced for some 16m. The diameters of these sub-circular features ranged from 0.2 to 0.3m. This line of post holes cuts across Ditch [1501] and was broadly at right-angles to Fence [1551]. These features probably date from the late 17th to early 18th century, and do not belong to the earlier ditched enclosure.

Post hole alignment 1552 (Fig. 31)

At the northern edge of the site, centred at TL 19206 04570, was a rough east-west alignment of features [1552], 4.2m in length (Fig. 31). This comprised three post holes, each 0.3m square, set at 1.4m centres, with two sub-circular features, each 0.2m diameter, offset 0.4m to the south. This group of features probably represents an earlier fenced boundary between the grounds immediately around the house and Field 'A'. Although no dateable artefacts were recovered from any of these contexts, they probably date from the later part of the post-medieval period.

Tree Avenues

Two alignments of shallow sub-circular features, [1557] and [1558], were observed in Field 'A' (Fig. 32). Initially these appeared to be alignments of post holes forming fence lines across the site. However, there was no evidence in any of these features for packing or the presence of a 'post-pipe'. Instead, it seems likely that they were pits for planting lines of trees, to form avenues or walk-ways. Although both lines are similar in nature, they represent different phases of activity.

Tree Avenue 1557 (Fig. 32)

The earliest line of tree-pits [1557] was traced for 132m, following a north-south alignment across the excavation area. The individual sub-circular pits were approximately 1.5m in diameter, and were positioned at approximately 6.0m intervals. This alignment was truncated by Wall [1546], and in one pit in the line cuts Kiln [1525]. Although no dateable material was recovered from these pits, their relationship to other dated features suggests them to be of late 16th to 17th-century date.

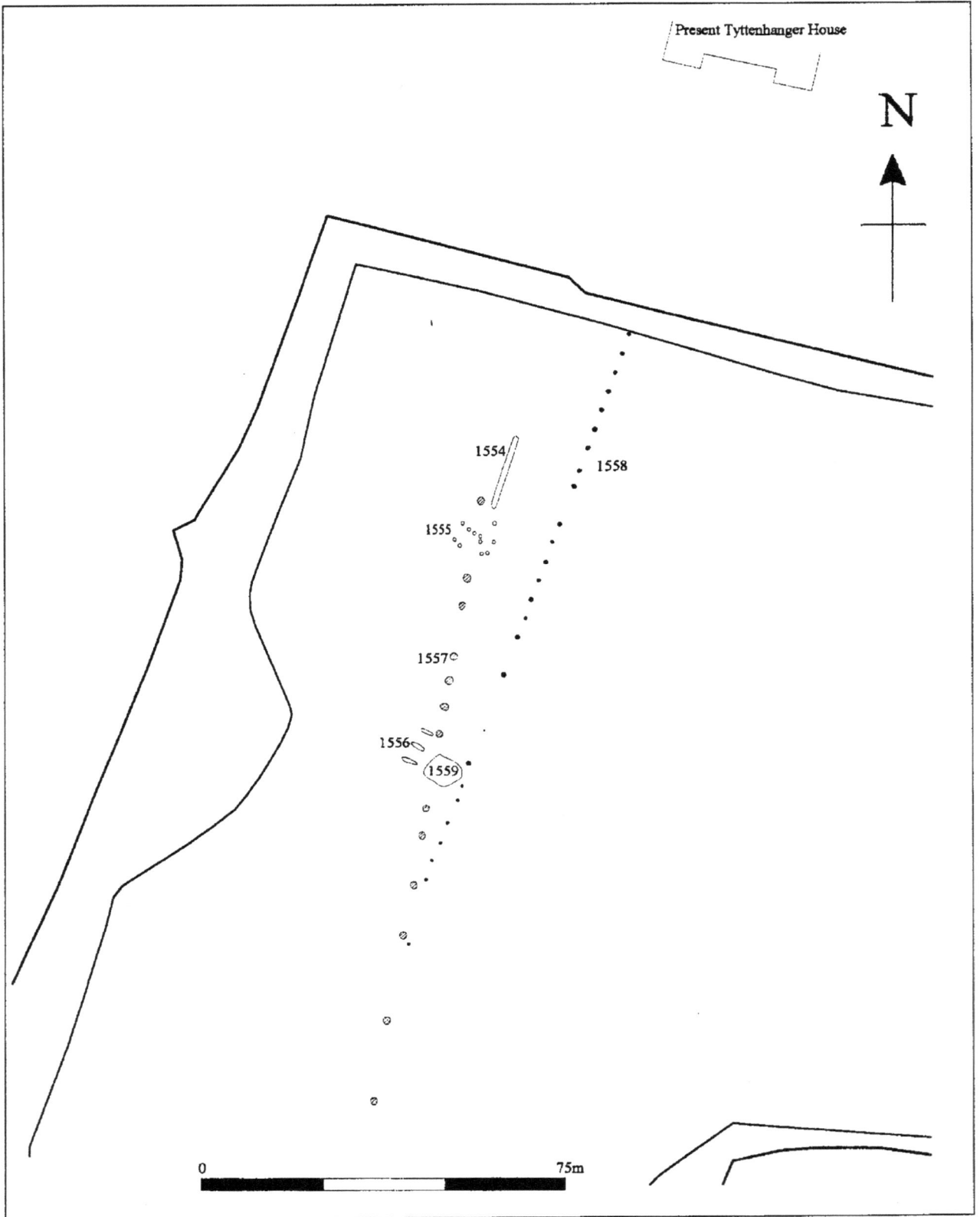

Fig. 32: Garden landscape groups

Tree Avenue 1558 (Figs 33 & 32)

Another line of sub-circular features [1558], following a NNE-SSW alignment, was also investigated crossing the excavation area for some 140m (Fig. 32). The features were 1.02m in diameter and 0.27m deep, regularly spaced at 5.0m intervals. The dark silty fills of these features displayed less evidence of leaching than the greyer fills of [1557]. Although no dating material was recovered from any of these features, pits in this line cut Ditch [1501], and Structures [1529], [1531] and [1536], suggesting that this alignment of features dates to the late 17th to early 18th century, predating the emparking of this land. Three similar pits were observed cutting through the east side of Structure [1529], possibly representing the east side of a tree avenue. Together with [1558], this avenue would have been 30m across.

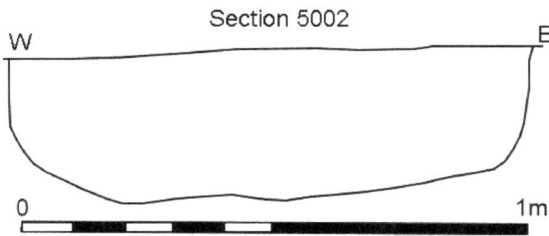

Section 5002

Fig 33: Section from Tree Avenue [1558]

Garden Features

Apart from avenues of trees, most garden features by their very nature are ephemeral and difficult to extrapolate from other archaeological features. However, several features in Field 'A' appear to relate to a formal garden south of the house:

Planting Bed 1554 (Fig. 32)

A linear planting bed [1554] was located to the west of Wall [1546] at TL 19092 04560 (Fig. 32). This feature was aligned NNE-SSW, and measured 18m in length and 1.4m in width. The orientation of this bed was similar to Avenue [1558]. The fill of [1554] was a dark humic silt, containing no archaeological finds.

Planting Beds 1556 (Figs 32 & 34)

A series of three smaller east-west planting beds [1556] was located in the middle of the excavation area, centred on TL 19080 04495. Each bed was linear, with rounded butt ends. The individual beds were 4.0m long, 0.47m wide and 0.14m deep, and were spaced at approximately 5.0m intervals. No dateable archaeological material was recovered from these features.

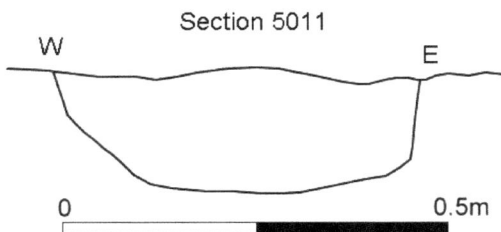

Section 5011

Fig. 34: Section of Planting Bed [1556]

Sub-circular features 1555 (Fig. 32 & Fig 35)

A group of eleven similar-sized sub-circular features [1555] was noted at the south-eastern end of Wall [1547], where it joins onto Wall [1546]. They were similar in nature to those in Avenue [1558] but, unlike the latter, they formed a discrete cluster, covering an area approximately 10m in diameter. These features ranged from 0.50 to 0.78m in diameter, and were 0.12m in depth. Unfortunately, all their fills were devoid of dateable material. These features do not appear to be structural, and probably formed a part of the formal gardens.

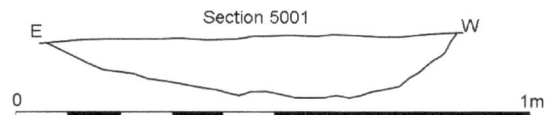

Section 5001

Fig. 35: Garden Feature [1555]

Sub-Circular Hollow 1559 (Fig. 32)

Another possible garden feature was [1559], a large sub-circular hollow which measured 11m in diameter and only 0.57m deep. This feature was located in the middle of the excavation area at TL 19088 04490 (Fig. 32). The hollow was located 2.0m east of the planting beds [1556], to the west of Avenue [1558] and possibly cutting into one of the tree holes of Avenue [1557] to the west. This feature also cuts through the corner of Ditch [1501]. The backfill of this feature was the product of both natural silting and deliberate dumps of dark grey silt containing some small fragments of post-medieval tile and brick. The primary fill of this feature appeared to be leached, suggesting that the hollow had held standing water for some time. Although no dating evidence was recovered from this feature, its stratigraphic relationship to others suggests it was in use during the 17th to mid 18th centuries. The hollow was definitely man-made, but appeared to be too shallow for an extraction pit. Furthermore, there was not enough rubbish observed within the backfill of this feature to interpret this hollow as a refuse pit. It appears more likely that it was part of the formal gardens, possibly a flower bed or a robbed-out water feature.

Brick Structures

Kiln?/Planting Bed? 1536 (Figs 6 & 30)

A rectangular structure [1536] aligned WNW-ESE, with the remains of a robbed out wall on its west side, was located at TL 19105 04548 in Field 'A' (Figs 6 & 30). It was 4.6m long, 2.8m wide and 0.8m deep. Its fill consisted of large flints and clay with some lumps of chalk, overlaid by dark humic silt. It might be the remains of a robbed-out kiln or the base deposit for a bed for garden plants. The pits forming Avenue [1558] cut into this feature. The robbed-out wall on the west side of this feature consisted of large irregular flints, poorly mortared together, and measured 2.65 × 0.40m.

Planting Bed 1533 (Figs 6 & 30)
Structure [1533] was located at TL 19119 04555 (Figs 6 & 30). It was orientated WNW-ESE, and consisted of a thin wall of decayed brick with no evidence of mortar bonding. The wall around the east side of this feature had been robbed out, but its plan was still discernible. The structure measured 6.00 × 3.08m, and was 1.8m deep (Richmond & Percival 1996, fig. 5, sec.033). Internally, it was filled with a highly mixed deposit of silt, clay, and cess dumps, with some flecks of charcoal. The poor quality of the surrounding wall indicated that this was not a very substantial structure. The nature of the fill suggests this may have been a bedding feature, in which had been buried some organic waste from the house. This feature was probably of 17th-century date.

Planting Bed 1534 (Figs 6 & 30)
In the north-west corner of Field 'A' at TL 19075 04571 was an 'L'-shaped structure measuring 3.55 × 2.20m (Figs 6 & 30), with walls 0.23m wide [1534]. It was poorly constructed of mortared tiles, and only its north and west walls survived. A deposit of sandy silt was observed inside the structure, with a deposit of burnt material butting up to the north face of the north wall. Its small size and simple construction may indicate that it was once the foundation for a raised garden bed.

Planting Bed 1535 (Figs 6 & 30)
A sub-rectangular feature [1535], aligned NW-SE, was located at TL 19065 04565, butting up to the south side of Wall [1547] (Figs 6 & 30). The southern and eastern sides of this structure had been extensively robbed-out, making it difficult to establish its full extent. The surviving walls were 0.4m in width, and enclosed an area 4.35 × 2.72m. These walls were constructed from large irregular flints, chalk and tile, set in a poor lime mortar. This feature may be a garden bed.

Column plinth 1539 (Figs 6 & 30)
A possible column plinth [1539] was observed at TL 19110 04588 (Figs 6 & 30). This square structure was 0.65m square, and consisted of single course of brickwork. The centre of the feature contained a dark silty fill, from which a sherd of 16th-century pottery was recovered. The insubstantial nature of this structure indicates that it may be a garden feature. Its small size was reminiscent of a base for a decorative column or statue.

Dovecote 1540 (Figs 7, 30 & 36)
Another similar but slightly larger feature [1540] was located at TL 19102 04490 (Figs 7 & 30). It appeared to be aligned with Building [1522] to the north, but was not directly related to it. The feature was 1.2m square and 0.3m deep (Plates 6 and 18). Its walls were constructed from large irregular flints, set in a lime mortar. The eastern wall extended south of the structure for 0.2m. The inside of the structure was filled with a dark sandy silt containing small bird bones (Appendix 1.8 Table 7). Charcoal flecks and corroded iron nails were also

observed in the top of the backfill. Animal remains of both juvenile and adult doves indicated that these birds were breeding here. It appears this may be a part of a structure for keeping birds, such as an exterior bird cage or dovecote, probably dating to the 17th to 18th centuries.

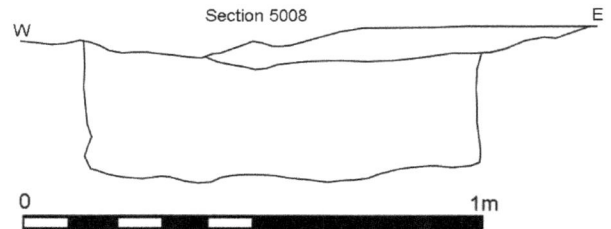

Fig. 36: Section from Structure [1540]

Miscellaneous Structures
During the project several structures additional to those described above were located and recorded. However, the function of some of these structures was difficult to determine from their form alone.

Structure 1541 (Figs 8 & 30)
At the south end of Wall [1546], was a 'U'-shaped arrangement of brick walls [1541] at TL 19060 04468 (Figs 8 & 30). This structure was aligned WNW-ESE, with walls surviving on the north, east and south sides. It measured 6.0m wide and over 5.5m in length: its walls were 0.4m wide, with only one course of brick surviving. At the west end of the north and south walls, large irregular flints had been used instead of bricks in its construction. There was no evidence of a floor surface inside the structure. Its size was indicative of a shed or storage area. An extensive sub-rectangular spread of late 17th and early 18th-century debris surrounded this feature.

Structure 1538 (Fig. 9)
A rectangular brick base [1538] measuring 3.3 × 1.6 m and orientated WNW-ESE was located at the northern limits of Field 'A' at TL 19221 04570 (Fig. 9). The brick base and the first course of the walls remained on its north, west and south sides. The interior of this feature was filled with post-medieval rubble and mortar fragments, which obscured the bonding patterns of the brick base. The individual reddish bricks forming the structure measured 230 × 110 × 50mm. An irregular spread of collapsed building debris was observed on the south side of this structure. This feature appears to be of a later date than most of the other structures on the site, and may represent a small base for a boiler associated with archaeologically ephemeral structures such as greenhouses.

Structure 1537 (Fig. 9)
A rectangular concentration of large flints [1537] was recorded in the north-east corner of Field 'A' at TL 19270 04560 (Fig. 9). This feature, measured 5.5 × 2.2m, and was orientated east-west. The flints were large and sub-angular, with no evidence of bonding or mortar. However, this feature appeared regular, compared to the

surrounding matrix of natural small sub-rounded natural gravels. It also appeared to relate to a large sub-circular pit, 3.0m in diameter, situated 3.5m to the south west. This feature lay outside the main area of the formal gardens, and appears to represent the base of a small outbuilding associated with the group of buildings that existed to the east of the present house in the late post medieval period.

Agricultural Buildings

Features at the south end of the excavation area in Field 'A' appeared to represent a series of agricultural buildings. These structures did not appear to respect the layout of the earlier ditch enclosures. It is thought that they belong to a small farmstead constructed sometime in the 17th century. This group of buildings was located in an area defined to the west by Ditch [1517] and to the east by Fence Line [1504]. The structures were located around a cobbled surface, covered by a large spread of demolition debris containing the bones of cattle, sheep, horses and pigs.

Building 1542 (Figs 8, 30 & 37)
The clearest evidence for a large agricultural building in the southern limits of the excavation area was Structure [1542]. This apparently square building overlay Ditch Group [1506] (Figs 8 & 30). The structure was defined by a series of large postholes on the east side, debris from a robbed-out wall on its south side and some smaller post holes on its west and north sides. The building measured 22m in length and 20m in width, and was on a similar alignment to Wall [1546]. Inside the structure were the remains of a robbed-out hearth, situated just north of the centre of the building. The hearth walls were 0.4m wide, consisting of lime mortar with some brick and tile debris, forming an 'H' in plan. The hearth measured 1.6 × 0.9m. A burnt reddish deposit was observed on the east side of this series of walls. A cobbled yard surface [216] was constructed against the west side of the building. This patchy surface measured 14.0 × 1.83m, and was constructed with a range of sub-circular cobbles and flints. A rectangular pit [193] had been cut through this surface. The pit was 2.50 × 1.15m across, and contained some tile fragments and cattle bone, the latter comprising leg bones from a wide age range of animals (Appendix 1.8). A drain ran along the north side of the building and around its west end, flowing westwards into Ditch [1506]. The drain was constructed from bricks bonded with mortar set on a tile base, forming a channel 0.46m wide. Only one course of brick survived. The cobble surface along the west side of the building overlay this drain run.

Section 5026, Building 1542

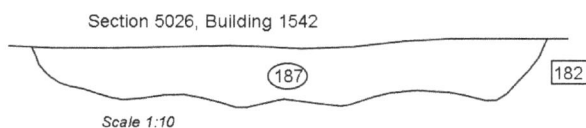

Scale 1:10

Fig. 37: Section from Building [1542]

Structure 1544 (Fig 8 & Fig 30)
A group of five post holes [1544] on the north side of Building [1542], extending northwards over a group of earlier pits, indicated the presence of another structure (Fig 8 & Fig 30). The post holes ranged in diameter from 0.3m to 0.6m: two of them contained tile packing around a central post-pipe. One post hole cut into Ditch [1505]. If this structure butted onto Building [1542], its estimated size would be 12 × 8m. To the east of this building was a cobbled yard surface [1545]. A narrow gully [1520] running along the western edge of the yard may have been intended to take 'run-off' water from the roof.

Structure 1543 (8 & 30)
The presence of a third possible building in this complex, centred at TL 19060 04460, was implied by two fragments of a wall [166 & 167] which survived where they had built with deeper footings to cross the infilled Ditches [1501] and [1504] (Figs 8 & 30). This possible structure [1543] was orientated WNW-ESE and measured 16 × 5m. The north side of this building may have been formed by Fence Line [1553].

Agricultural Yard Surface 1545 (Fig 30)
A patchy area of dense cobbling [1545] was centred at TL 19054 04445 (Fig. 30). It covered an area 6 × 5m, and appeared to be a yard surface associated with the surrounding post-medieval agricultural buildings. Alternatively, it could have been associated with the earlier ditch complex, as it extended between Ditches [1501] and [1505], which formed the entrance corridor. However, this cobbling was not present elsewhere in the length of the corridor, and finds from the layer of silt above the yard surface were dated to the late 17th century. Along the western edge of this yard a narrow gully [1520], 0.40m wide and 0.12m deep, was traced following a NNE-SSW alignment for a distance of 9.0m, towards the drain around Building [1542]. As well as draining the yard, this gully may have also taken rainwater run-off from the roof of Structure [1544].

Agricultural Pits 1564 (Fig. 39)
To the north of Building [1542] was a group of three pits [1564], centred at TL 19050 04466, (Fig. 39) which appeared to be associated with the adjacent complex of agricultural buildings. The largest pit [148] was rectangular, measuring 5.0 × 2.3m across and 0.4m deep. It was orientated north-south and had vertical sides and a flat base. Its backfill comprised a mixture of post-medieval brick and tile debris, with greyish-brown soil and a large amount of mortar. One metre to the north of this feature was a sub-circular pit [164], measuring 1.4 × 1.5m across. It had a very dark grey silty loam fill, which was devoid of archaeological finds. The third pit [159] was located 5.0m north of Pit [148], and was 2.5 × 2.3m across. It contained at least two fills: a band of loam 0.4m wide around the inside edge of the feature, with a deposit of sandy silt in the centre of the pit. It is possible that this pit was a well, serving the requirements of the adjacent buildings. Although few closely dateable finds were

recovered from these pits, the nature of the post-medieval building debris within their fills, coupled with their relationship to the adjoining buildings, suggest that these features are likely to date to the late 17th to early 18th centuries. A possible structure over these pits was indicated by the presence of five adjacent post holes [1544].

The Barn 1521 (Fig 9)
A large rectangular barn [1521] was located in Field 'A' at TL 19255 04540 (Fig. 9). This building was orientated NNE-SSW on a similar alignment to the present house, and measured 19.7 × 6.9m (Plate 6). Its walls were 0.4m wide, constructed of tile and bricks with little evidence of mortar. This relatively slight construction suggests that these walls probably formed the base for a timber-framed building. Tree root activity appeared to have undermined the south-western corner of the structure. The entrance to the building was 3.0m wide, and was located in the middle of its east wall. A coin dated 1700 was recovered from the soil within the entrance, consistent with the period of its use. This building was probably part of a group of outbuildings located to the east of the house. Some of these, to the north of the barn, survived into the late 19th century. However, this barn may have been demolished during the late 18th century, when the land to the south of the house was emparked.

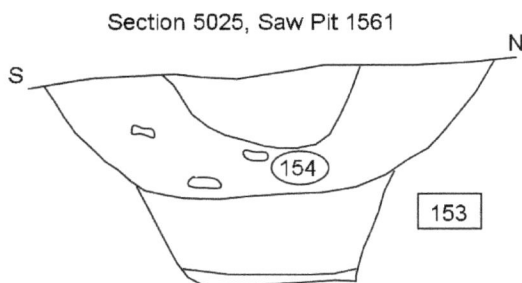

Fig. 38: Saw Pit [1561]

Saw Pit 1561 (Figs 38 & 39)
A large sub-rectangular pit with associated post holes [1561] was located at TL 19088 04449 (Fig. 39). It was orientated broadly east-west and measured 5.0 × 1.9m across and 0.8m deep (below the reduced level). The sides of the pit stepped down steeply to a flat base. A thin layer of silt had built up on the base of the feature, probably while it was in use. This was followed by deliberate backfilling of the pit, using redeposited gravel and silt. This feature is believed to have been a saw-pit. Pottery sherds, including large pieces of a glazed jug dating to between 1710 to 1760, and window lead fragments, were recovered from the base of this feature. This evidence is consistent with the area being converted into parkland in the second half of the 18th century. Two post holes, each 0.3m in diameter, were positioned to the west and south of the pit, at a distance of 2.0m its edge, suggesting the existence of a shelter, or possibly supports

for a platform for the sawyer to stand on. It was common for a house of the size of Tyttenhanger to have such features within their grounds, servicing the needs of the house and the estate. They were normally located close to workshops, rather than at-source in the woods (Wood 1968, 144).

Service Trenches 1566 (Fig 39)
A number of service trenches were located during the excavation. The oldest [1566] appeared to have carried a pipe supplying water to the mansion from the pump house, situated on the western boundary of Field 'A' (Fig. 39). This trench followed an erratic course, heading east from the pump house for 7.0m, then turning to the north-east for 72m, and curving northwards towards the house for the remaining 20m. It crossed eight other features: Wall [1547], Wall [1546], Structure [1531], Terrace [1529], Structure [1530], Flower Bed [1554], Avenue [1558]. This service trench pre-dates the 19th-century water pipe, and is probably of 18th-century origin.

PHASE 6 MODERN (1900 - PRESENT DAY)

Field boundary 1515 (Fig. 14)
Ditch [1515] formed the boundary between Fields 'A' and 'B'. It was orientated east-west and had been highly disturbed by tree root activity (Fig. 14). It was 2.0m wide, and was traced for 80m across the site, continuing beyond the limits of the extraction area. The orientation and nature of this feature suggests that it dates from the 18th century. However, cartographic evidence from the late 18th century shows this boundary but on a slightly different alignment, more in keeping with Ditch [1507]. The medieval ditch system observed in Field 'B' appeared to share the same orientation as this later boundary.

Pit 1562 (Fig 39)
A large irregular pit [1562] 16 × 6m and approximately 0.6m deep was located in the north-east corner of Field 'A' (TL 19210 04510; Fig. 39). Its dark silty fill consisted of a mix of burnt material and other soils. This pit had been used to dump domestic waste, including ceramic marmalade jars, glass bottles and various ceramic containers for pharmaceuticals. It appears to have ceased to be used in the early years of the 20th century (Appendix 1.7). This feature is probably one of many rubbish pits across the estate that served the house prior to the establishment of a formal refuse collection service in the 20th century

Burnt areas 1563 (Fig. 39)
Two roughly oval areas of burning [1563] were identified in Field 'A' (Fig. 39), 20m west of Pit [1562], at TL 19080 04514. The larger area measured 8m × 4m wide, and the smaller patch of burning was about 4m in diameter. Both areas consisted of patches of burnt gravel, and some of the stones in the centre of the patches were calcified, indicating an intense heat. However, there was

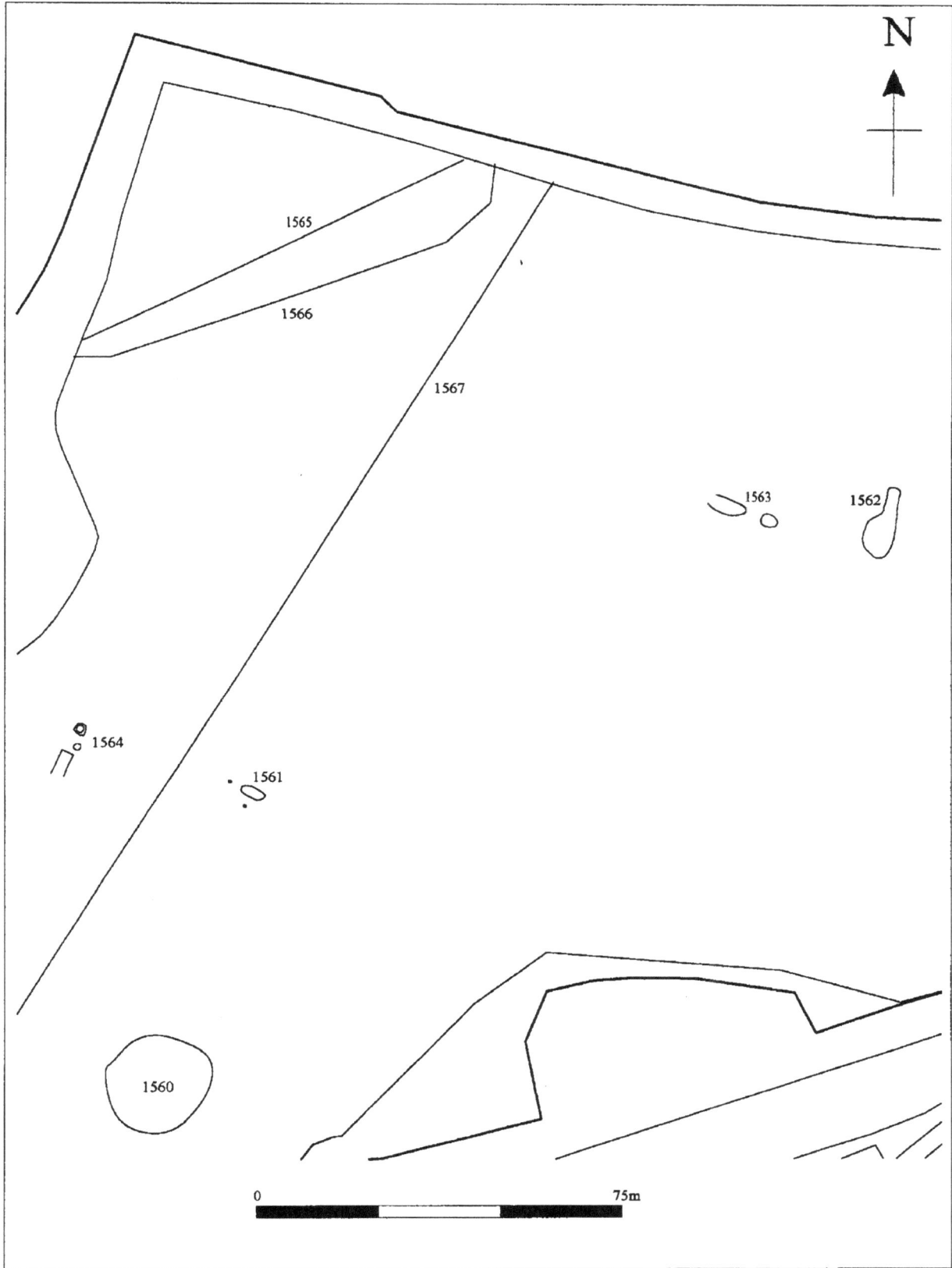

Fig.39: Miscellaneous groups

no evidence of residues associated with industrial processes. No archaeological artefacts were observed within either of these contexts, so dating was not possible. In addition, there was no structural evidence associated with these features. These could be the sites of 'brick clamps' for the firing of bricks or, alternatively, they could represent the sites of bonfires used to reduce the rubbish, prior to it being dumped into an adjacent pit [1562].

Services 1565 & 1567 (Fig 39)

The site was crossed by two modern service trenches, both of which related to the present house. The earlier water supply [1566] appears to have been superseded by a pipe following a more direct route [1565]. This trench was 0.4m wide, containing a cast-iron pipe of probably19[th] or early 20th-century date. It was located to the north of Trench [1566] and was orientated NE-SW, connecting the present house to the pump house. This feature was traced for a distance of 96m.

An electricity cable [1567], orientated NNE-SSW, crossed Fields 'A' and 'B'. The trench containing it was 0.5m wide, and was traced for some 365m, running from Bowmansgreen Farm across Field 'B and through the centre of the excavation area. The cable terminated at a sub station 20m east of the present house.

DISCUSSION

Interpretation of the evidence from this site has proved difficult, owing to the limited range of dateable finds recovered, and the absence of artefacts in the fills of many features. In addition, many features and structures on the site had been damaged by service trenches, agricultural activity and extensive phases of demolition and 'robbing' of building materials for sale or re-use outside the limits of the present site. However, it has been possible to establish a sequence of development from the relationships of the features and structures examined.

Early activity

Although the earliest archaeological finds on the site comprised various flint tools and flakes recovered from the periglacial gravel deposits, no archaeological features or artefactual assemblages associated with prehistoric settlement were observed within the confines of Field A. Similar finds were recovered during the evaluation trenches, and were also not associated with any occupational contexts (Percival and Richmond 1996, 17). The presence of these prehistoric flints equates to a background scatter of these objects carried to the area by palaeo-channels and river courses. Such artefacts are relatively common in gravel pits (Wood 1968, 256).

The landscape

In Field 'B', Ditches [1511-1516] represented a sequence of medieval field boundaries in an area that the evaluation showed as being devoid of archaeological deposits. These ditches formed a field system, consisting of long

narrow strips of land broadly orientated north-south. The process of enclosing strips of land for farming was common during the population expansion in the medieval period (Platt 1988, 42). In addition, the effects of partible inheritance could also lead to field sub-division (Roden 1969, 229). There was no evidence of occupation within these individual strip fields. The environmental evidence derived from the two corn dryers [1527, 1528] associated with this period indicates that wheat, oats and barley crops were being grown in the vicinity. It is plausible that this field system extended beyond the limits demonstrated in the archaeological record, as these features were difficult to identify within the disturbed gravel and brickearth subsoils. The eastern boundary [1514] associated with this system of ditches may have survived into the post medieval period.

Corn dryer [1528] was located in the south-east corner of one of these fields, and respects the orientation of the ditches around it. The two corn drying kilns appeared to be of a similar construction, but the northern dryer [1527] was less well preserved, having been truncated by Ditch [1507]. Both structures had a domed stoke-pit area on the east side of a narrow drying flue. The more complete kiln [1528] showed that the floor surface was supported by tiles above a duct. Both structures re-used Roman material in their construction and were dated to between the 1140-1300. The environmental analysis of the flue deposits pointed to wheat as the dominant cereal, but traces of barley, oats and possibly rye were also identified. A difference was observed in the type of fuel used for each of the dryers, with Kiln [1527] containing extensive evidence of large timbers of oak being burnt, while Kiln [1528] appears to have been fuelled by a variety of material including plants, straw and possibly the chaff from the cereals. There was also evidence that the cereals being dried in Kiln [1527] were cleaned before entering the kiln, but the cereals in Kiln [1528] may have not been fully processed. Snail shells extracted from these samples indicate that these structures stood in open country.

The kilns could have been used for two purposes, malting and/or drying the seed prior to grinding. This last process greatly facilitated the milling of corn, particularly in the case of hand milling (*quernpanes*). This practice was quite common in the medieval period, though the abbots tried to suppress the practice on their manors. For example, in his dispute with his manorial lord a certain Willemus de Tydenhangre claimed his ancient right of using 'manumolas' for a tenement in Holliwell Street in St Albans in about 1326-35 (Riley 1867, 249). In the survey of the manor of Tyttenhanger in 1331 there is specific mention of certain tenants who paid rent for the use of their own hand mills (B. Lib Add. Mss. 36237). It should be no surprise that these same tenants also possessed or shared their own crop drying kilns.

These structures may have been abandoned in the 13th/14th century, possibly in response to the many agricultural problems of this time, including poor weather conditions, low crop yields, and soil exhaustion (Platt 1988, 91-93), coupled with the series of plagues from 1348 to 1369, known as the 'Black Death' (Shrewsbury 1970). Destruction debris from the southern corn dryer was clearly visible within the medieval ditches around it, indicating that this early field system was also abandoned about the same time. Whether the demise of this field system and the abandonment of the kilns can be linked to a single event such as plague is debatable. Nevertheless, whatever caused this change it was of sufficient magnitude to break the traditional landholding pattern of the area. It might have been caused by the amalgamation of small landholdings on a piece meal basis or equally, by arrangement of the manorial lord. At present, we have only 'recovered' a fragment of the landscape at Tyttenhanger, so it is uncertain as to what extent this pattern may be applied to a wider area.

These early fields were superseded by a clearly defined field system [1507-10] on a different alignment, located in the west half of Field 'B'. The change of alignment of these later field boundaries is difficult to account for. It might reflect the presence of an earlier farm pre-dating that in Field B [1542], but this is by no means certain. This field system cut across the northern corn dryer. The ditches were deep, straighter, and wider than their earlier counter-parts. The north-eastern boundary of this field system appears to turn to avoid the large extraction hollow, suggesting that these fields were contemporary with, or later than, the tile production in the enclosure to the north. The establishment of a new field system may reflect the re-growth of agricultural prosperity in the late 15th century, or may simply be a response to the need to enlarge an existing holding (Platt 1988, 224: Roden 1973, 365).

THE MANORIAL SITE

The origins of the manor of Tyttenhanger, according to the *Victoria County History,* do not appear to pre-date the 14th century (Page 1908, 387). However, the earliest court roll material is dated to 1238 and it would be surprising if the estate was not even older (HALS: D/EB 2067.B M1). The fact that it was not mentioned in Domesday Book is not significant given that the majority of manors were recorded under the entry for St Albans. Nevertheless, if the manor was an Anglo-Saxon creation there is no direct evidence available. The parish of Rugge or Ridge, in which Tyttenhanger is situated, has all the characteristics of a typical pre-Conquest estate based upon a township unit. Ridge was originally a chapelry of St Peters and did not become a separate parish before the 14th century (Page 1908, 391; Youngs 1980, 241). The location of the church of St Margaret's would have been determined by the founding lord, in this case the abbot of St Albans. Interestingly, it was placed, more or less, in the centre of the parish. This is in contrast to the majority of lay endowments which show a strong preference for locating the new church close to an existing manorial centre. In the case of Tyttenhanger, the manor was situated towards the northern end of the parish and its territory extended into St Stephens, St Peters, Shenley and possibly North Mimms.

According to the historical record the manor was built between 1326-35 (Riley 1867, II, 371; Page 1908, 387). Whether this refers to an entirely new establishment is debatable, but until such time as any physical evidence is forthcoming the question must remain unanswered. The succeeding abbot (Michael) demolished the buildings and sold the materials (*ibid.*). To what extent that this involved the demolition of the entire manorial establishment is debatable. For example, while it is possible to demolish the living quarters, it is less practical to demolish the associated agricultural buildings. It makes sense to suppose that these would have been maintained for the purposes of managing the existing manorial estate. By the end of the 14th century there is mention of the construction of two barns and the commencement of rebuilding the manor by abbot John de la Moot (Riley 1867, III, 441). This work was completed in 1411 (Riley 1867, III, 448, 495). Contemporary sources say that 'hereupon' ditches and pools (fishponds) were dug out and stocked with fish: *'Deinde fossas et stagna erutare fecit, et copia diversorum pisciarum instauravit',* (*ibid.*). A survey of 1500 describes the site as a 'court' called '*le woolyard*' which is enclosed with park pales and contains dwellings, offices with stables and barns and '*le mote*' and '*fyshpond*'. The court with '*le mote*' contained 6.5 acres (HALS: D/EB 2067 B M.25; Appendix 1.13). This area coincides, almost precisely with the area recorded in the 1777 survey (HALS: D/ECd E39) and was first illustrated on a contemporary plan in the British Library (B. Lib Add Mss. 11317b). Also in the 1500 survey is mention of the first court called the '*lttzcort*' (little court) which contained buildings, barns, stables and others with a garden, which amounted to 3.5 acres.

The moat

During the course of investigating the area, it was apparent that there were some topographical features adjacent to Tyttenhanger House, which related to the archaeology of the site. Accordingly, it was felt desirable to undertake an earthwork survey in order to understand the site's landscape setting. The survey revealed an infilled moat to the west of the present house, some 5.0 to 6.0m in width. Another element of the moat was located to the east of the house in the old kitchen garden, where only the western side survived (Fig. 29). The presence of a moat gives credence to the theory that the earlier manor houses were situated in the vicinity of the present site, within the boundaries of the moat. The full extent of this feature is indicated on an estate plan of 1777 (HCRO PC 484). This shows water running around the west and north sides of the house, and beneath some outbuildings to the east, where it then re-emerges and flows northwards. The first record of fishponds at the manor dates to 1407, when Abbot William Heyworth completed the second manor house and stocked the fishponds (Riley 1869, 1495). The historical sources indicate that one fishpond, stocked with tench, was located 40m east of the present house in the kitchen garden by the east wall, and was in existence until the 19th century (Koughnet 1895,15). This pond was identified in the earthwork survey. The moat also appears to have been infilled at the beginning of the 19th century (Fowler, 1893, 35).

The deer park

Alongside such elements as fish ponds and moats, the deer park is a quintessential feature of the medieval seigniorial domain. They required a considerable amount of resources to create and maintain, and consequently were held by only the wealthiest individuals and institutions of medieval society. Their numbers, typology, function and distribution have been studied extensively in recent years (Birrel 1992; Cantor 1983; Rackham 1986; Stamper 1988). Nevertheless, despite the advances in research in recent years only a comparatively small number have been studied on an individual basis. Before proceeding to describe the boundary of the deer park at Tyttenhanger it is relevant to place it in its wider social and spatial context.

The abbot of St Albans was the premiere ecclesiastical lord in Hertfordshire and, arguably, perhaps only second to the Crown in status. The abbot was also a great lay lord who was involved in both local and national matters of government. It is therefore not surprising that he had several parks in the vicinity of St Albans (Hunn 1994, 72, 92, 176-79). The abbot is recorded as having a 'park for woodland beasts' at the time of the Domesday Survey in 1086 (Morris 1976, 135). There were at least four parks in the possession of the abbot apart from Tyttenhanger, including ones at Childwick, Eywood, St Albans and Redbourn (Hunn 1994, 179). The largest was probably at Eywood to the south of St Albans which enclosed 413 acres (167 ha). This was probably the park referred to in 1086. The 'Derefold' appears to have been located in the southern part the old Roman town of Verulamium (Hunn 1994, 178), and was possibly in existence until at least the later part of the 14th century (*ibid.*). The creation of a park at Tyttenhanger took place around 1427/28 and was, therefore, a comparatively late foundation. When the Tyttenhanger deer park was established in the early part of the 15th century it included an area of 30 acres, enclosed with a fence to the north of the house. There is a record that tenants close to the house were compensated and moved, so the meadow could be enclosed by a hedge and ditch (Riley, 1870, 257; Koughnet, 1895; 13; Page 1908, II, 387). This is recorded as having occurred around the late 1420s (Riley 1870, 254-60). The precise area of the first park is not known, but by the end of the 15th century the deer park was recorded as extending over an area of 310.5 acres (125 ha) (HCRO: D/EB/2067 B. M25). . Its extent was first recorded by Dury & Andrews in their *Topographical Map of Hartford-Shire* in 1766.

The boundary could have comprised a mix of different types of structure. All that was necessary to define a park enclosure was 'a wall or fence' (Petit-Dutaillis 1911, 151; Rackham 1986, 145; Stamper 1988, 141). The combination of a revetted bank and ditch would have created a vertical barrier over 3m in height, with a horizontal breadth of about 6m when calculated from the interior of the park. This accords with the view that a deer can leap up to 3m vertically and 6m horizontally (Stamper 1988, 140). It is difficult to make precise comparisons with other recorded park boundaries, but a few examples will suffice to illustrate the diversity of typology. The boundary at Paulersbury, Northants, comprised a rampart about 6.1 m wide by over 1.5m high (Webster and Cherry 1974, 216-17). The park pale at Pinner, Middlesex, consisted of a low bank between two ditches, but no dimensions were given (Youngs *et al* 1986, 140). At Slindon Park, W. Sussex, the park boundary consisted of a single phase bank and ditch which had the steepest face adjacent to the external bank, though not trace of a pale was found on top of the bank (Gaimster *et al* 1989, 214). At West Wood, Kent, a bank and ditch was located was 7-8m wide and the ditch 1.0m deep (Nenk *et al* 1995, 223). Finally, at Stoneham, Hampshire, an early pale was identified which had an internal ditch with a bank 2.6m high and 20 m broad (Nenk *et al* 1993, 264).

The warren

The farming of rabbits played an important role in the economy of medieval estates (Sheail 1971; Bailey 1988). They were a source of fresh meat in winter, and their coats were valuable for use on winter clothing (Bailey 1988, 1). However, rabbits, or *coneys* as they were called, required careful rearing involving purpose-built habitats and feeding (Rackham 1986, 47). In the St Albans area they are first mentioned in the 13th century (Hunn 1994, 179-180). At Tyttenhanger a 'Conygger' containing 42 acres of pasture and a 'Conygger wode' covering 28.5 acres was mentioned in the survey of 1331 (Brit. Lib Add Mss 36237). However, it was not until well into the 15th century that there was a reference to an inclosure being made around the 'Conyngere' (Riley 1870, 257-59). This foundation coincided with the widespread establishment of warrens in the post-plague years of the later 14th to early15[th] centuries in England (Bailey 1988, 2). Although the situation of the manor at Tyttenhanger was favourable from the point of view of water supply, *'ob aquarum copiam'* (Riley 1869, 441), much of its soils were relatively poor. This can readily be seen from the frequent references to moor and heath in the historical records. Such terrain was a natural focus for manorial lords who were interested in the economic potential of investing in breeding rabbits (Bailey 1988, 19). We do not know the precise extent of 'Tytenhanger hethe' in the early 15th century, but it must have been quite extensive. In 1427-28 the abbot inclosed a corner of the heath called 'le Conyngere', amounting to 30 acres near the mansion of Tyttenhanger, and converted into pasture land (Riley 1870, 257-59). The survey of 1500

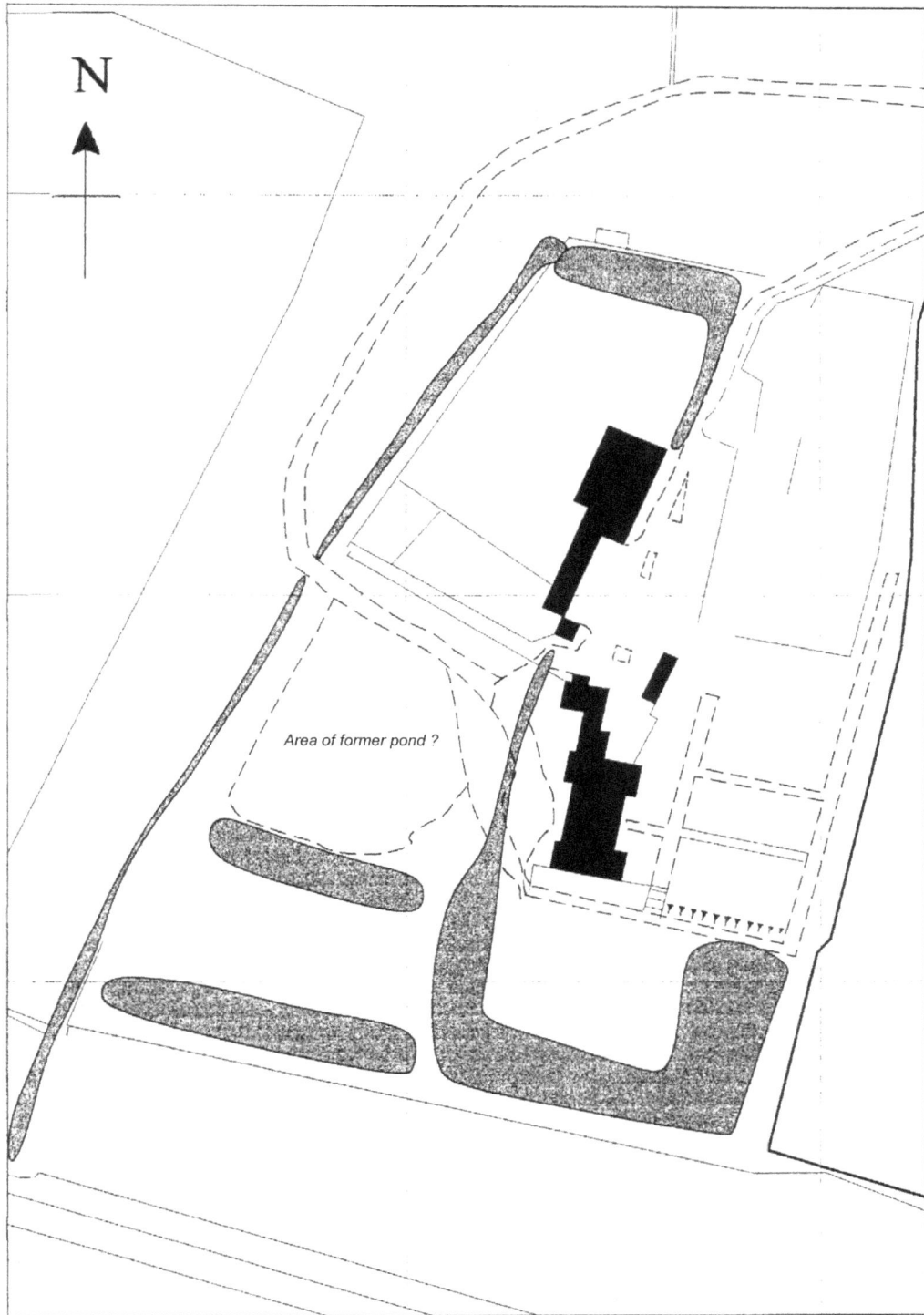

Fig. 40: Conjectured reconstruction of the moat and fishpond

only refers indirectly to 'warennesparke', so we have no description of its extent (HCRO D/EB/2067 B. M25). In 1532, the abbot leased it to John Bowman of Colney for 41 years (Page 1908, 387). At that date it adjoined *Crowchefield, Smartsclose*, the *Key Ground, Selwood* and *Catland* on the west, the farm of *Ridge* on the south, the farm of *Corsers* on the east and *North Mimms* on the north, though this last location does not make sense (*ibid*). The tenant was allowed 'firebote', timber to make his hutches and traps for destroying vermin; to cover, ditch, *plassh* and lay the burrows; he was allowed pasture for 1 gelding and 4 cows and received a coat worth 14/-; he was allowed meat and drink for himself and deputy whenever the abbot came to Tyttenhanger. At the end of his term the warren was to be left or 'stored' with 1000 coneys (*ibid*).

The warren continued to function into the 18th century, for it was referred to in a lease between Sir Henry Pope Blount and James Pilkington dated 1737. Apart from the lease of the park, the Lodge, Colney Heath farm and the right to dig for gravel and sell the timber, the tenant was to have use of the soil of the warren, 5½ acres of meadow taken out of a close called *Blounts* and 72 'hutch *trappes* for £60 per annum. The park was stocked with 2½ brace of bucks, 2½ brace of antlers, 2½ brace of *priickols*, with 26 does and their fawns and a 100 dozen rabbits. The location of the warren is indicated on the plan of 1767 (HCRO D/ECd P1). It is not surprising that it lay adjacent to the river Colne, since the river would have formed one boundary that the rabbits would have been averse to cross. We do not know when the warren went out of use, but there is no mention of it in the 19th century. Presumably, it ceased to be a commercial proposition when the old park was abandoned, and the new park was created on the south side of the house.

The dovecote

The dovecote was once a common feature of manorial sites, though their very ubiquity has been a cause of their relative neglect in the historical literature (Hurst 1988). No definite structure was identified during the course of the mitigation project, apart from the base of a small 'cage' or hutch [1540]. Nevertheless, there would have been at least one dovecote at Tyttenhanger, if not more. There is a mention of a dovecote belonging to the manor worth 13/4 in the survey of 1331 (B. Lib 36237). The term 'dovehouses' is used in an indenture of 1547, suggesting that such buildings were still in use (HCRO 56559). When this building and the tradition of rearing doves were abandoned remains unknown.

Function of the enclosures within the outer court

The function of these three areas is unclear, but the small south-eastern area covering a third of an acre does not contain the extensive spreads of tile and demolition debris observed within the other two areas. It is possible that this area may have had an agricultural use such as a small paddock. In the 17th and 18th centuries, agricultural buildings and a saw pit were established in this area, but

they do not respect the alignment of the enclosure ditches. The south-western area contained the well-preserved remains of a tile kiln, but no evidence of any other structures. The later agricultural buildings and pits were constructed over the south-east margins of this area. The largest of the three areas in the northern zone contained a domestic building [1532], a stable range [1522] and possible office or accommodation structure [1524] and tile kilns [1526 and 1525], but remained almost devoid of archaeology to the west. Later a walled enclosure and some garden features were established in this part of the area, but there was no evidence of the more extensive industrial features observed in the eastern half of this area. This northern area was divided down the middle by a long garden wall, probably during the late 17th century when this enclosure was no longer used.

The rectangular ditched enclosure does not appear to be aligned with the present house, and probably relates to the orientation of the early 15th-century manor. However, a number of 17th/18th-century garden features do not respect the orientation of these ditches. In particular, a series of post-medieval agricultural buildings cross the southern boundary ditches, narrowing the life-span of this complex to the 15th and 16th centuries, and was probably replaced when the present house was being built in the 17th century. Although not identical, a separate rectangular enclosure was also constructed in the mid 16th century at Helmingham, Suffolk. The area was very similar in size, being approximately 4.5 acres, compared to 4.2 at Tyttenhanger. The Helmingham enclosure appears to have been for gardens, located to the south-west and separate from the house, and is supposed to be unique (Thacker 1989, 14).

Buildings within the outer court

The largest single building within the outer court of the manor was [1522] which measured 37.4 m x 9m (122ft 6 ins x 29ft 6 ins approx.). The most significant feature of building [1522] was the difference in construction between the western wall and the other sides. It was evident that the western side of the building was of slighter construction. This suggests that this may have been due to considerations of design for a stable block opening onto the outer court. This building was originally interpreted at a possible 'tile house' for the drying and manufacture of tiles. However, one of the arguments against this was that it should have opened to the south rather than the north. Similar 'airing' buildings have been identified on other kiln sites, but they are often described as insubstantial timber structures (Drury 1981, 136). The building was divided internally into a series of bays, and a large pit was identified in the centre of the structure. The walls of this building are constructed largely of tile, similar in nature to those of Kiln [1526]. This suggests that tile production on this site pre-dated the construction of this particular building. Directly associated with this large structure was a smaller square building [1524]. The structure was brick-built, and appears to have had a suspended wooden floor. It is conceivable that the building could have been used as some sort of office or store room for equipment.

The second largest building was [1531] which lay at right angles to the barn or stable [1522 and 1523]. It had an overall length of 20m and width of 7m sub-divided into four relatively small rooms. The walls were 0.5m wide and composed flint and tiles bonded with a yellowish brown lime mortar. The presence of a substantially built garderobe at its western end suggests that it was a domestic dwelling. Despite the lack of ceramic dating evidence its style of construction and orientation looks to be broadly contemporary with the barn/stables to the south. It clearly predated the inner courtyard since it was cut by the foundations of the western gate tower [1210]. Other structures and foundations which shared a similar orientation were 1525, 1526, 1533, 1536 and 1540.

They are believed to belong to phase 2 (1400-1499) and probably associated with the building work undertaken by William Heyworth the abbot of St Albans Abbey in the early part of the 15th century (Riley 1867, III, 495). However, the possibility remains that these structures might have been built in the late 14th century by Abbot John de la Mote (Riley 1867, III, 448).

The entrance to the inner courtyard

The discovery of the rectangular gate towers flanking the entrance to the inner courtyard is significant in terms of understanding the architectural concept behind the manorial plan. These buildings appear to have been built of mainly brick with some courses of floor and roof tile and, to judge from the character of post-demolition back-fill, were embellished with moulded brickwork that had a thin plaster rendering. The exact date for the construction of the gate towers is not known but their character, if not ostentation, suggests a pre-Dissolution date. The eastern tower abutted on to foundations composed of 're-cycled' architectural blocks of clunch. These look to be of medieval date, possibly belonging to the 14th century manor house which was demolished by Abbot Michael (Page 1908, 387). The second period manor house was completed by 1411 (*ibid.*). The question is, could the gate towers be of 15th century workmanship? The type of bricks used and other building material could certainly belong to the late medieval period, though exactly when is difficult to establish. It is tempting to suggest that they might have been constructed in the early 15th century when the manor was re-built by Abbot John de la Moot (*ibid.*) but the only associated finds, albeit from deposits of burnt material are of Tudor date (Appendix 1.4).

The plan of the entrance to the inner court of the manor is remarkably regular in layout and appears pre-Tudor in concept. One might even go as far as to suggest that it has an almost Roman character in terms of its design. With its regular plan, massive foundations and external pale cream rendering it carries an unmistakable message of power and authority. Nevertheless, there was no defensive moat associated with this entrance, though it should be recalled

that the outer court appeared to have been defined by a wide ditch (4m wide x 2m deep). This was originally interpreted as a deer park boundary, but it is also possible that it defined the extent of the '*le woolyard*', which was mentioned in a survey of 1500 (HALS: D/ECd E39). The depth the foundations suggests that they would have contained an undercroft or shallow cellar. Above ground, it is conceivable that they were at least two, possibly three, stories high and roofed with tiles. The buttresses flanking the buildings at their northern ends were presumably to give them stability and perhaps to allow for some sort of internal stairway to reach the upper floors. Why the easternmost buttress of tower 1208 [1207] was deeper than its western counterpart [1209] is difficult to account for. The character of the architectural brickwork is not certain, but several fragments were retrieved from the post-demolition back-fill to give a hint what it may have been like (Appendix 1.4).

The recent gravel extraction phase at Tyttenhanger has permitted the first ever excavation of one of the many manorial sites that once belonged to the abbot of St Alban's Abbey. Although the core area, as defined by the 'inner court' has yet to be investigated, the excavations have revealed something of the status and quality of the late medieval site. In addition, they perhaps go some way to justifying the claim that Tyttenhanger was '*reputed to be the finest monastic country residence in the kingdom*' (Gesta Abbatum III, 495).

Tile production

The post-Conquest development of the tile and brick industry in England has been discussed by Salzman (1952), Wright (1972), Drury (1981). Regional studies have shown the considerable advances made in the tile industry during the later part of the Middle Ages in the Wessex area (Hare 1991). More local, shire-based studies have examined particular counties in greater detail. For example, to the east Essex has been studied (Ryan 1996) as has Bedfordshire to the north (Cox 1979) and Buckinghamshire to the west (Pyke 1995). In comparison, Hertfordshire remains relatively neglected, apart from the work of the *Victoria County History* (Page 1908, IV, 264-66) and a preliminary study undertaken by Branch-Johnson (1970). The place-name element 'tiler' is by no means uncommon in the county, but even so there is nothing like the number of references to 46 tile kilns being in production in Essex at the end of the 16th century (Drury 1981, 136). This deficiency cannot be addressed here, but it is relevant to discuss some of the potential sources which may be used in the study of the production of building materials in Hertfordshire.

Before the appearance of the 25" First Series Ordnance Survey maps of the 1870s, we are dependent on the numerous field-name elements that have been recorded on manorial and Tithe Apportionment documents. An adjoining area of 126 sq. km to the north of the parish of Ridge has been studied in some detail for such references (Hunn 1994, 252-318). In this area, 36 references to individual brick and tile production sites were found (Hunn 1994, 184), representing a density of one manufacturing site per 3.5 sq. km. However, out of all these references, which may be incomplete, only 3 (8.3%) referred to tile production (*ibid.*). If this figure was extrapolated for the county as a whole, then its area (1016.8 sq. km) might be expected to contain a total of 290 sites, of which only 24 sites would have produced tile. However, the author suspects that this figure is somewhat on the low side. The *Victoria County History* lists 7 sites as specifically producing tile in Hertfordshire (Page 1908, 264-66), and the *English Place-Name Society* lists a further 4 sites (Gover *et al* 1970, 43, 63, 129, 147). With the two listed by Hunn (1994, 313) this produces a total of 13 sites. The one site that all three sources have in common is a reference to a 'Tilehowsewik' belonging to the manor of Napsbury, in the parish of St Peters in the early 16th century and in 1569 (HCRO Gorhambury Deeds X.I.2). Interestingly, the 1569 reference also mentions a 'tyle pitt' (*ibid.*). There is a mention of the 'demesne warren and tyle kiln' in relation to Colney Heath, which could be interpreted as another site: however, this is by no means certain (HCRO 4727). Nevertheless, even if this last reference is discounted there still remain references to four 'tile houses' in the Tyttenhanger area. One is located in Shenley in 1386 (Page 1908, II, 265); one in Napsbury in the 1530s (Page 1908, II, 416); one at Coursers Farm in the early 16th century (Page 1908, II, 390), and one at Tyttenhanger (HCRO 56559). The latter is discussed below, and the problem of the documentary sources will be described further on.

The evidence for tile production on the site is perhaps the most important element of the fieldwork. Archaeologically, most features, such as workshops, that were associated with tile production, apart from the kiln itself, are less liable to survive due to their ephemeral nature. Only in the later medieval/early post medieval periods are the remains more substantial where production was less short-term (Drury 1975; 1981). At Tyttenhanger the evidence points to at least intermittent tile production. The location was good, the site being situated on well-drained gravels, 100m east of the river Colne (Fig. 1). Ample wood for fuel was available less than 300m north-west of the firing operations. Natural clay and sand deposits could be found only a few metres below the topsoil. Brickearth could also be easily extracted from the extensive deposit just over 100m to the south, buried immediately beneath the topsoil. These available resources satisfy the necessary criteria for tile production stated by Drury (1981, 135). In addition, the site is located close to London and St Albans, near to important road links of the medieval period and later. Another factor associated with the establishment of tile production is an immediate market for the products. In the early medieval period, tile production was a seasonal occupation to supplement an agricultural income, and sites were often ephemeral in nature. Two common reasons for a settled production site were the needs of large ecclesiastical land owners, such as the abbey at St Albans, and the erection of massive buildings in the late medieval period (Drury 1981, 32), like the construction of the manor in the late 14th/15th century. Elements of both of scenarios appear to apply at Tyttenhanger.

The rectangular tile kilns were situated in, and aligned with, the 15th-century enclosure. However, the 'tile' kiln [1526] was located in the south-western part of the enclosure, approximately 60m south-west of a large rectangular barn or stable, and the later 'kiln' [1525] was located only 20m to the east. Both kilns were relatively large: however, they have several differences. The possible kiln 1525 appears to have consisted of a brick-built chimney and single flue leading to a collapsed structure, whereas the tile built kiln was heated by a large stoke pit, feeding into a double parallel flue structure, constructed entirely from tiles. Thus, the technical name for [1526] is 'a double, parallel flued updraught kiln'. Examples of such structures have been excavated at Lacock, Wiltshire, where the interior of the phase 3 kiln had internal measurements of 3.0 × 1.8m or 5.4 sq. m (McCarthy 1976): at Norton Priory, Cheshire, where the tile kiln measured internally 1.2 × 0.85m or 1.02 sq. m (Webster and Cherry 1973, 154): at Lyveden, Northants, where the kiln had similar internal dimensions to the one at Norton Priory (*ibid*, 183): at Farnham, Surrey, the kiln was of early 13th-century date, and the floor of its furnace measured 2.6 × 2.35m or 6.1 sq. m (Youngs *et al* 1986). One of the most important tile producing sites was discovered at Beverley, S. Yorkshire, covering an area of over 4 acres (1.75 ha). The site comprised six kilns, of which two survived intact. There were also associated tile sheds and workshops (see below). The five rectangular kilns there were constructed of tile and were twin-flued: one measured 2.0 × 1.8m, or 3.6 sq. m (Youngs *et al* 1987). All these examples were of medieval date, and it may be significant that a similar kiln of late 17th early 18th-century date at Danbury, Essex, was over the twice the average size, measuring 2.1 × 4.8m internally or 10 sq. m (Drury 1975).

One of two late medieval tile kilns excavated at Little Brickhill, Buckinghamshire, was similar to Kiln [1526]. However, the Brickhill kiln was narrower and partly constructed from brick (Mynard 1975, 59). The roof tiles manufactured at this site were thinner and longer than those recovered from Tyttenhanger, measuring 165 × 275mm. In addition, the two fixing holes were closer together, being only 35mm apart, as opposed to 60mm in the examples from Kiln [1526]. A range of decorative tiles was made alongside plain roof tiles at Brickhill, with styles that were copied from a wide geographical area stretching from Wessex to the Midlands (Mynard 1975, 60-4). No such duality of manufacturing was evident from Tyttenhanger, where only one decorated tile recovered from Kiln [1525] had a simple incised decoration of a stag, which may have been a practice piece (see front cover).

As previously mentioned, the raw materials needed for tile production were available on the site. Brick-earth appears to have been extracted from the large hollow situated on the southern limits of Field 'A'. This sub-rectangular feature originally measured 60 × 20m in width. By the 19th century, this feature is depicted as a pond in the cartographic record. Today this hollow is overgrown and backfilled with a variety of modern domestic rubbish. At a later brick-and-tile kiln site in Runsell Green, Danbury, Essex, a similar 'pond' situated 60m from the kilns was the extraction point for raw materials (Drury 1975, 210). At Tyttenhanger, the evaluation identified shallow scoops backfilled with tile wasters around the margins of this extraction hollow (Percival & Richmond 1996, 15), also connecting this feature to tile production. Another extraction hollow, located 40m south of the ditch enclosure, measured only 20m in diameter. However, natural clay and sand deposits were observed in the base of this feature, possibly indicating that these resources were only sought from here. Another possible extraction pit exists approximately 300m to the west of the present site, located behind the present Red Lodge. This feature is marked on the 1777 estate plan in 'Pond Field'. Today it is sub-rectangular in plan and measures 40 × 20m. However, if this is an old extraction hollow, it may not necessarily have been used by the same tile makers. Documentary sources suggest that there may have been a kiln operating at Coursers Farm, 900m to the east.

The most significant feature of building [1522] was the difference in construction between the western wall and the other sides. It was evident that the western side of the building was of slighter construction. This suggests that this may have been due to considerations of design for a stable block opening onto the outer court. This building was originally interpreted at a possible 'tile house' for the drying and manufacture of tiles. However, one of the arguments against this was that it should have opened to the south rather than the north. Similar 'airing' buildings have been identified on other kiln sites, but they are often described as insubstantial timber structures (Drury 1981, 136). The building was divided internally into a series of bays, and a large pit was identified in the centre of the structure. The walls of this building are constructed largely of tile, similar in nature to those of Kiln [1526]. This suggests that tile production on this site pre-dated the construction of this particular building. Directly associated with this large structure was a smaller square building [1524]. The structure was brick-built, and appears to have had a suspended wooden floor. It is conceivable that the building could have been used as some sort of office or store room for equipment.

A series of walls [1549] appear to enclose a small compound to the north of these workshops, extending to the eastern boundary ditch [1500]. It is possible that this compound was used to store raw materials or finished tiles. Two other buildings, [1532] and [1531], appear to be on a similar alignment to the kilns and main workshops, but their function could not be ascertained. They clearly pre-date the large garden wall [1546], which cuts across Building [1532]. Structure 1536 could be the remains of a robbed-out kiln, but this was never confirmed.

Documentary sources

There are no sources relating to the production of tiles for the Tyttenhanger site. However, there are indirect references that indicate that tile manufacture was taking place on or in the general vicinity. The principal question concerns references to a 'tile-house' in the manors of Blackhide or Coursers and Tyttenhanger. This section describes the historical sources and the background to the site at Tyttenhanger, both in terms of the manorial establishment and references to the existence of tile manufacturing.

There is no mention or use of the prefix 'tile' in the 1331 survey or extent of the manor of Tyttenhanger (B. Lib Add Mss 36237). This neither proves or disproves the existence of such an industry, especially when the manor site itself is only referred to indirectly. According to the historical record the manor was built between 1326-35 (Riley 1867, II, 371; Page 1908, 387). Whether this refers to an entirely new establishment is debatable, but until such time as any physical evidence is forthcoming the question must remain unanswered. We do not know where the building materials came from for this first-phase historical manor, but the succeeding abbot (Michael) demolished the buildings and sold the materials (*ibid.*). To what extent that this involved the demolition of the entire manorial establishment is debatable. For example, while it is possible to demolish the living quarters, it is less practical to demolish the associated agricultural buildings. It makes sense to suppose that these would have been maintained for the purposes of managing the existing manorial estate. By the end of the 14th century there is mention of the construction of two barns and the commencement of rebuilding the manor by abbot John de la Moot (Riley 1867, III, 441). This work was completed in 1411 (Riley 1867, III, 448, 495). Contemporary sources say that 'hereupon' ditches and pools (fishponds) were dug out and stocked with fish: *'Deinde fossas et stagna erutare fecit, et copia diversorum pisciarum instauravit'*, (*ibid.*). There can be little doubt that this was referring to the construction of a moat which also formed an integral part of the fishpond system. It is possible that this rebuilding phase at Tyttenhanger may have acted as a catalyst to stimulate the development of the tile making industry in the area.

The corn-dryer in Field B [1528] was constructed using re-used Roman building material. Because of this, it seems unlikely that there was any surplus waste building material available from local medieval tile or brick producing sites at the time this dryer was constructed. The corn dryer contained pottery dating to between 1140-1300, indicating that tile production must post-date the 14th century. The earliest use of the prefix 'tile' first occurs in the mid-15th century in the reign of Henry VI (HCRO D/EB 2067B M1). There is mention of 'Tylerswyke' in 1442/43, 1447/48, 1455/56 and 'Tylerslonde' in 1444/45 (*ibid.*).

The next important source concerning information on the manorial site and the manufacture of tiles dates to 1500/01, when a survey was undertaken of the manor of Tyttenhanger (HCRO D/EB/2067 B. M.25). This document is unquestionably the most important source concerning the landscape of the late medieval estate. It itemises each parcel of land, describing its land-use, acreage, tenant and juxtaposition to other land units. Although it is complete there is evidence that parts of it, such as the occasional field name, were meant to be added at a later date. Here we will be concerned with a brief summary of its principal components, and a description of those elements that are relevant to the manorial site, including mention of tile production. In 1500 the manor of Tyttenhanger had a total area of 1391.74 acres, concentrated mainly within the parish of Ridge. However, it seems that there were also scattered holdings in the parishes of St Peters and St Stephens. There was even one croft recorded as lying adjacent to Barnet Wood, to the north of St Albans (*ibid.*). Although the area of the park is itemised, it is not always clear what was the land use of each of the separate land parcels (Appendix 1.12). The park was recorded as covering an area of 310 acres, which contained both woodland, pasture and arable land. The precise proportion is not certain, but it would be a mistake to interpret the use of the term 'park' as denoting a particular type of land use. The largest single unit of land was the manorial 'waste' of Colneyheath which covered an area of some 400 acres. As its name implies and as future documents attest, the area comprised open heath land, of which only a small proportion survives today.

Of particular relevance to the present study are the references to the moat and adjoining parcels of land. There is mention of a 'court' called '*le woolyard*' which is enclosed with park pales and contains dwellings, offices with stables and barns and '*le mote*' and '*fyshpond*'. The court with '*le mote*' contains 6.5 acres. This area coincides, almost precisely with the area recorded in the 1777 survey (HCRO D/ECd E39) and first illustrated on a contemporary plan in the British Library (B. Lib Add Mss. 11317b, Fig. 16). Also in the 1500 survey is mention of the first court called the '*lttzcort*' (little court) which also contained buildings, barns, stables and others with a garden, which amounted to 3.5 acres.

The next item mentions one '*campus*' (open field) next to '*le tylehowse*' lying between *lobwell* and the way to Coursers on one side and abutting on the edge of '*harepathe*' (London Road) and the other on the way leading towards the manor, containing 33.5 acres. There are several other references to '*le tylehowse*', '*tylehowsfelde*' in the document, which seem to point towards this structure being in the general vicinity of

Coursers road, to the south of the present day extraction area.

Following the dissolution of the monasteries by Henry VIII in 1539 the manor of Tyttenhanger, including its park and a tile house, were granted to Sir Thomas Pope and Elizabeth his wife on March 18th 1547 (HCRO 56559-64; Page 1908, II, 388). In a companion document there is also a reference to both a *tyle howse and brewhowse* (HCRO 56563). The former reference accords with our current interpretation of the archaeological evidence. There seems to have been some confusion over an additional reference to a tile kiln which was, until recently, believed to refer to the same item (Page 1908, 388, 390). It now appears that the two references should be seen as quite separate and that the latter appears to refer to a second tile-producing site which Page (*ibid.*) describes as being '*in decay and ruinous*'. However, in an indenture dated November 6th 1547 the manor of Blackhide, otherwise called Coursers, was granted to Sir Thomas Pope and Elizabeth his wife by Sir Richard Lee, including '*all lands, meadows, pastures, woods, commons and cows with six acres of pasture lately inclosed within the park of Tittenhanger being before the gate of the said manor. Land called Hiksons, a toft and 2 croftes called Cobbys, another lately called Grubbes with the tyle kyll and all other lying... rent of £4 15s. 4000 of good tyles, 2 quarters of stone lyme and 23 couple of coneys*' (HCRO 79423). This suggests that the kiln at Coursers was still capable of producing tiles at that date. In 1594 there is a further mention of a kiln which was leased to Harry Brock for a rent of £5 (Page 1908, 390). To date this document has not come to light, although it is listed among the Caledon Deeds deposited at the Hertfordshire Archives and Local Studies Library. The last reference concerning a tile kiln occurs in 1639 when it was listed among the possessions of Sir Thomas Pope Blount of Tyttenhanger (Page 1908, 390; Inq. p.m. vol 490, no. 90). These last references to tile kilns should be seen as quite separate from those relating to the site at Tyttenhanger. There are no direct or indirect references to tile production among the estate documents for the manor of Tyttenhanger after the mid 16th century.

Garden features and landscape

Garden features are archaeologically difficult to detect because of their ephemeral nature and, in this case, these features could have been easily removed from the archaeological record in highly disturbed ground. However, a number of elements did survive and were identified. No record of the layout of the gardens at Tyttenhanger exist, but historical accounts of the house indicate that there were kitchen gardens, a large shrubbery and pleasure ground, glade and formal flower gardens around the house in the post-medieval period (Koughnet 1895, 52). Chauncy, who published the first work on the history of Hertfordshire in 1700, recorded that Sir Henry Pope Blount became sheriff of the county in 1661, and '*built here a fair structure of brick, made fair walks and gardens to it*' (Chauncy 1824, 388). Although no illustration of the mansion appeared in Chauncy's work, other houses of contemporary date were illustrated, giving a flavour of what they might have looked like. For example, Bushey Hall near Watford (Chauncy 1824, vol II, 454-455) indicates the sort of arrangement, which would have existed to the south of the house.

The scant archaeological evidence for garden features reflects a continuous process of change during the medieval and post-medieval period. These range from medieval ecclesiastical gardens, deer park and formal gardens, giving way to the more natural 'landscaped approach' in the 18th century. Nevertheless, some of the evidence for these changes has survived and, although fragmentary, does permit certain elements to be distinguished. At present, our understanding of the late medieval gardens at Tyttenhanger remains poor. When Henry VIII and his court arrived from Hatfield in 1528 he was said to be very pleased with the estate (Koughnet 1895, 17). Whether this reflected his pleasure at the change of venue, and therefore hunting, or whether he was pleased with the quality of the buildings and their setting, is impossible to know. We do not know the condition of the Tyttenhanger estate some twenty years later, when it was acquired by Sir Thomas Pope (Page 1908, 388). However, he was attested to be one the wealthiest commoners in the realm and would, presumably, have had the resources to maintain if not embellish the surrounding grounds (*ibid.*). If he did, there is nothing in the historical record to suggest that this was the case. There is a record of a visit by Queen Elizabeth in 1578 to Lady Pope (Elizabeth Powlett) at Tyttenhanger (Koughnet 1895, 37) so it may be assumed that the accommodation was suitable for a queen.

Most of the surviving garden features appear to date to the 17th and 18th centuries. It was not uncommon for early gardens to fall into disrepair for long periods, then to be renovated at a later date (Thacker 1989, 18). Several small structures, mainly dotted around the west half of Field 'A', have been tentatively interpreted as garden features. Some of these appear to be formal beds, others may be gazebos or summerhouses, but this type of feature often leaves little in the way of archaeological remains. Another 16th-century country house, Haddon Hall in Derbyshire, had a system of garden walls, lodges and garden houses (Thacker 1989, 18). The fact that many of the garden structures appear to have used tiles in their construction may be indicative of the range and quantity of material that became available after production had ceased on the site. Although these features may be part of a formal garden, 'formal' does not mean 'uniform' (Thacker 1989, 34).

Down the centre of an old ditched enclosure in Field 'A', a large brick wall [1546] was constructed. This cut through the western end of the possible terrace feature and some of the late medieval outbuildings. This wall runs from the house to the northern end of a group of late 17th or early 18th-century agricultural buildings. The wall

was subsequently rebuilt on a slightly straighter alignment. Furthermore, at a later date, probably in the early 18th century, most of this wall was robbed out and only the northern portion remained. Another wall [1547] was constructed to the west of [1546] to form an irregular walled enclosure in the north-west corner of the field. This enclosure is shown on the 1777 estate plan. At least one long flower-bed was also identified within this zone. This walled area would have offered some seclusion from the avenue to the east.

A well-documented feature of the landscaped garden was an avenue, bordered by trees on either side, running southwards from the house across the site (Koughnet 1895, 52). Avenues of trees were common elements on large estates during the late 17th and early 18th centuries (Thacker 1989, 34). The avenue at Tyttenhanger was not marked on the 1777 estate plan, but is illustrated on Dury and Andrews survey of Hertfordshire in 1766. The southern end of this avenue was also shown on a survey of 1767 (HCRO D/ECd P1). It is clear from the illustration that the avenue flanked a driveway that went from near Bowmansgreen Farm of the 'Homestall' to a gated entrance on the London Road. This formal avenue appears to have disappeared in the late 18th century (Koughnet 1895,140). It is unclear whether this refers to the entire length or just the northern end. Judging from an 1835 reference to the '*coach drive*', it appears that the southern end, amounting to 2.5 acres, was '*now laid into five other customary closes*' (HCRO: D/Ecd T.29). The archaeological remains of the western margins of this avenue were identified as a line of regularly spaced sub-circular features. The eastern side proved to be more elusive and only a few elements were observed at the north edge of the site. The avenue was about 30m wide, and was traced over a length of 140m. Its full length from the mansion to the London Road would have been about 1000m, but its southern end had been eroded by agricultural activity. The alignment of this avenue follows that of the earliest phase of Wall [1546]. A second smaller avenue, situated to the west of the main avenue, was also indicated on the Dury and Andrews' map of 1766. On site, evidence survived for a NNE-SSW tree-pit alignment (Fig. 32).

As well as forming avenues, clusters and small clumps of trees were also planted for different effects, sometimes with a symbolic meaning, such as representing troops or ships (Wood 1968, 215). The discrete cluster of trees [1555] placed at the junction of Walls [1546] and [1547] may have had such a function.

Sometime between 1767 and 1777 the land to the south of the house, essentially that now forming Field 'A', was turned into open parkland with gravel walks. This echoes the fashion of the time for a more naturalistic form of gardens, pioneered by Lancelot 'Capability' Brown between 1750 and 1780 (Lasdun 1991, 95). A small irregular rectangular enclosure survived in the north-west corner of the field, and is depicted on the 1777 estate plan. This feature appears to have been removed by the second half of the 19th century. The land to the south of the present house remained in this state until the present day, while other areas of the site continued to be farmed.

Agricultural activity

The evidence for agricultural activity on the site was varied in nature and spans the medieval period to the present day, including the field systems observed in Field 'B'. However, a number of out buildings were erected during the 17th and 18th centuries on the estate (Koughnet 1895, 52-53, 143). On the southern margins of the ditch enclosure in Field 'A', a series of farm buildings were erected across these ditches. These features were located within a spread of destruction debris dating to the late 17th early 18th century (Figs 8 & 30). This area was defined by a gully to the west and a ditch and fence line to the east. A long brick wall extended from the house down through the field to the northern margins of these buildings. The main structure [1542] was constructed from brick walls and large posts, possibly leaving the eastern side open. A brick and tile built drain conduit ran around the margins of this structure and drained into one of the old enclosure ditches towards the river. On the western side of this building a cobble surface had been constructed over the drain and square pit containing exclusively cattle bone was also associated with this building. A possible hearth was located in the middle of the structure. A cobble courtyard lay to the north east of this building around which were some agricultural pits [1564] (possibly covered) and a smaller walled outbuilding [1542]. A gully helped to drain the western margins of this cobble yard. These buildings appear to be associated with livestock, with animal remains of cattle, sheep, horses and pigs recovered from demolition contexts. This activity is believed to belong to the home-farm of the estate referred to as the 'Homestall' on a plan of 1767 (HCRO D/ECd P1). The plan shows eight structures, three of which were no more than between 4 and 5m square. The other five buildings were much larger of which two will survive on the western edge of the extraction area. The layout of the farm suggests a gradual sequence of development rather than being the product of a formal plan. The map was surveyed in 1767 by Joseph Cole on behalf of the Honorable Charles Yorke to a scale approximating to 1:2500. The farmstead is also illustrated on Andrew and Dury's survey of Hertfordshire in 1766. The more detailed survey records that the 'Homestall' covered an area of 2.0.20 acres (0.85 ha). By the time of the 1777 estate plan this farmstead no longer existed (HCRO PC 484). Nevertheless, not all agrarian buildings were concentrated at a particular location. There was an isolated barn [1521] in the north western corner of Field 'A'. Its function is not known but it might have served for the storage of winter feed or for stabling of the occasional cow in calf or horse.

CONCLUSION

The investigations carried out at Tyttenhanger have identified a sequence of archaeological remains that reflects the changing nature of the landscape from the medieval period to the present day. Excluding a few isolated prehistoric flints, the historical and archaeological sequence commences in the medieval period. An early medieval field system consisting of strips of land delineated by ditches was identified in the southern part of the site. Associated with this field arrangement were several corn dryers. A historical reference to a 'malting' lane suggests that these features were used for malting as well as drying crops prior to grinding. In the later medieval period this field system underwent a dramatic change, when a more regimented arrangement of land divisions was imposed, on a different orientation.

The first house was established at Tyttenhanger in the early 14th century: after only a generation or so it was apparently demolished. Construction of its replacement was commenced in the later part of the 14th century, and was completed in the early half of the 15th century. The site of these houses appears to have been to the north, beyond the area of investigation. The earthwork survey around the present house recorded the presence of a moat and fishponds, which were associated with the 15th century house. The preliminary results of the investigation suggest that this establishment extended well into the north side of Field A.

A complex of ditched enclosures was established to the south of the house. Within the enclosure was evidence of domestic, agricultural and tile/brick kilns. One parallel-flue kiln survived in an excellent state of preservation. Tile production on this site was probably initiated by the construction of the 15th-century manor house, and continued intermittently, until well into the 16th century.

During the 17th century, the second house was demolished and the present house constructed (Smith 1993, 148). Part of this demolition may have included the courtyard-type building to the south of the present mansion. There was some evidence for a formal garden layout, created probably about 1660. This layout may have included brick enclosure walls, with possible associated garden structures and flower beds. A number of trees also appeared to have been planted, including an avenue forming a corridor across the site from the house towards the main road. At the same time a farmstead was established to the south and west of the garden features. Finally, between 1767 and 1777, the land south of the house was turned into parkland. Apart from the intrusion of some service trenches, the grounds have remained in this state until the present day.

APPENDIX 1: FINDS

APPENDIX 1.1: FLINT OBJECTS

Table 1: List of flint objects

Context	SF: No	Type	Quantity	Date
u/s natural gravel	6000	Unfinished axe	1	Prehistoric
u/s natural gravel	-	Scraper	1	Prehistoric
u/s natural gravel	-	Flake	1	Prehistoric
u/s natural gravel	6004	Blade	1	Prehistoric
u/s natural gravel	6007	Flake	1	Prehistoric
u/s natural gravel	6008	End scraper	1	Prehistoric

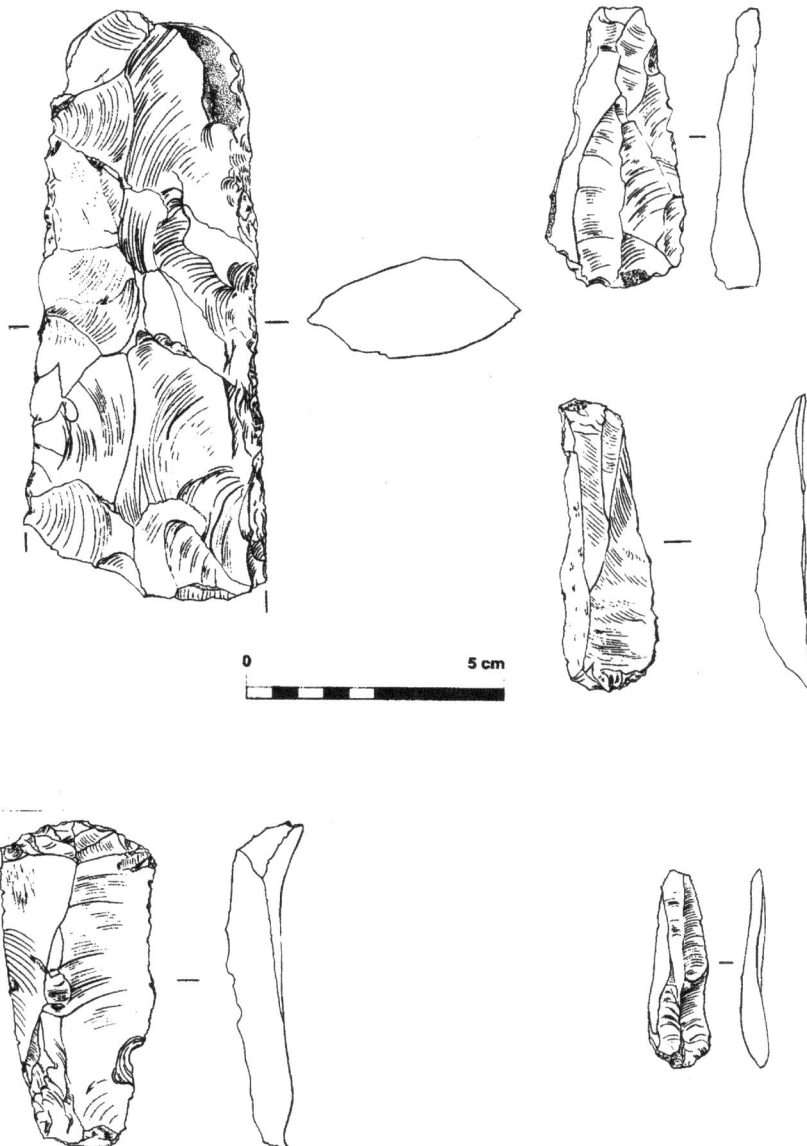

Fig. 41: Flint objects

APPENDIX 1.2: SMALL FINDS

Ten small finds were recovered over the duration of this project (Fig 42). In addition, a further 61 metallic finds were recovered from a metal detector survey of the site (Appendix 1.6).

Table 2: Small finds

SF no.	Context	Group	Material	Type	Date	Phase
6000	U/S	-	Flint	Axe -unfinished	Prehistoric	
6001	1004	1521	Copper alloy	Penny	1700	3
6002	1018	-	Copper alloy	Farthing	1635-49	3
6003	1029	1529	Copper alloy	Buckle	17th	3
6004	U/S	-	Flint	Blade	Prehistoric	
6005	110	1545	Lead	Fragment	Post-medieval	3
6006	110	1545	Cu alloy	Pin	17th/18th	3
6007	U/S	-	Flint	Flake	Prehistoric	
6008	U/S	-	Flint	End scrapper	Prehistoric	
6009	95	1525	Tile	Stag decoration	Early post-med	2/3

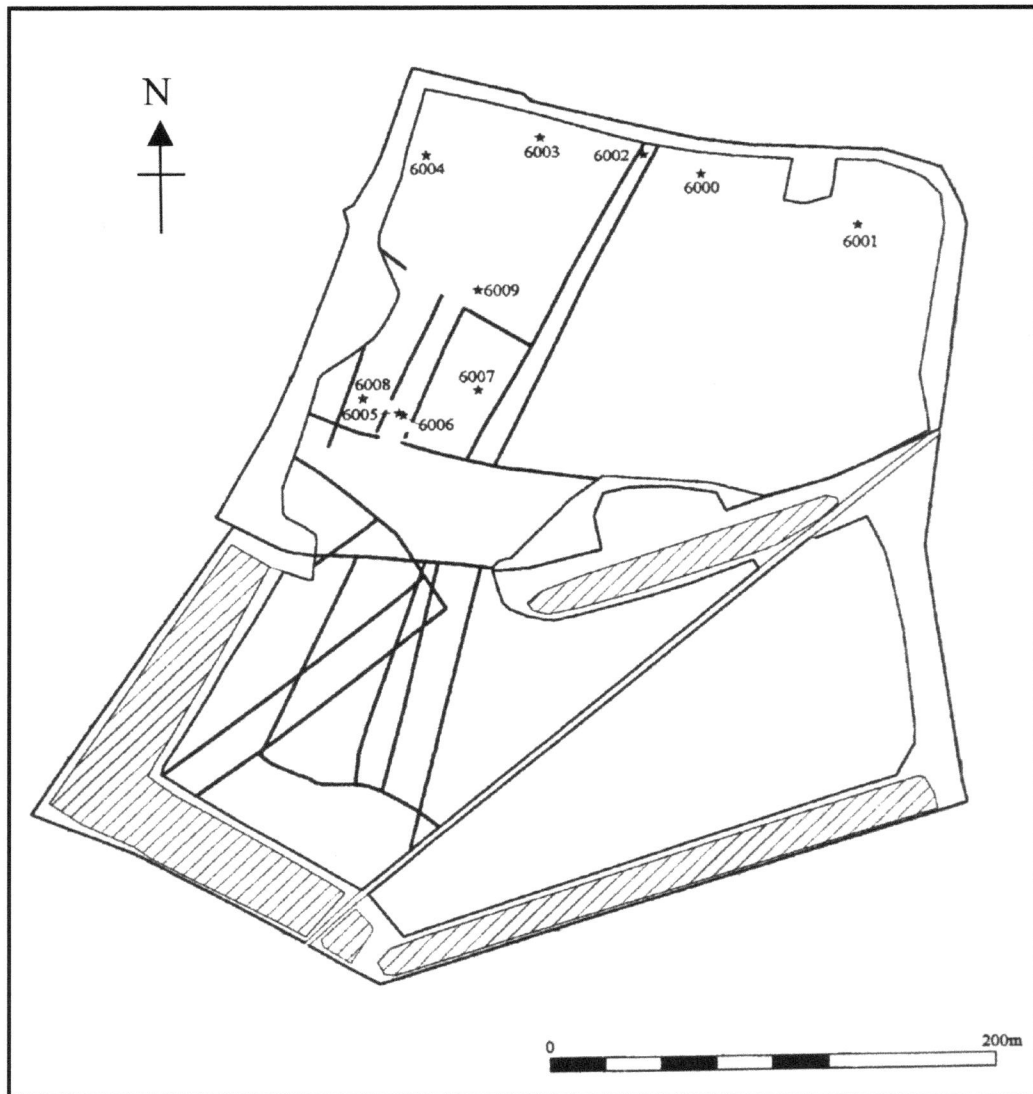

Fig. 42: Distribution of small finds

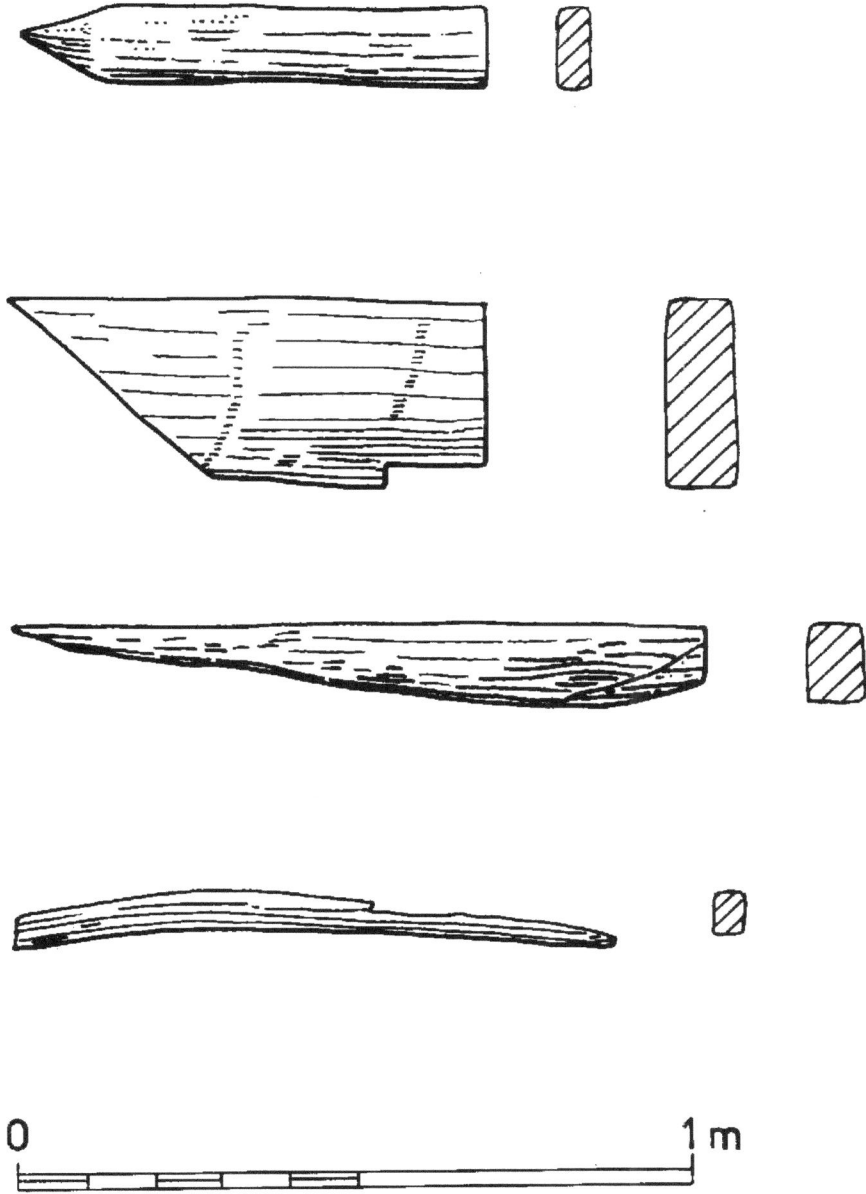

Fig. 43: Timbers from lower fill of garderobe [1532]

APPENDIX 1.3: POTTERY
by Lucy Whittingham

The pottery assemblage recovered during the first phase of the project was relatively small, amounting to 112 sherds from 367 contexts. The sherds were reasonably well-preserved, with many contexts containing multiple fragments of the same vessel. This assemblage consisted mainly of fragments of various jugs or tankards, reflecting the agricultural /domestic nature of the assemblage. The wide date ranges for some of the fabrics recovered on this site, particularly greywares, are due to long and often overlapping chronologies of styles, and local traditions during this period.

Table 3: Pottery

Context No.	Group No.	Feature Type	No. Sherds	Provisional Date	Phase
1027	1539	Garden Structure	1	1550-1700	4 / 5
1054	1557	Tree Avenue	1	1630-1800	5
1058	debris	Spread	1	1800-1900	5
1079	1511	Curved Ditch	26	970-1100	1
1133	1528	Corn Dryer	1	1140-1300	1
1136	1528	Corn Dryer	6	1140-1300	1
1139	1528	Corn Dryer	7	1140-1300	1
bund?	debris	Spread	1	1480-1550	2/3
12	1500	Ditch	3	1140-1300	1
77	1540	Building	5	1550-1700	4 / 5
110	1545	Debris	5	1580-1700	4 /5
110	1545	Cobbled Yard	1	1720-1780	5
110	1545	Debris	10	1630-1800	5
137	1507	Ditch	7	1140-1300	1
144	1500	Ditch	1	1140-1600	1 / 4
144	1500	Ditch	1	1140-1600	1 / 4
154	1561	Saw Pit	18	1580-1700 1710-1760	4 / 5
187	1542	Post hole	2	1550-1700	4 / 5
196	1506	Gully	3	1480-1600 1600-1700	4 / 5
203	1527	Corn Dryer	12	1140-1300	1

POTTERY FROM THE BUND EXCAVATION

The assemblage has been quantified using sherd count and weight and identified with reference to the fabric type series established by the Museum of London specialist services.

RESULTS

An assemblage of 143 sherds (45.5kg) were recovered from four contexts. With the exception of those in contexts 1200 all are of an early post-medieval date and contemporary with each other. The sherds are from an estimated 24 vessels, the majority of which are from context 1204 (Plate 24). Smaller assemblages of similar material are found in contexts 1213 and 1215.

Stoneware
The most prominent of the wares is Raeren Stoneware (RAER) imported from the Rhineland between 1480 and 1610. All of these vessels are examples of plain, sometimes large, drinking jugs in common use in this country between 1480 and 1550. In fact the lack of decorated Frechen stoneware which flooded the market in 1550 suggests that this assemblage pre-dates c1550.

Redware
The second most common of fabrics in this assemblage are jugs in London-area early post-medieval redware (PMRE). These are all large rounded jugs with pinched spouts, characterised by the dark brown external finish of the pottery surfaces. These are a common jug form dating from the late 15th and 16th centuries.

Cistercian ware
More unusual forms are the substantial part of a multi-handled Cistercian ware (CIST) cup that looks as if it is a second from a relatively local industry.

Surrey-Hampshire border ware
The complete bottle-shaped costrel in Surrey-Hampshire border ware with olive green glaze (BORDO) is the only example of this ware found at the site that might also suggest that the assemblage is from the earlier part of the 16th century (Plate 24). Surrey-Hampshire Border ware becomes common in use after c. 1550. This particular barrel-shaped costrel form is usually dated in London assemblages as 17th century.

Context [1200]
The assemblage in context 1200 differs from the others in being of a mixed date. Six sherds from the same jug in late medieval Hertfordshire glazed ware (LMHG) date from 1340 to 1450 and are contemporary with the Langerwehe stoneware (LANG) jug sherd of 1350 to 1500 date. The one sherd of London-area early post-medieval redware (PMRE) is later in date (1480 to1600) and similar to the other PMRE jugs in contexts 1204, 1213 and 1215.

APPENDIX 1.4: CERAMIC BUILDING MATERIAL
by Jonathan Hunn

The undiagnostic nature of many of the bricks and roof tiles from this period make analysis of the assemblage difficult (Salzman 1952, 230). However, sizes of the material can give an indication of the period of manufacture. However, assumptions based on the dimensions of materials alone are not entirely dependable: for example, 'Tudor' style bricks were manufactured into the 18th century. The standardisation of building materials is a relatively modern phenomenon, but in the middle of the 15th century a statute addressed concerns over poorly made and erratic-sized tiles (*ibid.*). Whether or not this was followed to the letter everywhere is unknown. In general, the bricks and tiles from the site were a reddish brown colour, 5YR 5/3 on the Munsell chart. Where mortar was observed, it was lime-based. Historical evidence indicates that re-use of building materials was a widespread practice at Tyttenhanger during the medieval and post medieval periods. The presence of Roman material [200] in a medieval corn dryer, and the robbed-out state of many structures demonstrates this practice in the archaeological record. The material from the first phase of excavation on the site has been combined with material from the bund excavation (below). However, three pieces are worthy of mention here: The first was a roof tile, which bore the impression of a stag sketched on it (220 x 140 x 15mm). The drawing is a good likeness, which suggests that whoever drew it had a detailed knowledge of the animal. The tile was incomplete and was found unstratified in the middle of the site among other building material (Fig.44). The second object was a decorated 14th century floor tile, which came from one of the work shops at Penn near Amersham, Buckinghamshire (Plate 23). Its dimensions are given below and its decoration is similar to those that survive at Windsor castle (Keen 2002, 223, Fig. 5 no. 8).

0   100 mm

Fig. 44: Stag tile from Tyttenhange

The third object was another floor tile and though badly worn its design was sufficiently discernible to identify it (Keen 2002, 223, Fig. 5 no. 12). A few other fragments of 14th century floor tile were observed during the watching brief but these were too fragmentary and poorly preserved to be worth recovering from the site. It is probable that the tiles came the abbot's chapel which if so the foundations for this structure may still survive in the vicinity of Tyttenhanger house.

Material from the bund excavation

Hearth/kiln [1201]

A single tile and sample of mortar were retrieved from this structure. The tile was a reddish yellow colour (Mun 5YR 6/6) and measured 290mm x 180mm x 14mm. It was slightly bowed and had two nail or peg holes (11mm dia). It had been set in a light yellowish brown mortar (Mun 10YR 6/4) to fix it securely in position.

Garderobe [1217]

This was mainly built of flint and mortar but tile was used in the levelling courses and in the arched recess; in addition brick was used at the base of the structure. The tile was predominantly a yellowish red colour (Mun 5YR 5/6) and measured 215mm x 170mm x 14mm. The brick was red and unfrogged (Mun 2.5YR 4/6) and measured 225mm x 105mm x 50mm. The size of tile was the same as that used in the tile kiln [1526]. The mortar was yellowish brown (Mun 10YR 5/6).

Eastern gate house/tower [1208]

From the post-demolition fill [1203] came three pieces of building material. The brick debris was mostly broken and fairly soft. Several complete unfrogged bricks were recovered and these varied from a soft red fabric (Mun 2.5YR 4/6) to a harder reddish brown (Mun 2.5YR 5/4). They measured 230mm x 120mm x 55mm and wall [1205] was bonded by a brownish yellow mortar (Mun 10YR 6/6). An incomplete tile was recovered which was slightly bowed and reddish brown in colour (Mun 2.5YR 5/3). It was at least 230mm+ x 170mm x 14mm. The third piece was a fragment of a floor tile which was originally, probably square (208mm by 30mm thick. It had a greenish black glaze sealing a light red fabric (Mun 2.5YR 6/6).

Western gate house/tower [1210]

From a robber trench [1214] came three incomplete moulded brick fragments (Plate 22). The fabric was a fairly hard, red colour (Mun 2.5YR 5/6). The most common pieces were a round edged type or mullion (110mm wide by 47mm thick). The rounded end was sometimes slightly fluted and rendered with a fine thin, very pale brown mortar (Mun 10YR 7/4). The second piece was a simple chamfered brick (110mm wide by 55mm thick) with a darker type of rendering, possibly due to weathering. The third piece was both stepped in profile and with an angled end (at least 200mm long by 110mm wide and 58mm thick). It was also rendered by a very pale brown mortar (Mun 10YR 7/4).

The tiles from Beverley were in two sizes: 270 × 165-80 × 13-15mm and 310 × 190-205 × 15-18mm with a single pulled suspension nib (Youngs *et al* 1987, 146). The tiles from the 2nd phase kiln at Tylers Green, Penn, Bucks) were 290x170x12mm, which were dated by archaeomagnetic dating to between 1445-85. The tiles belonging to the 1st phase kiln were 270-80x170x13mm. Bricks in the blocking of the 3rd phase kiln were 225x120x48mm. Brick from the floor of the 4th phase kiln 230x110x40mm. Brick (reddish brown, unfrogged) from the 5th phase kiln, which had an archaeomagnetic date range of 1535-1670, was 220-228mmx110x54mm

Phase 1: Early medieval (1066-1399)
Phase 2: Late medieval (1400-1499)
Phase 3: Late medieval/early Tudor (1500-1539)
Phase 4: Early post-medieval (1540-1620)
Phase 5: Later post-medieval (1620-1775)
Phase 6: Modern (1900-present day)

Table 4: Summary of brick and tile

Context	Group	Feature Type	Decoration	Tile (floor)	Phase
U/s	north of 1524		A quarter design of foliage in circular bands	112 x 112 x 24 with chamfered side	U/S
U/s	On spoil heap		A quarter design of roundels at each corner with central fleur de lys	104 x 107 x 24 with chamfered side	U/S
U/s	north of 1524		Green glaze	270/163/22	U/S
			Brick	**Tile** (roof)	
U/S	nr. 1542		Length? x 105mm x 35mm		U/S
95	1525	Kiln ?	240 x 120 x 60	290 x 172; 223 x 140 x 20	3
120	1526	Tile Kiln	No brick present	215 x 160/170 x 15	2
170	1542	Drain	230 x 115	-	4
57	1522	Building	230 x 115; 235 x 119 x 60	250 x 170	2/3
1026	1546	Garden wall	220 x 100 x 65; 230 x 100 x 60	-	4
1084	1529	Courtyard	? x 135 x 60 ; 230 x 120 x 60	-	3
200	1527	Corn dryer	150 x 150 x 40	-	1
72; 1071	1547	Garden wall	210 x 110 x 80; 230 x 110 x 50	-	4
1006	1538	Brick base	230 x 110 x 50	-	4
1203	1570	Fill of 1208	230 mm x 120mm x 55 mm	230 + (?) x 170 x 14mm	3
1205	1570	Eastern gate house wall	230 x 120 x 55mm		3
1217	1532	Garderobe	225mm x 105mm x 50mm	215 x 170x 14mm	2
1201	1534	Tile hearth	No brick present	290 x 180 x 10mm	2/3
	Buildings	Existing out buildings	230 x ? x 58mm; 193 ? x 62mm (some 115mm wide); ?mm x 110 x 50mm;		4
	Tytt. house	Existing roof		270 x 155 x 11mm	5
	Tytt. house	Chimney stack (W)	230mm x 110 x 60mm		4

* The minimum size of tiles decreed in the statute of 1477 was 266 × 158 × 16mm, or 10½" × 6¼" × ⅝" (Salzman 1952, 230).

APPENDIX 1.5: ARCHITECTURAL STONE

by Nicholas Doggett

Description

Of the four fragments of architectural stone retrieved during the excavation, two [6012 & 6013], were recovered from unstratified context. Both are of Jurassic limestone. [6012] is heavily abraded and may have been part of a paving slab; [6013] is roughly dressed on its top flat surface with a slightly concave chamfered edge giving way to another roughly dressed vertical surface. It is possible that this fragment formed part of a roughly dressed stone coping on top of a rubblesone or more probably brick wall.

The two other fragments [6010 and 6011] were excavated from the fill of Ditch 1500. [6010] is of Totternhoe clunch and has a roughly dressed top flat surface with a steeply chamfered edge giving way to another roughly dressed vertical surface. While it may, like [6013] simply have formed part of a wall coping, irregularities to one corner of the flat top surface may

indicate that it formed part of a window sill. [6011] is the most obviously 'architectural' of the fragments. It is composed of Oolitic limestone and its top flat surface is undressed and was clearly not exposed to the elements; on the exposed side the presence of a moulded 'cornice' above a concave-chamfered vertical surface indicates that the fragment may have formed part of a moulded window head.

Interpretation

None of the architectural fragments is easily datable, although the moulding of the apparent window head suggests a late 15th or early 16th century date. All, however, support the idea that some of the re-cuts of Ditch 1500 were associated with the removal of building material from a wall that ran along this boundary. It is possible that the clunch fragment was re-used from an earlier phase of building than the others.

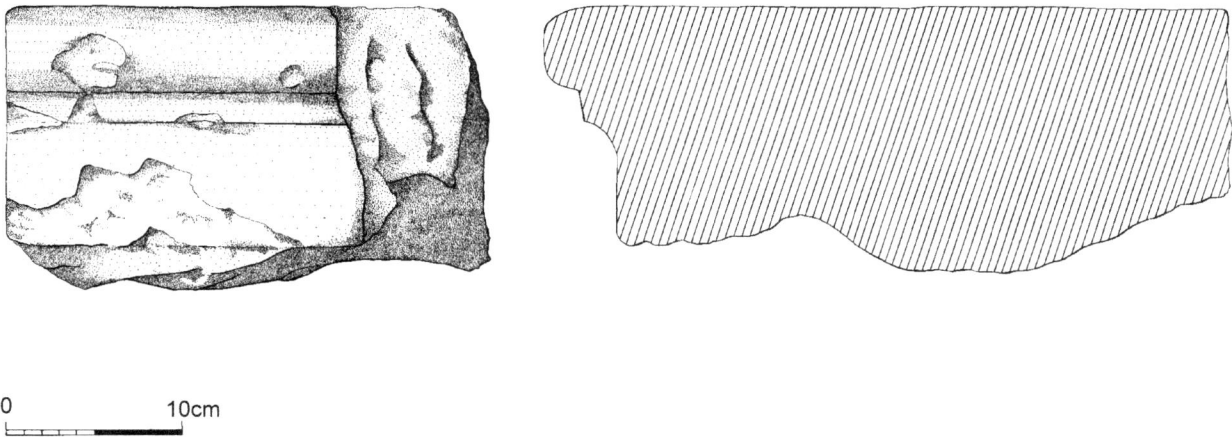

0   10cm

Fig. 45.1: Architectural fragments

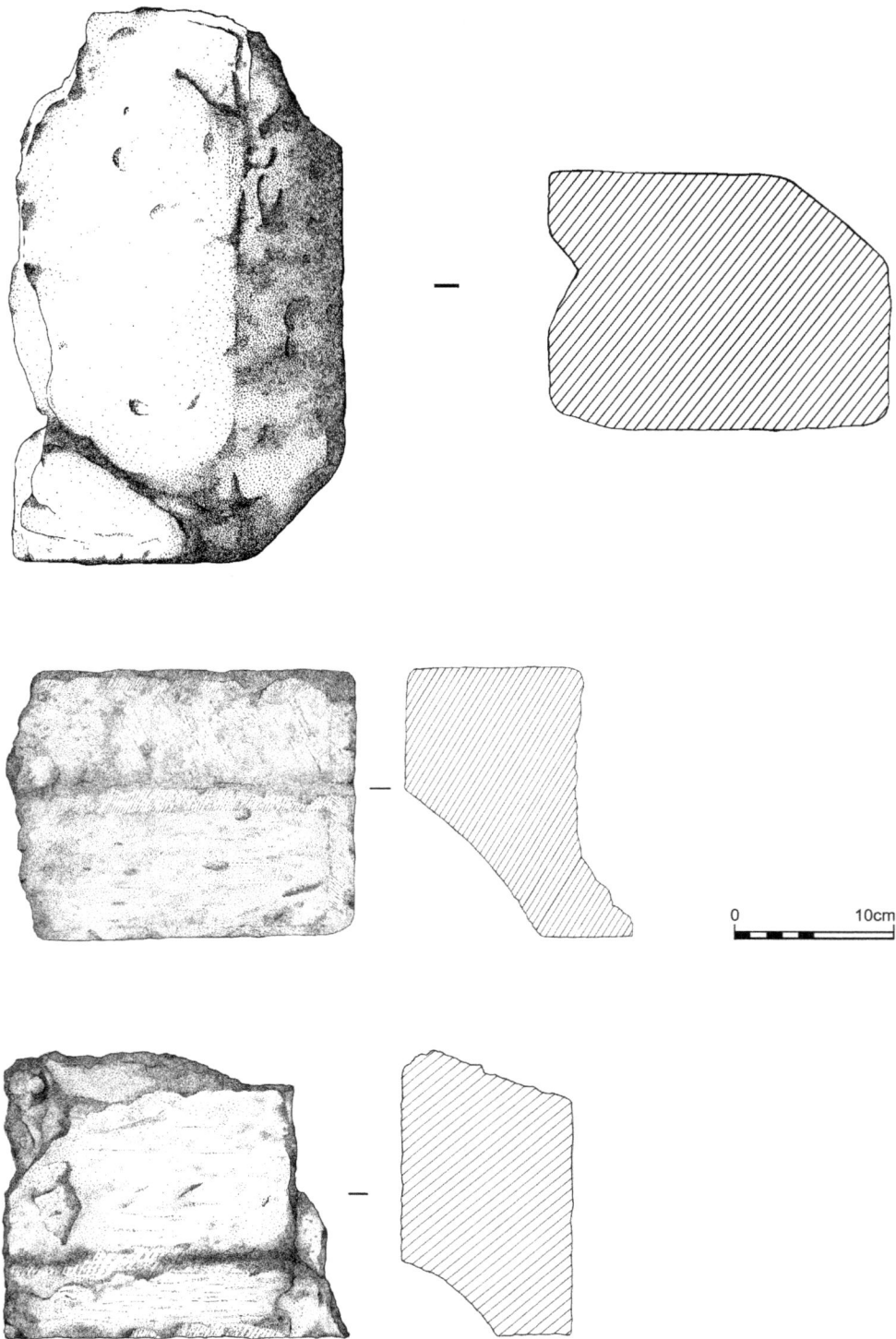

Fig. 45. 2: Architectural fragments

APPENDIX 1.6: METAL DETECTOR SURVEY

A total of 61 metal artefacts were recovered by C. Ribbans and R. Paul using metal detectors on the site after the topsoil was removed. The assemblage consisted mainly of coinage and buckles, with some occasional domestic objects. Of all the artefacts recovered during this phase of the work, 60 % of both assemblages were dated to the 15th and 16th centuries, highlighting the main period of activity on the site. Spatially, the distribution of the finds reflected the concentration of archaeological features in the area to the south of the present house (Fig. 46).

The results of this survey reinforce the interpretation of the archaeological deposits.

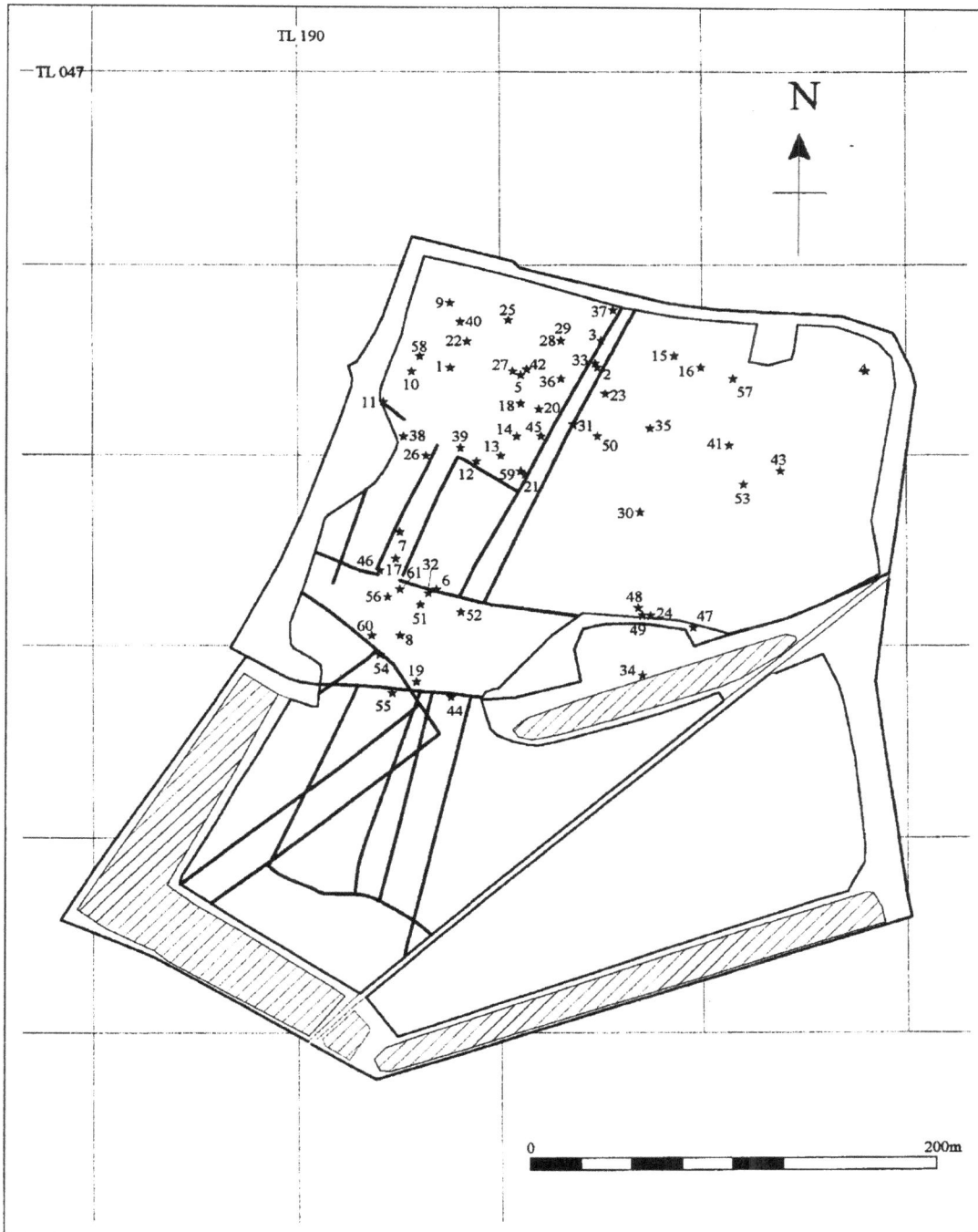

Fig.46: Distribution of finds recovered by the metal detector survey

Table 5: Metal finds from the metal detector survey

No	SF No.	Type	Additional Description	Monarch	Date	NGR
1	6010	Half groat	-	Edward IV	1461-85	19075/04524
2	6011	Penny	Sovereign type	Henry VIII	1509-47	19148/04546
3	6012	Penny	-	Henry VIII	1509-47	19150/04560
4	6013	Groat	-	Elizabeth I	1558-1603	19280/04544
5	6014	3 pence	-	Elizabeth I	1558-1603	19110/04542
6	6015	Groat	-	Elizabeth I	1558-1603	19068/04430
7	6016	Shilling	-	James I	1603-1625	19050/04460
8	6017	Half groat	-	Charles I	1625-1649	19050/04406
9	6018	Rose farthing	-	-	17thC.	19075/04580
10	6019	Cu alloy disc	Marie de France	-	18thC	19056/04544
11	6020	Jetton	-	-	16thC	19042/04528
12	6021	Jetton	-	-	-	19088/04497
13	6022	Jetton	-	-	-	19100/04500
14	6023	Jetton	-	-	-	19108/04510
15	6024	Bronze dagger chape	62mm	-	16thC	19186/04552
16	6025	Bronze sword chape	50mm	-	16thC	19199/04546
17	6026	Bronze ring	-	-	15/16thC	19048/04446
18	6027	Ornate buckle	34mm	-	Georgian	19110/04527
19	6028	Handle fragment	-	-	-	19058/04382
20	6029	Cu alloy buckle	-	-	Medieval?	19119/04524
21	6030	Cu alloy buckle	Plus pin	-	Tudor	19112/04490
22	6031	Cu alloy buckle	-	-	Tudor	19078/04560
23	6032	Cu alloy buckle	D-shaped	-	Medieval	19152/04532
24	6033	Brooch	30 mm circular	-	-	19174/04416
25	6034	Crotal bell	-	-	18thC	19104/04571
26	6035	Ring brooch/buckle	Fe pin intact	-	Late med/Tudor	19063/04500
27	6036	Bronze crossbow bolt	Tip broken off	-	16thC	19106/04544
28	6037	Decorative lead fragments	Leaf-like fronds; Yorkist sun	-	-	19130/04560
29	6038	Window leading	-	-	16thC	19130/04560
30	6039	Spectacle buckle	18mm and strap plate	-	16thC	19169/04470
31	6040	Cu alloy button	Long shank	-	Tudor	19136/04516
32	6041	Bronze artefact	Dagger quillon?	-	-	19064/04428
33	6042	Bronze circular mount	17mm	-	-	19147/04548
34	6043	lead token	O: Crude quadruped R abstract design	-	-	19170/04385
35	6044	Iron key	191mm long	-	-	19174/04514
36	6045	Iron handle fragment	102mm long	-	-	19130/04540
37	6046	lead weight	Pyramidal shape	-	-	19156/04576
38	6047	Lead weight	Circular shape	-	-	19052/04510
39	6048	Lead bag seal	-	-	-	19080/04504
40	6049	Lead letter	'A'; 60mm high	-	-	19080/04570
41	6050	Penny	Bishop Wolsey type / Durham mint	Henry VIII	1520	19213/04505
42	6051	Penny	London mint	Henry VIII	1545	19113/04545
43	6052	Groat	Bristol mint	Henry VIII	1540	19238/04492
44	6053	Nuremberg jeton	Sceptre type	-	1570	19075/04374
45	6054	Nuremberg jeton	Sceptre type	-	1570	19120/04510
46	6055	Nuremberg jeton	Ship type	-	1550	19040/04440
47	6056	Denarius	Fragments of; forgery	?	Roman?	19195/04410
48	6057	Half penny	Copper	William III	1700	19168/04420
49	6058	Jetons (x2)	Copies of coins of Louis XIV	?	-	19170/04416
50	6059	Farthing	Royal/Richmond; copper	Charles I	1625-1649	19148/04510
51	6060	Groat	Damaged	Edward IV	1465	19060/04422
52	6061	half penny	Leaf-pellet issue	Henry VI	1450	19080/04418
53	6062	Cu alloy buckle	Large double loop	-	16/17thC	19220/04485
54	6063	Dress fastener	Hook type	-	16/17thC	19040/04396
55	6064	Cu alloy bell	Hawking bell?	-	16thC	19046/04376
56	6065	Cu alloy thimble	Squashed	-	15thC	19044/04426
57	6066	Cu alloy buckle	Decorated rectangular type	-	17thC	19215/04540
58	6067	Cu alloy buckle	Single loop of Saxon type?	-	-	19060/04552
59	6068	Folding knife	Iron with bone handle	-	Post-med	19110/04492
60	6069	Iron axe head	-	-	Pre-conquest?	19036/04406
61	6070	Maiden head decoration	Decoration from priest's laver bowl	-	1450	19050/04430

APPENDIX 1.7: CONTENTS OF HOUSEHOLD DUMP
(pit 1562. Fig 39)
by Andy Richmond

Introduction:
Following soil stripping of Phase 1 at Tyttenhanger Quarry an isolated pit [1562] was identified which upon excavation was seen to contain a quantity of refuse. It is believed to represent a small rubbish pit dating to the earlier part of the 20th century. The primary matrix of the pit's fill was grey ash (from the rake out of fires), and this contained a variety of utilitarian glass and stoneware containers. The following items recovered enable us to identify the date of the feature and the nature of the refuse contained within.

Mineral water bottles:
Fragments from at least ten mineral water bottles were found. Five were of undetermined provenance, but three were identified as originating from the Company of Caley, Norwich, and another two were from *Adey & White* of St Albans. The Caley bottles were each of aqua glass and are known as 'flat-bottomed hamiltons' with cork closures. This company had retail outlets throughout eastern and southern England during the earlier years of the 20th century and its bottle are regular finds on refuse tips of this age. The local Adey & White bottles were both damaged, but it was possible to see they were 'Premier' patent bottles of a 6oz and a 10oz capacity in aqua glass with internal stoppers made of glass. This variety of bottle closure works upon a similar principle to the codd marble-stoppered bottle popular at the turn of the century, and is known as a patent variation, of which hundreds were developed. The date of the Adey & White bottles is *circa* 1900-15.

Cream Jugs
Several whole and many broken cream jugs were recovered, none with company names impressed or stamped. Each was of stoneware with a treacle glaze. The majority originally had handles, all of which were broken at the time of recovery.

Ginger Beer bottles
Considering the high quantity of ginger beer which was consumed at the turn of the century it was perhaps surprising that only a single bottle of this type was recovered, perhaps representing a worker's throw-out after a hard mornings work. The bottle was a standard-shape cork-closure stoneware bottle in all-over brown glaze impressed *Temple Mineral Waters, Barnet*. Blob-top cork closure bottles were used between the years 1900 to 1912. As with the majority of ginger beer bottles, this one had a potters mark stamped near the base showing it to be from the Bourne, Denby factories. The number 4 on the stamp indicates the date of manufacture of the bottle (not the contents) in 1904. This date should not necessarily indicate the date of the pit deposit, for such bottles were to be returned for re-filling and re-sale. The life of a bottle may therefore cover many years until its breakage or the closure of the company.

Ink bottles
Numerous (c 20-30) bulk ink containers were recovered from the pit, each being of plain salt-glazed stoneware. Various sizes were recorded, the smallest being of *c* 2oz size and the largest of *c* 30oz size. Several of these ink bottles displayed the pottery mark of Doulton & Co, Lambeth close to the base indicating the manufacturers of the vessels. One of these stamps displayed the number 12, indicating a date of 1912. In addition to the stoneware bottles, several small aqua glass inks were found, one having the

embossing of *Blackwood & Co, Patent, London*, a company still making inks today.

Paste pots
Several stoneware paste jars and pots were recovered, the majority having no impressing or stamping. Most were of simple salt-glaze, but several were of two-tone, having a lighter slip applied to the rims. Various sizes were recorded, the largest having a capacity of 60 oz. Approximately 10 (several being broken) mustard jars from the same company were recovered, clearly representing a favoured product. These were of stoneware covered in a white slip and carrying an under-glazed transfer reading *Moutard de Maille, Vinaigrier Distillateur, Fournisseur, des premieres Cours, De L'Europe, PARIS*. These are known to have been a popular product from *c* 1910-1930 available at several outlets in London. A possible stoneware caviar pot with no markings was found and two pot lids were recovered (both damaged) one advertising cherry tooth powder (J Gosnell & Co) the other anchovy paste (Burgess's, Hythe Rd, London) both dating to *c* 1910.

Poison bottles
Several broken poison bottles were recovered from the pit, each being of cobalt blue glass, rectangular in shape and with vertical ribbing down the front and sides, with 'Not To Be Taken' embossed on the front. The ribbing on the glass was used to inform blind or poorly sighted people that the bottle contained poisonous liquid. All manner of substances were contained in such bottles, including arsenic and cyanide.

Others:
A variety of other items were recovered from the pit including fragments of at least one water filter and numerous broken pieces of china, both kitchen and decorative wares. Fragments of items of kitchenalia included mugs, plates, butter crocks and preserve jars. Three varieties of preserve jars were recovered being from the firms of *James Keiller* of Dundee, *John Moir & Sons* of Aberdeen and London and *The Army & Navy Co-operative Stores* of London. A fragment of a large (1 gallon) two-tone stoneware flagon was found, being impressed on the neck *Thomas Oakley & Compy, St Albans Supply Stores, St Albans*. This perhaps represents a local hardware company who will have sold a variety of liquids from such vessels. Usually flagons contained ginger beer or beer, but examples are known which advertise vinegar, olive oil, varnish, and medical substances. Many aqua glass bottles were found (*c* 50), the majority un-embossed, but those with embossing advertised sauces, bath salts, hair preparations, medicines and embrocations. In addition, several broken bottles which contained maraschino liquor were identified. These so-called Zara bottles were very popular at the turn of century, being imported from the continent and sold throughout numerous outlets in Britain. Many pieces of rusty metal were also contained by the pit, the majority being unidentifiable. Two large metal water tanks formed, perhaps, the primary fill of the feature, before the remaining refuse was filled in around.

Concluding Statement:
The pit is a small refuse tip, no doubt associated with Tyttenhanger House, but not representing the main tip for the property. The small size of the pit suggests it was used for the disposal of household refuse over a short period, perhaps on no more than five to ten occasions. It may be that is it was used by workers on the estate to fill a hole (made for other purposes such as to obtain gravel) with rubbish available at the time it required re-instating. The items recovered from the pit show it was filled in the years *circa* 1900-15.

APPENDIX 1.8:
ENVIRONMENTAL EVIDENCE
by James Rackham

Three environmental samples were taken during the course of the project, all from corn drying kilns.

Table 6: Environmental samples

Sample No	Context	Group	Feature Type	Description	Volume (l)
7000	1137	1528	corn dryer kiln	Ashy layer on the floor of stoke hole	9
7001	1135	1528	corn dryer kiln	Fill of the middle section of flue	10
7002	203	1527	corn dryer kiln	Ashy fill of flue	9

Samples 7000 and 7001 contained little artefactual material with a few fragments of brick/tile from 7000, three sherds of pottery from each sample and a few fragments of animal bone. Both residues were largely chalk, with some small flint gravel and sand. A higher proportion of flint and pebble gravel was present in 7001. The samples from Feature [1528] were dominated by charred plant remains in which charcoal, charred cereal grains and charred weed seeds were abundant. Chaff remains, although common in 7001, were only represented by a few fragments in 7000. The abundance of charred cereal in both these samples supports an interpretation of the kiln structure as a corn-dryer, but the character of the botanical remains present in 7001 suggests that a partly processed crop was being dried, not a cleaned one. It is however, possible that the chaff from winnowing the crop was being burnt on the fire that heated the kiln. Detailed analysis of the botanical remains is required to address what stage the crop processing these remains reflect. 5.0g of charred cereal grains from 7001 were retained for radiocarbon dating at a later date. Both samples from feature [1528] included abundant terrestrial mollusc shells. Both open country and shaded habitats were represented in these taxa, although the latter may have reflected the shaded environment afforded by the kiln or its ruins, rather than extensive woodland. The residue from feature [1527] indicates the character of the context was different from the samples from [1528]. A high proportion of the sample was composed of flint and pebble gravel, with some pebbles up to 80mm in diameter, with a little burnt stone but no chalk. The environmental remains were dominated by charcoal, much of it oak, from large timbers as well as smaller roundwood of 30mm diameter. Charred cereal grains were abundant, but unlike the samples from [1528] very little chaff and very few weed seeds were present. The cereal remains in this feature had been already cleaned before they were burnt. The concentration of cereal in all three samples is suggestive of both structures being corn drying kilns, although the character of the cereal remains and other charred material in each was different. Although not specifically identified, wheat appears to dominate the grain assemblages, with barley and oats (possibly rye) in much lesser quantities.

ANIMAL BONE

Thirty-three bones and the partial skeletons of at least six juvenile feral doves and three adult doves were collected from Feature [1540]. The partial skeletons of juveniles suggest a location where doves were breeding, and this structure may be associated with a dovecote or similar suitable building.

Pit fill [193], associated with agricultural Building [1542], contained five cattle metapodial bones and no other bones. This assemblage included one extremely large metatarsus with a greatest length of 267mm. This corresponds to an animal with a withers height of 1.45m.

The layer of demolition debris [110] associated with the collapse of a group of agricultural buildings contained evidence of cattle, horse, sheep, and pig bones, some of which were dog gnawed.

The bones in general were in good condition of preservation, except for fragments from Contexts 12, 1002 and 1003, which showed a greater level of surface erosion than other fragment.

Table 7: Animal bone

Context	Group	Feature Type	Species	No. of individuals	Butcher Marks	Phase
12	1500	Ditch	Sheep/ goat	1	-	3
52	1558	Tree avenue	Cattle	1	Yes	4
76	1540	Dovecote	Dove	1	-	2/3
77	1540	Dovecote	Frog/ toad	1	-	2/3
77	1540	Dovecote	Mole	1	-	2/3
77	1540	Dovecote	Young and adult Doves	8	-	2/3
110	-	Demolition Layer	Cattle	6	Yes	3
110	-	Demolition Layer	Cattle sized	3	Yes	3
110	-	Demolition Layer	Horse	2	-	3
110	-	Demolition Layer	Sheep/ goat	2	-	3
110	-	Demolition Layer	Pig	1	-	3
110	-	Demolition Layer	Unknown	1	-	3
154	1561	Saw pit	Cattle	1	Yes	4
193	1542	Pit	Cattle	5	-	4
1002	1537	Flint Platform	Cattle	1	-	4
1002	1537	Flint Platform	Cattle sized	1	-	4
1003	-	Pit	Cattle	1	-	4
1003	-	Pit	Cattle sized	1	-	4
U/s	-	-	Cattle	1	Yes	-

APPENDIX 1.9: CHARRED PLANT REMAINS
by John Giorgi

INTRODUCTION
During excavations at the site, three bulk soil samples were collected for the recovery of biological remains, including charred plant material, from two features interpreted as corn driers. The initial assessment suggested that the botanical remains could provide evidence on the use of these two features and possibly information on aspects of crop husbandry and processing.

SAMPLING, RECOVERY AND IDENTIFICATION METHODS
Three samples were collected, processed and assessed. Two samples were from kiln [1138] consisting of a nine litre sample <7000> from an ashy layer [1137] on the floor of the stoke hole and a ten litre sample <7001> from the fill [1135] of the middle section of the flue. The other sample (nine litres) was from a deposit [203] associated with a similar shaped feature. Both features are considered to be of medieval date and radiocarbon dating of cereal grain from kiln [1138] has produced an early 14th-century date.

The flots were divided into size fractions using a stack of sieves for ease of sorting. The richest charred plant assemblage from [1135] sample <7001> (kiln [1138]) was not sorted but only scanned because of the density of the plant remains; items, however, that were not readily identifiable were extracted for further examination. The charred plant remains from the other two samples from [1137] (kiln [1138]) and [203] were sorted and quantified with the exception of small cereal fragments (less than 2mm), charcoal and indeterminate items; estimates of their frequency, however, were made. Identification of the plant material was carried out using a binocular microscope together with modern and charred reference material and reference manuals. The habitat information was obtained from Clapham *et al* (1987).

RESULTS
The results are shown in Table 8. The three samples all produced rich charred plant assemblages with the richest assemblage being from [1135] sample <7001> (kiln [1138]) with a high frequency of cereal grain, chaff, stem fragments, and weed seeds. The other sample <7000> from this kiln from [1137] contained a fairly similar and rich charred plant assemblage with cereal grains and weed seeds but virtually no chaff or stem fragments. The sample from [203] contained mainly cereal grains. A large amount of fragmented wood charcoal was present in all the samples with particularly large fragments in [203]. A small number of seeds preserved by waterlogging and representing wild plants were found in all three samples and included elder (*Sambucus nigra*), brambles (*Rubus* spp.), nettles (*Urtica* spp.) and celery-leaved crowfoot (*Ranunculus sceleratus*); these seeds are probably intrusive. There follows a discussion of the range of cereals and weed seeds.

The cereals
Cereals were represented in the samples mainly by grains although chaff and ?straw fragments were found mainly in [1135]. Wheat (*Triticum* spp.), barley (*Hordeum sativum*), rye (*Secale cereale*) and oats (*Avena* spp.) were all identified in the

samples although the condition of the cereal grains was not good particularly in the samples from [1137] and [203] and the majority of the grains could not be identified.

Wheat was the best represented cereal in the samples with the well preserved grains being identified as free-threshing wheats, either hexaploid, e.g. bread wheat (*Triticum aestivum* s.l), or tetraploid wheats, e.g. rivet wheat (*T. turgidum*), durum wheat (*T. durum*). These species are distinguishable by their rachis fragments and the presence of hexaploid wheat rachis fragments in sample <7001> from [1135] confirmed the presence of bread wheats. A number of wheat rachis fragments, however, could not be identified. Oats were well represented in the samples although no floret bases were recovered. Thus, it was not possible to establish whether these were wild (*Avena fatua*) or cultivated (*A. sativa*) oats. Oats, however, were widely grown and used during the medieval period. Barley grains were not particularly abundant although the presence of both straight and twisted grains indicated the presence of six-row hulled barley in the samples; a few barley rachis fragments in sample <7001> from [1135] were also identified. Only several rye grains were found in the three samples.

Charred stem fragments were present in large numbers in sample <7001> from [1135]; the well preserved fragments were large, ribbed and hollow and included nodes and internodes. It is difficult to distinguish between the straw of cereals and large wild grasses (van der Veen 1991, 353) although the association of these remains with rich charred grain assemblages suggests that they are probably from cereals.

The four cereals found on the site, free-threshing wheat, barley, rye and oats, are the four main cereals represented as archaeobotanical remains on medieval sites in southern England (Greig 1991, 321). The representation of the different cereals in the samples corresponds well with the historical evidence. Thus, the predominance of wheat in the samples is reflected in the historical records showing that it was the main crop cultivated in the London region in the 14th century and also the main bread grain (Campbell *et al*, 1993, 38). Oats, which were also well represented in the samples, was almost as widely grown as wheat because of its many uses both as human food (for brewing, pottage) and animal fodder. Barley, the main cereal used in brewing, was cultivated on a smaller scale (ibid, 38). Rye was also an important bread grain although it was not well represented on the site.

Pulses
Pulses were represented by a moderate number of seeds and fragments in the two samples from kiln [1138]; the condition of the remains was such, however, that no definite cultivated species could be identified. Some of the larger fragments were classified as vetch/vetchling/pea (*Vicia/Lathyrus/Pisum* spp.), which may include cultivated species although the smaller leguminous seeds probably belong to wild species, possibly cereal weeds. Pulses did however, have important uses in the medieval period for restoring nitrogen to the soil and were used as both animal and human food.

Table 8: Charred plant remains

Species		No. of specimens		
		kiln 1138	**kiln 1138**	**?kiln -**
Cereal grains				
Triticum aestivum s.l..	free-threshing wheat	34	+++(+)	21
*T.*cf. *aestivum* s.l..	?free-threshing wheat	61		35
Triticum spp.	wheat	65	++	58
Triticum/Secale cereale L.	wheat/rye			
Secale cereale L.	rye	1	+	1
cf. *S. cereale*	?rye		+	1
Hordeum sativum L.	barley	2	++(+)	3
cf. *H. sativum* L.	barley	1		4
Avena sp(p).	oat	8	++(+)	36
cf *Avena* sp(p).	?oat	29	++	50
indeterminate cereals	indet. grains	313	++++	211
indeterminate cereal frags	indet. grains <2mm	+++		+++
Cereal chaff				
Triticum aestivum s.l..	hexaplod wheat rachis frag		++(+)	
Triticum spp.	wheat rachis fragments		+++	
Hordeum sativum L.	barley rachis fragments		+	
indet. cereal	cereal rachis fragments	1	+	
indet	stem frags		++(+)	
Other plants				
Brassica/Sinapis spp.	-		+	
Silene spp	campion/catchfly	6	+	
Silene/Stellaria spp	catchfly/stitchwort	4		
Agrostemma githago L.	corncockle		+	
Stellaria media gp	chickweed	1		
Caryophyllaceae	-		+	
Chenopodium sp(p).	goosefoots etc.	1	+	
Atriplex spp	orache	24	+	
Chenopodium/Atriplex spp	goosefoots etc./oraches		++	1
Malva spp.	mallow	12		
Medicago sp(p).	medick	1	+	
Vicia/Lathyrus spp.	vetch/tare/vetchling	3		
Vicia/Lathyrus/Pisum spp.	vetch/vetchling/pea	5	+++	
Fabaceae indet.	indet. legumes (frags & small rounded seeds)	23	+++	
Rumex sp(p).	dock	65	++	1
Lithospermum arvense L.	corn gromwell	11(m)	+++	
Euphrasia/Odontites spp.	-		++(+)	
Plantago major L.	great plantain	1		
Galium spp.	bedstraw	3	+	
Sambucus nigra L.	elder		+	
Valerinella dentata (L.) Poll.	narrow-fruited corn salad		+	
Anthemis cotula L.	stinking mayweed	111	+++	1
Anthemis spp.	-	33	+	
Lapsana communis L.	nipplewort	2	+	
Cyperaceae	-		+	
Festuca/Lolium spp.	fescue/rye-grass	6		
Lolium spp.	rye-grass	7	+	
Bromus sp(p).	brome	1	+	
Poaceae	indet small grasses	6		3
indet plant items(charred)	-	+++	++	+
charcoal fragments	-	+++	++++	++++

key: +=1-10 items; ++=11-50 items;+++=51-100 items;++++=100+ items

Wild plants

Wild plants were well represented in the two samples from kiln [1138] and included a wide range of species. Many of the weed seeds, however, could not be identified to species which limits the ecological information because species within a genus may have significantly different habitats. Nevertheless, the majority of the charred weed seeds were from plants of disturbed (including cultivated) ground and waste places; characteristic arable weeds included stinking mayweed (*Anthemis cotula*), a cereal weed of heavy clay soils, corn gromwell (*Lithospermum arvense*) (which was represented by mineralised items), narrow-fruited corn salad (*Valerinella dentata*), corncockle (*Agrostemma githago*), bedstraw (*Galium* spp.) and brome (*Bromus* spp.).

The remaining seeds were from wild species that may grow in a range of habitats including disturbed ground and waste places but also grassland environments; this includes docks (*Rumex* spp.) which were well represented, *Euphrasia/Odontites* species, catchfly/stitchwort (*Silene/Stellaria* spp.), goosefoots etc./oraches (*Chenopodium/Atriplex* spp.), great plantain (*Plantago major*), mallow (*Malva* spp.), leguminous plants, eg. medick (*Medicago* spp.), and various grasses, eg. fescue/rye-grass (*Festuca* spp/*Lolium* spp.). The association of these weed seeds with the cereal grains, however, suggests that many of these plants were probably growing as arable weeds and imported onto site with the harvested grain. There were very few woodland/hedgerow plants represented as charred seeds except a few elder (*Sambucus nigra*) and nipplewort (*Lapsana communis*).

DISCUSSION

The quantity of charred plant remains in the three samples was high with the greatest density of remains per litre of soil being in the scanned sample <7001> from [1135]. The two quantified samples from [1137] and [203] produced 94 and 47 items per litre of soil respectively (excluding charcoal, small cereal fragments and indeterminate material).

There were significant differences in the composition of the plant assemblages with the two samples <7001> and <7001> from kiln [1138] containing both cereals and weed seeds while the sample from [203] contained a virtually clean deposit of cereal grains. There were also differences between the two samples from kiln [1138] with [1135] sample <7001> containing not only cereal grains and weed seeds but other parts of the cereal plant with chaff and stem fragments. These parts of

the cereal represent by-products from the early stages (threshing, winnowing and raking) of crop-processing of free-threshing cereals. The other sample <7000> from [1137] contained virtually none of these early crop-processing by-products. The majority of the small weed seeds in both samples from kiln [1138] would have been separated by sieving although larger

weed seeds found in the samples, e.g. bedstraw, corncockle, brome, and have a similar size to the cereal grains would have been more difficult to separate other than by hand-sorting.

The kilns would have been used for drying grain either before storage or milling. Grains would have been cleaned if intended for human consumption but not for animal fodder. The main crop, however was free-threshing wheat, which was used exclusively as human food. Much of the by-products (i.e. the chaff) was also from wheat. It is likely therefore that the plant assemblages represent a mixed product with the chaff, straw and weed seeds representing residues from tinder (from crop-processing by-products) used to fuel the kiln; indeed the recovery of the two samples from the stoke-hole and flue would support their use as such. This material was mixed with cereal grain which may have been accidentally charred during drying. The kiln would have been cleaned between operations. The mixed assemblages may represent the residues from the final operation of the kiln used to backfill the feature once it was no longer in use. The sample from [203] contained virtually no by-products and therefore probably derives from the accidental charring of the cleaned cereal grain.

CONCLUSIONS

The three charred plant assemblages from the kiln samples provide useful information on the range of cereals used at the site with free-threshing wheats being particularly well represented followed by oats and then barley. This corresponds well with the historical evidence for this period although little comment may be made on the few rye grains. The majority of the wild plant seeds probably represent arable weeds with stinking mayweed suggesting the cultivation of clay soils around the site. The presence of by-products from the early stages of crop-processing (the chaff, straw fragments) as well as from the later stages (e.g. weed seeds) suggests that the site was producing its own crops. The plant assemblages in kiln [1138] is probably a result of mixing of the cleaned cereal grains and weed seeds, chaff and straw from their use as tinder, possibly used as backfill once the kiln went out of use.

APPENDIX: 1.10: CONTEXT GROUPS

Over the duration of the project 223 contexts were recorded in the excavation area and 144 from the enhanced and normal watching brief. From these 367 contexts, 68 feature groups were identified from the archaeological record. Most of the groups (27) consisted of walls from buildings and structures. Ditches and gullies accounted for 21 of the group types. The remainder of the record consisted of fences, pits, flower beds and tree avenues.

Table 9: Context groups

Group	Type	Date	Phase
1500	Enclosure Ditch	15th -17th	2/5
1501	Enclosure Ditch	15th -17th	2/5
1502	Enclosure Ditch	15th -17th	2/5
1503	Enclosure Ditch	15th -17th	2/5
1504	Ditch	17th/18th	4/5
1505	Enclosure Ditch	15th -17th	2/5
1506	Enclosure Ditch	Early 15th	2
1507	Field Boundary Ditch	14th-16th	1/4
1508	Field Boundary Ditch	14th-16th	1/4
1509	Field Boundary Ditch	14th-16th	1/4
1510	Field Boundary Ditch	14th-16th	1/4
1511	Field Boundary Ditch	10th/11th	1
1512	Field Boundary Ditch	10th-14th?	1
1513	Field Boundary Ditch	10th-14th?	1
1514	Field Boundary Ditch	10th-14th?	1
1515	Field Boundary Ditch	10th/14th-18th/19th	1/6
1516	Field Boundary Ditch	10th-14th?	1
1517	Ditch	17th/18th	5
1518	Enclosure Ditch	15th -17th	2/5
1519	Ditch	?	?
1520	Drainage Gully	17th/18th	5
1521	Barn	Early 18th	5
1522	Barn/stables	15 –16th	3/4
1523	Extension to barn	16th	3/4
1524	Building	15th/16th	3/4
1525	Tile Kiln	16th	3/4
1526	Tile Kiln	15th-16th	3/4
1527	Corn Dryer	12th -14th	1
1528	Corn Dryer	12th -14th	1
1529	Inner courtyard	1500-1539	3
1530	Building	15th/16th	2/4
1531	Building	Late medieval	2
1532	Building	Late medieval	2
1533	Garden Structure -Bed	17th/18th	4/5
1534	Hearth/kiln	1540-1620	4
1535	Garden Structure -Bed	17th/18th	4/5
1536	Garden Structure -Bed	17th/18th	4/5
1537	Flint Platform	17th/18th	4/5
1538	Brick Base	18th-19th?	5/6
1539	Garden Structure - Plinth	17th/18th	4/5
1540	Dovecote/ rookery?	16th-18th	3/5
1541	Shed	17th/18th	4/5
1542	Agricultural Building	17th/18th	4/5
1543	Agricultural Building	17th/18th	4/5
1544	Agricultural Building	17th/18th	4/5
1545	Yard Surface	17th/18th	4/5
1546	Garden – Main Wall	16th-18th	3/5
1547	Garden – Wall	17th/18th	4/5
1548	Wall	?	?
1549	Compound Walls	15th/16th	2/4
1550	Fence line	15th/16th	2/4
1551	Fence line	17th/18th	4/5
1552	Fence line	17th/18th	4/5
1553	Fence line	17th/18th	4/5
1554	Garden – Flower Bed	17th/18th	4/5
1555	Garden - Tree Cluster	17th/18th	4/5
1556	Garden – Flower Beds	17th/18th	4/5
1557	Garden - Tree Avenue	17th	5
1558	Garden - Tree Avenue	17th/18th	4/5
1559	Garden – Hollow	17th/18th	4/5
1560	Extraction Hollow	15th/16th	2/4
1561	Saw Pit	Early 18th	5
1562	Rubbish Pit	Early 20th	6
1563	Burnt Areas	?	?
1564	Agricultural Pits	Late 17th-Early 18th	5
1565	Service Trench - Water	19th	6
1566	Service Trench - Water	Late 18th	5
1567	Service Trench - Electricity	20th	6

APPENDIX 1.11: CONCORDANCE LIST OF FEATURES

Table 10: groups, contexts, sections and photographic numbers

Group no.	Type	Feature	Fill	Section number	Photo archive no.
1500	Ditch	14, 15, 16, 24, 26, 28, 30, 32, 34, 36, 39, 41, 44, 48, 144, 146, 151	12, 13, 27, 31, 35, 25, 29, 40, 42, 47, 49, 88, 145, 152	5005,5006, 5007,5023, 5024,	117, 123, 124, 129, 146
1501	Ditch	108	107	5010	131, 132
	Ditch	111	112	5014	
	Ditch	115	116	5016	
	Ditch	132	133		140
1502	Ditch	146	147		116
	Ditch	150	147		
1503	Ditch	141	143		147
	Ditch	142	143	5022	144
	Ditch	197	198	5027	
1504	Ditch	130	131	5018	139
1505	Ditch	134	135		141
	Ditch	117	118	5017	138
1506	Ditch	174	194	5029	100
	Gully	195	196	5028	
1507	Ditch	136	137	5030, 5031	93, 142
	Ditch	138	137		
1508	Ditch	199			
1509	Ditch	1130			
1510	Ditch	1129			
1511	Ditch	1079			
	Ditch	1126			
1512	Ditch	1125			
1513	Ditch	1128			
1514	Ditch	1127			
1515	Ditch	1032			
1516	Ditch	1131			
1517	Ditch	192			
	Ditch	207			
1518	Ditch	113	114	5015	142
1519	Ditch	1025			
1520	Ditch	168	169		
1521	Building	1004			10
1522	Building	55			66
		56			
		58			
		59			
		64			89
		66			
		67			
		68			
1523	Building	60			
		61			
		62			
1524	Building	1		5003	120 – 122
		2			
		3			
		4			
	Post-Hole	10	9	5004	
		11	6, 5		
		8	7		
1525	Kiln	89-94	95-98, 119, 140	5012, 5013	
1526	Kiln	120	123-129		7-9, 85-88
		122	121		
1527	Corn dryer	200	201	5030	90-93
1527	Corn dryer	202	203	5032	
1528	Corn dryer	1124, 1138-44	1133-1137		74-77
1529	Inner courtyard	1109-1113,1028-32, 1061-2, 1083, 1202-14, 1221-23		Bund exc.	51, 54-57, 59, 81

Group no.	Type	Feature	Fill	Section number	Photo archive no.
		1080-88, 1111-15			
1530	Structure	1116-21			52
1531	Structure	1037-40, 1060			37, 81
1532	Structure	1033-34, 1041, 1051, 1214-1217		Bund exc	
1533	Structure	1035			
1534	Hearth/kiln	1068, 1201		Bund exc	
1535	Structure	1075			
1536	Structure	70, 71			
1537	Structure	1002			
1538	Structure	1006			24, 25
1539	Structure	1027			
1540	Structure	72, 73, 74, 75,	77, 76	5008	66, 130
1541	Building	155, 156, 157			
1542	Building	176-88, 204-5	187	5026	25, 96-98, 151
		170-3, 193,			
1543	Building	166, 167, 217-22			
1544	Building	158, 160-63			152
1545	Cobbles	216			
1546	Wall	206, 1026			34, 42
1547	Wall	1059, 1067, 1071-74			
1548	Wall	1076			
1549	Wall	54, 1095-6, 1101			60, 61
		1103, 1106, 1107			
1550	Fence	208, 209, 210			
1551	Fence	211, 212, 213			
1552	Fence	110, 1008, 1009			1- 4
		1011, 1022			
1553	Fence	165, 217-23			
1554	Garden feature	1052			
1555	Garden feature	51	50	5001	
1556	Garden feature	100	99	5011	118
		109			
1557	Avenue	140, 1027			
1558	Avenue	53	52	5002	119
1559	Garden feature	106	101-105		
1560	Extraction hollow	87	78-86	5009	84
1561	Saw pit	153	154	5025	148-150
1562	Pit	1023			
1563	Burnt area	1000, 1024			
1564	Pit group	148	149		137, 143, 153
		159, 164			
1565	Water pipe	1036			
1566	Water pipe	1053			
1567	Electric cable	1099			

APPENDIX 1.12: MEDIEVAL FIELD AND PLACE NAMES

Table 11: Medieval field and place names surviving on the manor of Tyttenhanger from the 14th to the 19th century

Name	Type	No. of acres in 1331	Court Record Extracts	No. of acres in 1500	No. of acres in 1777	No. of acres in 1838
Adamesland		7 acres called				
Aldewyk				1		
Almyscroft, lytill						
Amysgretcroft				6.25		
Amyscroft, Litil				2		
Ampsheth				***		
Arkley Field						12.78
Arkeleyslond						
Arnolds				0.75; 1.26; 0.25; 0.75		
Arnolds				Mess, 0.95		
One assart				2.25		
Astmareslond	A	18.1				
Astmerlond						
Ayleswardeslond						
Barleycroft				7.25		
Barleycroft				4.6		
Barley Lands, Upper	G					3.6
Barley Lands, Little	G					1.5
Barley Lands, Lower	G					4.5
Barnettewode		1 croft on			***	***
Bernardeslond		10				
Blundels				***		
Brache, le	A	9				
Brasiers croft				3.5		
Brasyers lane				***		
Braysiers Wyk				***		
Breche, le	A	10.3				
Breche, le	A	8 (h&d)				
Broad Field	A				20.8	21
Brodefeld, le	A	209.1 contra portum				
1 heath in (see heath)	H	5.6				
Bowman's Green Fm					***	***
Bromfeld, le	M	0.5				
Bromfeld	A	70.5				
Broom Field, Great	A				12.3	24.6
Broom Field, Little	A				13.76	14.6
Browgars				11.6		
Browngers	A			***		
Brongers, lytil	Pyg			0.6		
Bushcroft				2.9		
Busshcroft				2.25		
Bush Field	A				5.8	
Bush Field, Little	A				4.75	
Bush Field, Great	A				6.8	
Bush F, Lower High					21.1	
Bush F, Upper High					16.5	
Busshefelde			1478/79			
Bussheyfelde						
Bydell/Bidelles	M		1442/43			
Calmscroft				0.5		
Chalfremed	M	0.5				
Chapelslonde			1435/36			
Charnelcroft				***		
Chirchestrat		1 croft next to	Cherchestreet			
Chyrchehyll			1442/43			
Colneycroft				7.75		
Colneyheth				400		***
Colneygat				***		
Coyengers			1468-80			
Conygger*	P	42				
Conygger wood#	W	28.5				

Name	Type	No. of acres in 1331	Court Record Extracts	No. of acres in 1500	No. of acres in 1777	No. of acres in 1838
Cosuars/Cosmers				Mess.+0.5	1.55	***
Culverscroft	A	4.5				
Curmafelde				1		
Curmesfeld				2.5; 2.6; 1; 0.5;1.1; 0.5;		See Scurms
Daslond						
Delle, le	P	1.25				
Dewslade	P			22.5	Deeves Field ?	
Dichefeld			1468-80			
Dogescroft (4 acs)			1400/01			
Doggettscrofts			1435/36			
Domelslane croft				***		
Dommesfeld	A			65.5		
Dunsmoor Field					28.2	27.6
Donells homecroft				***		
Ducketscrofte	P/w		1468-80			
Dycteylane			1478/79			
Erkefordemed	M	4				
Efeld, le	A	41				
Eselde	A	36				
Estefelde			1442/43			
Eyfelde				27.25		
Felgatecroft				4.75		
Flexwike	T			0.3		
Foldingat				Adj. Park		
Forsterslond			1400/01			
Fouracres			1468-80			
Frankefled			1478/79			
Freezfelde				***		
Fyshpond				See manor		
Gardyns ground						
Grovecroft + coppice				14.8		
Grovefeld				3.5		
Grynders				Toft 0.9;		
Gryders croft				4.6		
Hadhamslond (2 acs)			1468-80			
Halefeld	A					
Halefeld lane				***		
Hammespond**						
Hanhamstudlond	M	8 + 6				
Hareparthe				***		
Hattheslade	NL	8				
Hatheslade	P	13.7				
Heath	H	18				
Heathey Field	A				16.5; 17.5;	17.9; 20.5
Helderscroft	A			***		
Helescrofte			1244			
Hernebarns			1442/43		Hornbeams ?	
Hethfelde	A			63.5		
Hethfelde	A			44.5		
Hilles	P/w		1468-80			
Hillfelde				5.6		
Hodyfeld	A	6				
Hogmore (in park)				3.75		
Homecroft				3		
Homefelde, le			1455/56			
Homwyke	T			1.5		
Hornbeams	M				4.5	3.3
Horn beams, lower	M				4.3	
Horn beams, upper	M				6.8	
Kilns				***		
Knollysground				***		
Jargenyles			1400/01			
Jargeules			1435/36			
Litiloldfeld			1468-80			
L(l)tt(le)cort				3.5		
Litilmidylfelde	A			66.75		
Lobwell				***		
Lobwellecrof	A	5.2				

Name	Type	No. of acres in 1331	Court Record Extracts	No. of acres in 1500	No. of acres in 1777	No. of acres in 1838
Lobewellehulle + #		67.7				
Lobbys, Great					22.8	2/20
Longefelde (8 acs)			1400;1435/36			
Longcrofte (2 parcls)			1447/48	3.8		
Madeland Croft	A				11.5	11.1
Manor + le mote				6.5		
Marlecroft	A			2.25		
Medecroft				1.6		
Medeplot				4.75		
Mershe, le	P			15.25		
Midilfeld	A			86.5		
Middelfeld	A	80.35				
Mireslond						
More, le				38.5		
Mote, le				See above		
Newlonde				***		
Neyfel				***		
Nodiscroft				10.15		
Nodyscroft hegge				1 hedlond inxta		
Nolleslond		10				
Odecroft		6.3				
Olde Housewyke, le			1455/56			
Oldefeld			1468-80			
One campus	A			33.5		
One croft	A			6.3; 5;		
One croft				8.75		
One messuage	Ms			1.5		
One parcel				0.5		
One piece of land				0.5		
Oxelese, le	P	See Conyngger				
Oxelese, le	P	14.5				
Pegeslond						
Palmers Field,Lower	G					9.9
Palmers F, Middle	G					7.8
Palmersgrove						
Park, Tittenhanger	G					56.9
Park lane, le				***		
Park pale, le				***		
Park, parcel of (see hammespond)	A			16.25		
Parcel in same place	A			31.25		
Parcel of park	A			7.5		
Parcel of park	A			7.25		
Parcel of park	A			18		
Parcel of park	A			18		
Parcel of park	A			18		
Parcel of park	A			6.75		
Parcel of park	A			7		
Parcel of land				1.1;3.75; 0.8;		
Parcel of wood				6.5		
Parsonnescroft			1478/79			
Pasture				5.3		
Perstecrofte			1442/43			
Perycroft				6.15		
Perygrove				18	Coppice 18.3	Coppice 18.3
Pease Croft	A				2.6	
Pease Croft, Little	M				1.7	
Pesecroft				4		
Pesecroft				1.8		
Pesecroft (x2)				3		
Piece of land				0.1		
Pirifeld	A	49.2				
Popes			1442/43			
Popescroft			1478/79			
Portefeld		4				
Preestesfeld (16 acs)			1400/01			
Prescroft (assart)				9		
Prestfelde			1435/363			

Name	Type	No. of acres in 1331	Court Record Extracts	No. of acres in 1500	No. of acres in 1777	No. of acres in 1838
Presteswyk						
Puttock field					24.2	
Puttuke hill	A			***		
Pyryfelde				46.75		
Raisoneslond						
Riponsbrad				4.6		
Ripns whetcroft				7.5		
Ripons lane						
Rugge, eccl de		1 messuage next to				
Rugge hill				***		
Rugge Lane			1442/43			
Rugge Dyke			1478/79			
Rypons lane				***		
Salissground				***		
Salysburnfeld	A			Next Dommesfeld		
Scurms, Little/Great	G					3.8; 4.8
Scryvins	M			0.3		
Seecroft				4.5		
Saffron Green	G				***	11.3
Shapham Green	C				2.6	
Schep(r)ds grove	W			1.6		
Shepsecotesfelde			1442/43			
Shrobbes, le			1468-80			
Smartnolcroft			1468-80			
Smythescroft	A			***		
Southehawe	W		1468-80			
Southstubefeld			1478/79			
Stankefelde lane		Half acre on				
Startholes, Great	A				30.1	27.35
Startholes, Little	A				5.5	7.2
Startholes	A				16	15.7
Stertefeld	A	111.5		5.8		
Stexslonde			1435/36			
Sweterycheslonde			1442/43			
The iii crof				1		
Thangefeld				***		
Thangton wood		3 acres on				
Thaynesinefeld	A	161.5				
Themerefeld	NL	8				
Theymer	M	0.5				
Tholyrscroft (3acs)			1468-80			
Tilers Croft	A					7.5
Trossereslond		10				
Tryangle, le				With dewselade		
Tydenhangre grene	T	1 tenement on				
Tydenhangre grene	T			2 cotts; 0.8 ac		
Tylers	M				4.8	
Tylers, Great					21.1	
Tylers, Little					15.75	
Tylehowsfelde				***		
Tylerelonde			1444/45			
Tylerswyke			1442/43			
Tylhows, le				Way going to		
12 (Twelve) akers				0.6; 1.75; 0.25; 0.5; 0.25; 1; 2.76;		
Valentyneslond			1435/36		Valentines Fm	
Waylward	T			***		
Warrennesparke				***	Warreners Closes	
Westfeld			1468-80			
Westgate			1478/79			
Westrete			1468-80			
Whetfelde, lytil				1.25		
Whitcroft						
Whitelfeld			1468-80			
Widgate				Next to le more		
Williamscroft, lytil				1.5		
Willyamscroft	A			4.5		
Williamswyke				1.25		
Winchefelde			1244			

Name	Type	No. of acres in 1331	Court Record Extracts	No. of acres in 1500	No. of acres in 1777	No. of acres in 1838
Wynchefeld				2.5; 1; 6.25; 16.5; 1.1;		
Woolyard, le				A court called		
Wood; near le more				42.5		
Wood	W	12				
Wormedel felde				8.6; 0.77;0.5; 0.6; 0.3; 1; 0.5; 0.3; 0.8; 0.5; 0.5; 0.95; 1;		
Wormesfeld						
Wrobbleylane			1468-80			
Wrobbelslond	A	26			Rabley ?	Rabley?

Key
*** mentioned at that date, no acreage
A- arable
G- grassland
H- heath
M- meadow
Ms -messuage
P- pasture
Pyg- pyahtle (small enclosure)
W –wood

APPENDIX 1.13: SURVEY OF THE MANOR OF TYTTENHANGER C.1500/1501 (HALS: D/EB/2067 B. M.25)

Extent of the manor of Tyttenhanger, its rents and services of all its tenants both free and villeins in the same *renovata* (burgbote or domain) in the reign of Henry VII in the XVI year in the time of the venerable Abbot Ramrygg.

A measure of the abbot's manor and park and waste of *Colney Heth*.

Manor of the Abbot with court called *le woolyard* which is enclosed with park pales and said court contains dwellings, offices with stables and barns and *le mote* and *fyshpond*
The court with *le mote* contains VI and a half acres.

A parcel of park with *hammespond* and the other parcel adjoining lying between Colney heth and the aforesaid manor and the way going to *le tylhows* and contains 16 acres 1 rod.

There is another parcel in the same place called........... lying between *hammespond* and the wood of the same *Colneyheth* on one part and contains 31 acres 1 rod.

One wood called...........lying between the aforesaid manor and *le more* besides *widgate* to *colneyheth* on the one part and contains 42 and half acres.

There is another parcel of park called *le more* next to *widgate* lying besides the manor and aforesaid wood on one side and abutting on *le wydgate* and contains 38 and half acres.

Another parcel of park called *hogmore* lying between a parcel called.........next to the gate towards the manor and lane containing 3 acres 3 rods.

Another parcel of park called....... next to the gate next to the manor and lying between *hogmore* and *periory* next to *foldingat* containing 7 and half acres.

Another parcel of park next to *foldingat* called *pyryfelde* containing 46 acres and 3 rods.

In the park there is a grove called *perygrove* which lies next to le park pale and contains 18 acres.

Another parcel in the park which lies between the aforesaid grove and *le park pale* and contains 7 acres and 1 rod.

Total 247 acres

There is another parcel lying next to *peryfelde* on one side and abutting towards *le more* next to the manor containing 18 acres.
One parcel next to the aforesaid and abutting on the same containing 18 acres
One parcel abutting on the same (or first) containing 18 acres
One parcel on the same containing 6 acres 3 rods

One parcel on the same containing 7 acres

Total within the park 310 and a half acres

At the same place cora? Called *Colneyheth* lying between *Tyttenhanger Park* and *Knollysground* on one side and abutting on *newlonde* and the other on *freezfelde* containing 400 acres

Measure of lands and rents

In the first court called the *lttzcort* (little court) with dwellings......... buildings, barns, stables and others containing and garden 3 and half acres.

One campus (field) next to *le tylehowse* lying between *lobwell* and way to Cosuars on its side and abutting on one end on *harepathe* and the other on the way leading towards the manor containing 33 and a half acres.

A parcel of pasture called *le mershe ~ warennesparke* lying between *dewslade* and *lobwell* on one side and the other side next to *Neyfeld* and *le park lane* and abutts on one boundary on *warennespark* and the other on *Colneygat* and contains 15 acres and 1 rod.

A parcel of pasture called *dewselade* with lane and *le tryangle* lying between *lobwell harepath lane ampsheth ~ tylehowsfelde* on the one part containing 22 and half acres.

In the same place one field called *midilfeld* and lying between *selwood harepath pinfol hill, lytilmidylfelde* and *domnesfeld* on the one part containing 86 and a half acres.

Another field called *dommesfeld* lying between *Salysburnfeld ~ hethfelde* on one side abutting on the boundary on *midilfelde* and the other towards *Rugge* and contains 65 and a half acres.

And has one croft in the same place called.........towards *Rugge* and lies next to *hethe felde* and contains 8 acres and 3 rods.

And has a field called hethfelde against one side between *dommerfelde* and one side towards *Rugge* containing 63 and a half acres.

A field called *litilmidylfelde* lying on one side next to *mydylfeld* and one side on *puttuke hill* and also on *bussheyfelde* containing 66 acres and 3 rods.

A field called *hethfelde* lying between *lytylmydelfelde ~ Stertefelde* and *Stertefeldelane* going towards *Rugg hill* on the one part containing 44 and a half acres.

A field called *Eyfelde* lying between *colney* and *parklane* and on one side abutting *on le marsche* containing 27 acres 1 rod.

Tenants of Tyttenhanger

William Gardyn of Tyttenhanger Green one messuage and garden between *Tyttenhanger Green* Willismyth browngers and one croft called *Smythiscroft* cont ....

One croft called *Smythescroft* lying between the messuage on aforesaid *halefeld lane*, marlecroft and *Amysgretcroft* on one part and containing............

One croft called *Amysgretcroft* lying between *browngers smythescroft Thangefeld* on *Tyttenhanger park* and containing 6 acres, 1 rod 5 poles.

One croft called *litil Amyscroft* lying *between marlcroft, halefelde* land and a parcel of wood called *willyamscroft* containing 2 acres.

The same holds *Williamswyke* and a croft adjacent lying between messuage on aforesaid Tyttenhanger lane ~ *lytill browngers* containing 1 acre, 1 rod and 3 poles.

Total.......

Thomas Flenes one croft called *marlecroft* lying between *smythscroft, halefeld lane, lytill almyscroft* containing 2 acres 1 rod and 5 poles.
One parcel of land lying between *halelane, charnelcroft ~ salissground* containing half an acre.
One field called *Curmafelde* and one portion of land lying between house *called waylward* which on one side abuts on *astmerlond* containing 1 acre.

Total 3 acres 3 rods and 25 poles. Rent 12d

Garden of St Peters in Sain Albans held by same.

One croft next to land of Thomas Smythe and lies between *Tyttenhanger Green, Salysground* and *halelane* containing 6 acres 1 rod and 11 poles. Rent 8d.

In the same location called *Tyttenhanger grene* one tenement which has pasture in same...... 2 cottages containing 3 rods 8 poles.
John Donnell one messuage called *Scryvins* lying between *Tyttenhanger Green , helderscroft donells homecroft* and *homwyke* on the one part containing 1 rod and 12 poles

And holds one toft called *homwyke* abutting on *brasyers lane* containing 1 and half rods

And one toft called *flexwike* abutting on the aforesaid *brasierslane* and containing 1 and half rods and 4 poles.

A croft called *homecroft* lying between land of John repo, John prirst, *heldercroft* and aforesaid messuage containing 3 acres and 5 poles.

One toft called *brasiers croft* lying between messuage of John Repo, *braysiers lane* towards *Tytten Grene* containing 3 and a half acres and 7 poles.

2 crofts called *pesecroft* lying between land of John Repo and *braysierscroft* on the aforesaid *Titng grene* containing 3 acres and 7 poles.

One pyghtill called *litil browgars* lying between *williamswyk, gardynars pond* and *gardynars feld* containing half an acre and 14 poles.

One croft called *browgars* lying between *Tyttenhanger lane, gardyns ground* and *Tyttenhanger parke* containing 11 and half acres and 14 poles.

One croft called *hillfelde* lying between *wormedel felde* and a *field of 12 acres* and *Stertefelde* on one part containing 5 acres, half a rod and 20 poles.

One field called *Stertefelde* between *Nodiscroft, hilfelde, grovefelde* and Tyttenhanger lane on one part containing 5 and half acres, 1 rod and 5 poles.
One field called *grovefeld* lying between *Stertefeld, lytilwelfeld, Segipdsgrove ~ wormefeld* on one part containing 3 and a half acres.

One field called *lytilwhetfelde* lying between *Tyttenhanger lane* and land of John Ripon and *grovefeld* containing 1 acre, 1 rod and 6 poles.

One grove called *Schep®ds grove* lying between *wormesfeld*, Ripons *whitcroft* and *grovefelld*
from *kilns* he has and contains 1 and half acres and 20 poles.

John Donnell one croft in two parcells called *longcroft* lying between messuage of john Ripon, *wormefelld, Rypons lane* from the park and contains 3 and half acres and 28 poles.

Lands held of the Almonar
The aforesaid John Donell holding a field called *12 acres*, one piece of land lying between land of john Ripon and land called *blundels* on one side and contains one hedlond next to *nodyscroft* hegge containing half an acre, half a rod and 12 poles.

And the other piece of land is between the land of John Ripon and Ayleward on one side containing half an acre.

Lands held of the Almonar

John Ripon has one messuage lying between *braysiers wyk, felgatecroft, domelslane croft* and *Ripons lane* containing 1 and half acres.

One croft called *aldewyk* lying between *Curmefeld, donells longrove, feldate* and *whetfeld* containing 1 acre

One croft called *felgatcroft* lying between *carterscroft, pesecroft, whetfeld, aldwyke* containing 4 and half acres and 1 rod.

One croft called *Ripons whetcroft* lying between *Seecroft donell, lytill whetcroft, Schepard grove, felgatcroft* on one part and containing 7 and half acres.

One croft called *Seecroft* lying between Tyttenhanger Green lane and whetcroft aforesaid and abutting on land.........towards.......... and containing 4 acres, half a rod and 2 poles.

One croft called *the medeplot* lying between *donells homefelde, colnerscroft, Pirnottrndyng, ripons lane* containing 4 acres 1 and half rods.

One croft called *colneycroft* lying between the aforesaid croft called *medeplot, astmerlond* and at one end next to *Curmesfelde* conatining 7 acres 1 and half rods and 6 poles.

A field called *Curmesfeld* and lying between land w mane , J. Donell, Ayleward on one side and on of W mane and John aforesaid containing 2 and half acres.

Another piece of land lying between the land of Aylward and Elizabeth Wigge called *Arnolds* containing half a rod and 5 poles.

A piece of land lying by W. Man and Elizabeth Wigge called *Arnolds* lying on by side on land of J Smart and John Ripon containing 3 rods and 4 poles.

Another piece of land lying between the land of Walter Aylward and land of Elizabeth Wigge called *Arnoldes* and extending to *Wychefeld* containing 1 acre and 10 poles.

Another piece of land lying between land of Aylward on the Aylwards and Arnolds containing 1 acre, 1 rod and 8 poles.

And the aforesaid John copyhold on one croft called *perycroft* which lies between land called *browgars, peren? de Tyttenhanger* and *Tyttenhanger grenelane* containing 6 acres and half a rod and 10 poles.

One croft called *Nodycroft* lying between *Tyttenhanger grenelane, Stertefeld,* a field called *12 acres* and *groplane* containing 10 acres , half a rod and 15 poles.

A croft called Williams croft lying between land once Richard Chappell, *Brasereycroft, homefeld* and *honicroflane* and contains 4 acres, half a rod and 10 poles.

One croft called *lytilwilliamscroft* lying next to *homieroslane* and *Riponsbrad* containing 1 and half acres and 10 poles.

One croft called *Riponsbrad* lying between *hillond* land of John purs called *gardynarsfellde* and *lytilwilliamscroft* containing 4 acres and a half and 16 poles.

Copyhold land in *wormedelfelde* on *mote* [2 abreviation marks above p. 8 1st line] lying between land of w. man, John Donell's *Alwik* containing 8 and half acres, half a rod and 10 poles.

In the valy towards the *grenlane* another piece lying between land of John Smart and Elizabeth Wygge called *Arnolds* containing 1 rod.

In the same place another piece lying between land valtezi Aylward and thomas Palmer on one side and extends towards greenlane containing 3 rods and 22 poles.

Another parcel lying between land of valtrey Aylward and John Smart on one side and abutting on *grene lane* containing 3 rods.

John Ripon in field called *12 akers* one piece of land lying next to *hilfeld* and *Stertefelde* and extending towards *wormdel feld* and on *the hedlond* next *to wormdelfeld* containing 1 acre and 3 rods.

One other piece of ground between the land of John Donel and land called *blundel* on one side containing 38 poles.

One other piece of land lying between land of John Smart and other side containing half an acre.

One hedlond next to *Nodycroft hegge* and extending to donel hedlond towards *gropelane* containing 1 rod.

A piece of land lying between land of John Donell and John Smart on the other side containing 1 acre

Another piece of land lying between the land of John Smart and *gropelane* on the other side containing 2 and half acres, 1 rod and 10 poles.

John Purs holds by copy one *assart Salis*, one parcel of wood lying next to *Salis mede, Busshecroft* and *pescroft* and land called *cosmers* containing 2 acres 1 rod.

One croft called *Busshcroft* lying between *Salis wood, Chapell grove, pescroft* and aforesaid assart containing 2 acres 1 rod and 2 poles.

One croft called *pesecroft* lying between the land (of) *dethe charnell howse* in St Albans on one side and on the other on *Busshecroft* containing 1 acres, 3 rods and 14 poles - 1 acres, 3 rods and 14 poles.

One messuage with a garden of half an acre called *cosmers* and pasture lying between *Saliswood assart, pesecroft* of aforesaid parcel of land of Thomas Flenys and *halelane* - 5 acres, 1 and half rods.

One croft of assartlond *prescroft* lying between *Colneystreet, Turmersfelde* and same croft held on *helderstret* containing 9 acres.

The other croft of land called *the iii croft* lying between the land of Wigan and the other aforesaid croft against *Arnoldes grove* and the other on *helderscroft* containing 1 acre 8 poles.

A piece of land in *Wynchefeld* lying between one croft and one piece of land in the same field held by Elyzabeth Wygge called *Arnoldes* and abutting on *helderscroft* containing 2 and half acres.

And holds in the same field *in the valy* one piece of land lying between terram Arnolds on one side containing 1 acre.

Elizabeth Wigge holds by copy one messuage called *Arnolds* and lies between the same land in the same tenure (with) a garden – 3 rods and 26 poles.

One toft called *grynders* and lies next to croft called *pesecroft* in the same tenure containing 3 rods and 24 poles.

One croft called *grovecroft* which extends to said messuage and contains with a coppice 14 acres 3 and a half rods.

The aforesaid Elizabeth holds one croft called *medecroft* which abutts on aforesaid messuage on south – 1 acre and half and 18 poles.

The same holds one croft called *Calmscroft* abutting on said messuage containing half an acre and 21 poles.

One croft called *barleycroft* which extends to *martonsfelde, brodfeld* and aforesaid messuage – 4 and half acres and 21 poles.

One croft called *barleycroft* which extends to *gardynars* feld containing 7 acres 1 rod and 7 poles.

One croft called *pesecroft* lying between *marmaslane* and toft called *gryders yarde* and *honie Croslane* containing 4 acres and 4 poles.

One croft called *gryders croft* lying on one side next to the toft aforesaid called *gryders yard* and the other on *honycroslane* containing 4 and a half acres and 21 poles.

One croft next to *wynchefeldgat* lying between *gardyners feld, honycroslane* and on a lane going to the messuage containing 5 acres and 10 poles.

One croft called *bushcroft* next to honycroslane and the other on the lane going to the aforesaid messuage. – 2 acres 3 and a half rods.

One croft called Wynchefeld croft lying between messuage of W man wynchefled and honycroslane containing 6 acres 1 rod.

One field called Wynchelfeld *in the valy* parcel of land called a Schot and is all the land in *wynchefeld* next between *Curmesfeld, aylwards* and lane going to St Albans and one parcel of land in the tenure of J. purs and the other parcel in the tenure of J rypon containing 16 and a half acres.

And in the same field on *mote* (?) one parcel of land between land of J. purs and w man on one side abutting on *helderstret* containing 1 acre and 24 poles.

On mote other parcell of land between land of w man on one side abutting on croft held ciggs W called *longecroft* – 1 acres 14 poles

And on motem other parcel between land of w man ~ *Arnoldesgrove* on one side abutting on aforesaid croft in tenure of w man - 3 acres, 3 rods and 5 poles.

And holds one parcel of wood called *Arnolds grove* lying between *Asmerslond* and *wynchfeld* on one side and on land of W man called *Curmersfeld* containing 6 and half acres.

In the same field called *Curmesfelde* one piece of land lying next to *Wynchefeld* abutting on *Arnolds grove* containing 2 and a half acres and half a rod.

In the same field a piece of land lying between of W. man ~ *grenlane* on one side – 1 acre, 1 rod and 4 poles.

In the same field a piece of land next to the land of Walter Aylward containing half an acre and 12 poles.

Another piece of land next to land of J. Smart and W. man on one side containing 1 acre and 24 poles.

Another piece of land next to land of J. Rypon on one side containing half an acre and 12 poles

Another piece of land between *wormedelhegge* and land of W. Man on one side abutting on land of W. Man on west and abutting on *wormedelfeld* containing 3 rods and 26 poles.

Total acres in *Curmetfeld*

And in same field called *Wormedelfelde* between land of W Man on one side abutting on lane of J. Smart contains 3 rods and 12 poles.

One piece of land between land of W. man and Walter Aylward on one side and abutting on land of W. Man containing half an acre

A piece of land between land of W. man ~ *grenlane* containing half an acre and 25 poles.

Piece of land between land of W. man and Walter Aylward on one side and abutting on *Rypons lane* containing 1 rod and 12 poles.

One piece between land of J Smart on one side containing 1 acre and 4 poles.

One piece between land of W. man and j. Smart on one side containing half an acre and 12 poles

Another piece of land between land of W. Man and J. Smart on one side containing 1 rod and 22 poles.

Another piece of land between land of W. man containing 3 rods and 15 poles.

Another piece of land between land of W. Man and J. Smart containing half an acre.

Another piece of land between land of W. man and J. Smart on one side containing half an acre.

Another piece of land between land of W. man and J. Rypon on one side containing 3 rods and 32 poles.

Another piece of land between land of W. man and Walter Aylward on one side containing 1 acre and 16 poles.

Total of acres in *Wormedelfelde*..........

PHOTOGRAPHIC PLATES
(ARCHAEOLOGICAL MITIGATION PROGRAMME
SOUTH OF TYTTENHANGER HOUSE)

Plate 1: View of corn drier 1528 looking north

Plate 2 : General view of the northern half of the mitigation area

Plate 3: North west view across Structures 1531 and 1210

Plate 4: South side of inner courtyard area 1529-1530

Plate 5: Detail of foundations belonging to 1530 looking south

Plate 6: Structure 1540 in foreground and 1522 beyond

Plate 7: Detail of foundations belonging to 1529 looking east

Plate 8: Foundations of 1530 looking westwards

Plate 9: Building 1524 looking south west

Plate 10: Structure 1532 (garderobe?)

Plate 11: Foundation of eastern gate-house/tower 1208

Plate 12: Detail of junction of foundation 1205 with 1209

Plate 13: Remains of foundation 1205

Plate 14: Elevation of foundation 1205

Plate 15: Detail of foundation 1207

Plate 16: Entrance [1222] into inner courtyard area

Plate 17: Detail of western gate-house/tower foundation 1210

Plate 18: Detail of structure 1540

Plate 19: View of tile kiln 1526 looking west

Plate 20: Detail of support arches belonging to 1526 and remains of unfired tiles

Plate 21: Kiln 1526 being conserved by John Price

Plate 22: Examples of moulded brick from 1214

Plate 23: Building material recovered during the watching brief phase

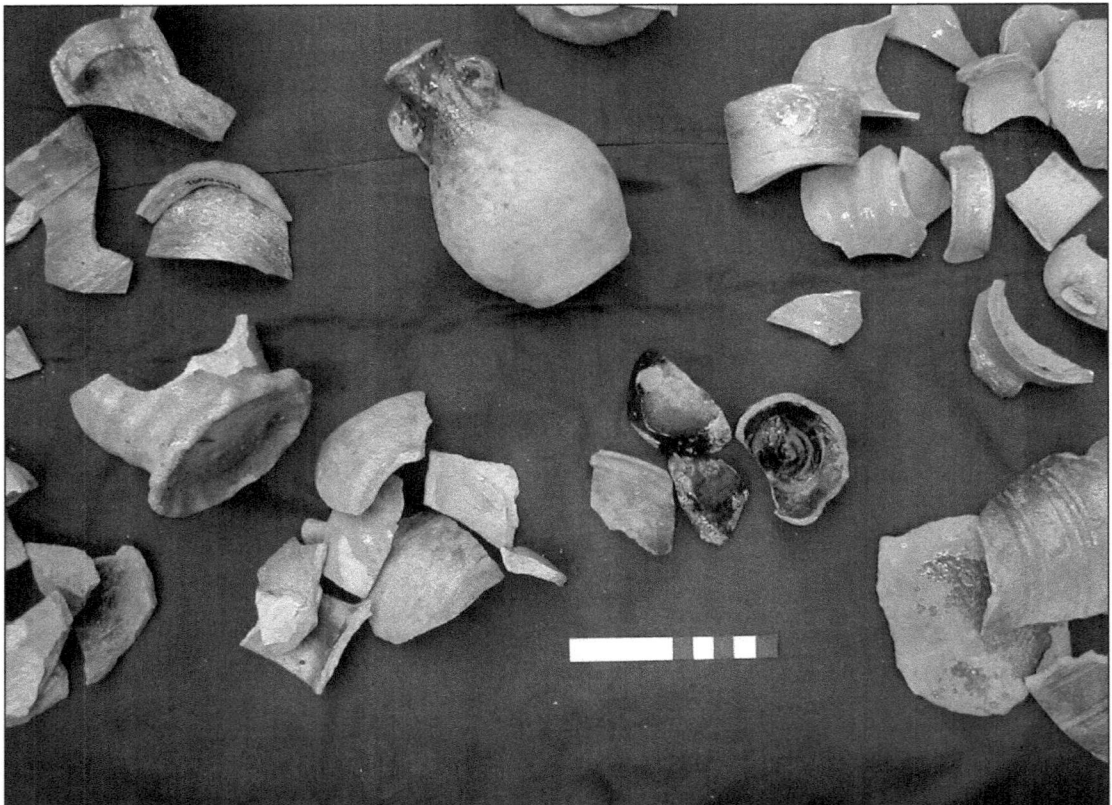

Plate 24: Pottery from hearth deposit 1204

PART 2

MESOLITHIC SITE
by Martin Lightfoot

SUMMARY

Between mid summer and early autumn 2001, an archaeological evaluation and survey was undertaken on a field to the south east of Tyttenhanger House. A total of 173 flint objects were recovered. The finds were predominantly blades, flakes, cores and core fragments, with some retouched forms. Typologically these almost certainly date from the Mesolithic period, though it is possible that some pieces represent later Neolithic or Bronze Age activity.

INTRODUCTION

During late October 2001 *Archaeological Services and Consultancy Ltd* (ASC) carried out an archaeological excavation on a site at Tyttenhanger Quarry (NGR TL 193 041). This followed an evaluation by ASC on 30th July 2001, which established the presence of scattered Mesolithic flint. The project was commissioned by Andrew Richmond of Phoenix Consulting on behalf of Lafarge Aggregates, and was carried out according to a programme of archaeological works devised by Phoenix Consulting and approved by the Hertfordshire County Archaeology Office, and a written scheme of investigation prepared by ASC (ASAC/TQ/SA/H98/1r). This report presents the findings from the July evaluation and the October excavation, and includes an analysis by Philippa Bradley of the flint artefacts recovered from the site.

SETTING

Tyttenhanger quarry lies within the Vale of St Albans, between the River Colne and the South Hertfordshire Plateau. The terrain varies from flat to gently undulating, lying between 71 and 75m OD. The bedrock of the area is chalk, which is at a depth of between 8-14m (Turner and Hunn 2000). Overlying this bedrock are various glaciofluvial and alluvial deposits of clay and gravel. According to Dr P. G. Hoare (1996) the gravel, which consists predominantly of angular to well rounded flints, within a medium to coarse sand matrix, is thought to have been laid down by a westward flowing precursor of the River Colne during the Anglican II period of the Quaternary. Above the gravel deposits a 'brickearth' appears to have accumulated during the periglacial conditions of the Devensian stage of the Quaternary, between 120 and 10 thousand years ago (*op cit*). Cryoturbation may have been responsible for the patchy mixing of this layer with the underlying gravels apparent in much of the area. The topsoil of the area is described as the Hamble 2 soil association ('typical argillic brown earths') by the soil survey of England and Wales (1983a, 1983b)

ARCHAEOLOGICAL & HISTORICAL BACKGROUND

SITES & MONUMENTS DATA
SMR data indicates the finding of two Mesolithic flint axes near Colney Heath Farm and the presence of a ring ditch in a field just south of Coursers Farm. There are earthwork features in the area around Colney Heath, which on morphological grounds may relate to Bronze or Iron Age land usage (Howlett and Lisboa 1996, 10), though this has not been confirmed by excavation.

DESK BASED ASSESSMENT & FIELD WALKING
During 1995/1996 a programme of archaeological evaluation was undertaken by *Tempvs Reparatvm* (Percival and Richmond, 1996). This comprised a desk-based assessment and a programme of fieldwalking, whereby flints, sherds of medieval and post medieval pottery, and fragments of tile were recovered.

The flint objects were interpreted as 'background noise or plough scatters' (*op cit*, 8). Geophysics was inconclusive in the area currently forming the object of this report, (Field C, areas 1, 2 and 4), (*op cit* fig 3). Test pitting, while providing useful geomorphological data (Hoare 1996), failed to find any artefacts or archaeological deposits. Trial trenching of field C (trenches 19-22) failed to locate any archaeological features, though 'a light scatter of worked flint' was recovered (*op cit*, 16).

In December 1997, ASC carried out a fieldwalking survey on land immediately to the south of Coursers Road (Hunn and Coxah 1997), 104 flints were recovered. Tentative that of these, 5 were cores, 8 scrapers, 3 blades and 73 flakes, with 15 pieces of unworked natural. The overwhelming majority of artefacts recovered during this exercise were flint (70% of the total finds recovered).

ARCHAEOLOGICAL EVALUATION
Prehistoric features were identified during an archaeological evaluation on land to the South of Coursers Road (Hunn 1999, 42): these appear to date to the Bronze and Iron Ages.

ARCHAEOLOGICAL EXCAVATION

During the autumn and winter of 1999, *ASC Ltd* carried out a programme of archaeological excavation (Turner and Hunn, 2000). This focused on fields 'A' and 'B' (*op cit*, 6, Figure 2). The findings of the excavation were predominantly medieval and post medieval, though six flint tools were recovered. The flints were unstratified and consisted of one unfinished axe, one 'scraper', two 'flakes', an end scraper, and a blade. The conclusion of the excavators was that 'excluding a few isolated prehistoric flints, the historical and archaeological sequence commences in the medieval period' (*op cit*, 42).

AIMS & METHODS

The overall objective was to assess the character and nature of the archaeology within the area designated for aggregate extraction and associated activities. The work was carried out in line with the general strategy in relation to the *Scheme of Archaeological Mitigation* (SAM), and the *Detailed Methods Statement for Watching Brief and Related Archaeological Work* (Zeepvat 1998), and arose out of the intermittent archaeological watching brief covering this area, which was thought to be of peripheral archaeological interest (Percival and Richmond, 1996).

In late July 2001 an area to the west of the road to Tyttenhanger House was stripped of topsoil to allow the construction of a roadway for the passage of vehicles to the landfill site. During the course of the watching brief a concentration of typologically Mesolithic worked flints were recovered, and an evaluation, was undertaken by ASC to attain some spatial information, and to collect more examples (Trench 1).

Following confirmation that the finds were of probable Mesolithic date, it was decided by the consultant that a further programme of archaeological work be carried out in an adjacent area, where the topsoil was to be stripped in advance of gravel extraction. An area of 30 m² adjacent to the road and following the route of a proposed footpath was subjected to detailed excavation.

The entire threatened area was rapidly fieldwalked after the topsoil had been removed, and all finds of Mesolithic flint were individually numbered and their precise location was recorded. The area adjacent to the road (Trench 2) was methodically cleaned back and flint artefacts recovered were recorded in the same way.

RESULTS

The topsoil (01) consisted of friable, dark brown, silty clay and was approximately 0.2m thick in the area of detailed excavation (T2). The natural sub-soil (02), which overlay the alluvial sandy gravel, consisted of firm reddish-brown silty clay, containing some small sub-angular pebbles, and almost certainly relates to the brickearth (Hoare, 1996). Deposit (03) was a thin archaeological layer, roughly 0.05m thick in T2, lying immediately below the topsoil and above the cleaner reddish-brown sub-soil (02). This deposit consists of a firm, mixed brown / reddish-brown silty clay, disturbed significantly in places by root action and cryoturbation. In total 274 flint artefacts were recovered from the site. Of these the precise spatial position of 173 were recorded. The substantial number of unstratified flints was recovered from spoil heaps or from the surrounding excavated area.

CONCLUSIONS

The distribution of flint artefacts revealed in the plot (Fig . 48) corresponds with the impression of the excavators that there was a concentration on the western edge of the site, and justifies the more detailed examination of this area, with the opening up of Trenches 1 and 2. However, the mere fact that these areas received much greater attention and were carefully cleaned, compared with the large stripped area, which was only field walked, may have skewed this data.

The impression from the density plot is that flint finds thin out in a north and easterly direction. This may accurately represent a true fall in density, though it is also highly probable that this fall off is due to the excavation of top-soil being deeper towards the north and east of the site, consequently removing much, or in some areas, all of the archaeological layer (03). The impression of the excavators was that this might probably be the case, as the layer associated with the artefacts was thinner to non-existent in the north and east of the site.

A comparison between the flints recovered from Tyttenhanger with the published findings from the site of Hampermill, Watford (Derricourt and Jacobi 1970), shows similarities in the range and type of artefacts recovered. The site of Hampermill (TQ 098941) lies on the Pleistocene gravels on the flood plain of the River Colne. A synthetic treatment of the Mesolithic flint industry along the River Colne and other nearby rivers would shed significant light on this period.

It has been apparent for at least forty years that the Colne valley might provide significant evidence of Mesolithic activity (e.g. Lacaille, 1961). Indeed, work on the lower Colne valley near Uxbridge has borne this out, with high quality environmental and artefactual data (Lewis, Wiltshire and Macphail 1992). The area immediately surrounding the site currently under investigation has been subjected to periodic archaeological works relating to the programme of archaeological evaluation (Percival and Richmond 1996) and subsequent archaeological mitigation, which has indicated the presence of some Mesolithic flints. Sites of this type along the Colne valley have the potential to tackle the many questions surrounding Mesolithic activity regionally and in riverine areas nationally.

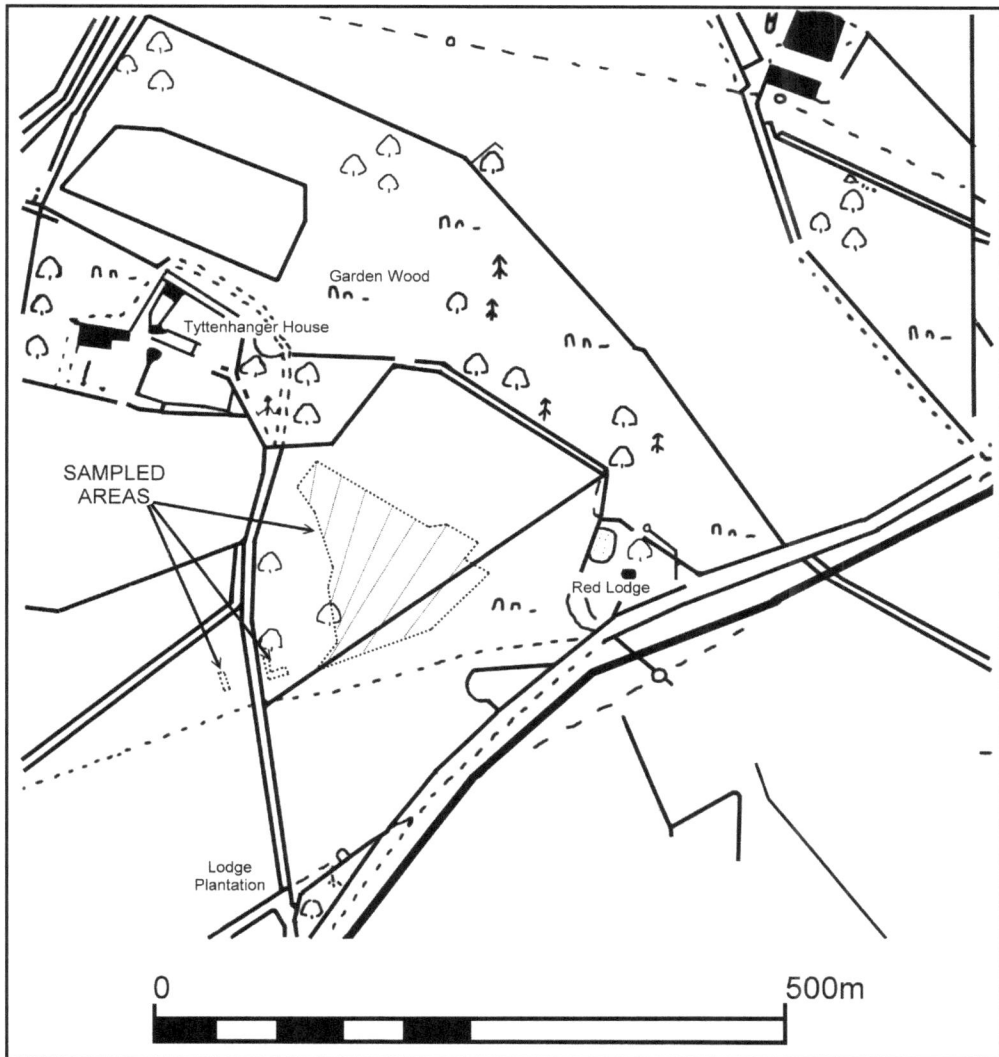

Fig. 47: Location of trenches and sampled area

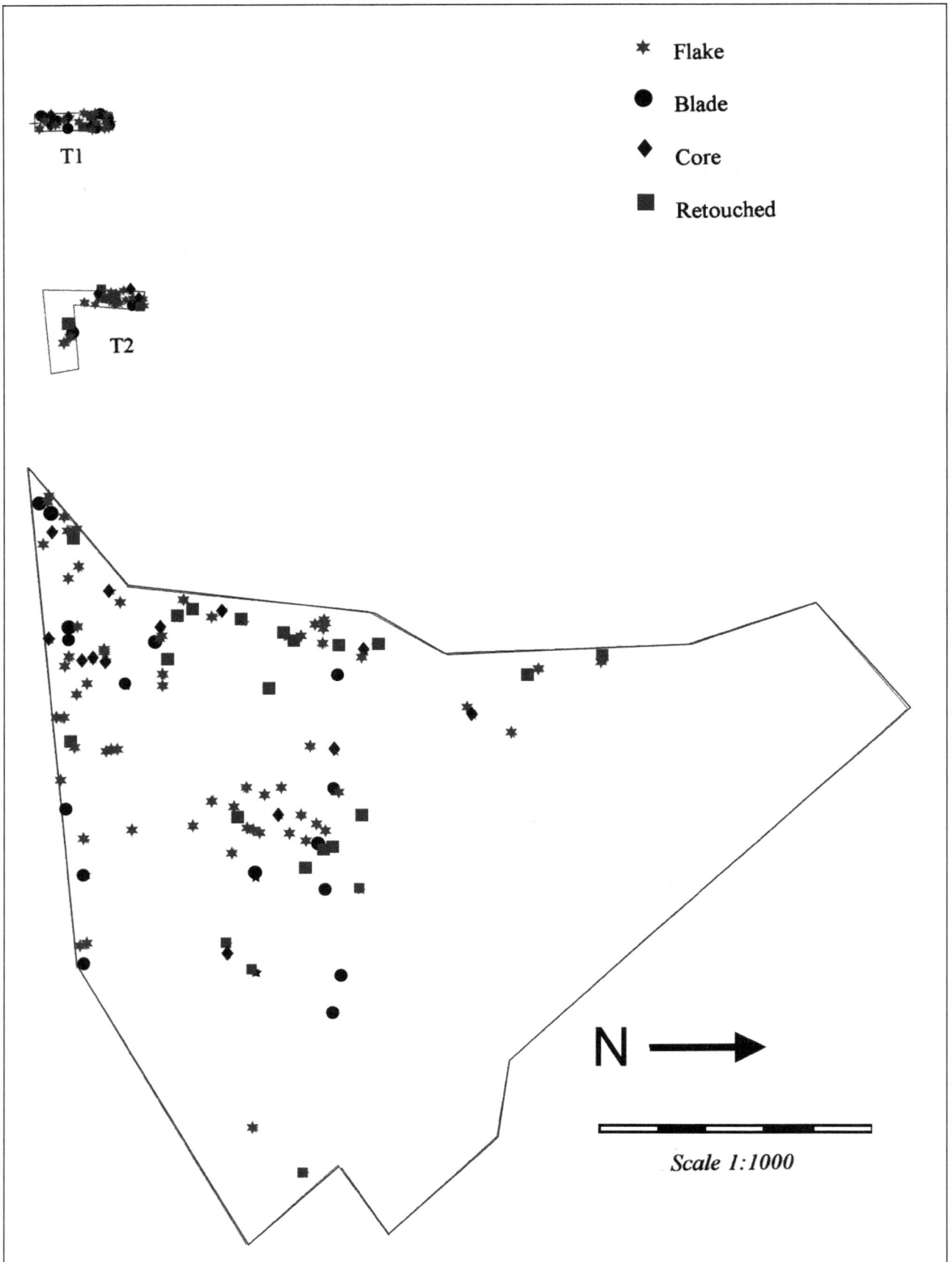

Fig. 48: Distribution plan of worked flint

APPENDIX 2.1: WORKED FLINT FROM TYTTENHANGER QUARRY WEST

by Philippa Bradley

INTRODUCTION

A total of 274 pieces of worked flint and a single piece of burnt unworked flint came from the archaeological investigations. The flint is summarised in Table 12, a selection of material is described in the catalogue and illustrated in Fig. 49. Further details of the assemblage may be found in the site archive.

The assemblage consists of debitage and a range of retouched pieces (Table 12). A few pieces of flint (for example a discoidal core and some crude core fragments) suggest possible later prehistoric activity but the bulk of the material is of Mesolithic date. However, there is little that is definitely later either technologically or typologically, so this possible later element remains tentative.

METHODOLOGY

The flint was examined and the assessment database used as a basis for the analysis. The assessment had highlighted refitting and usewear analyses as being potentially helpful for understanding the assemblage (Bradley 2001). To this end a refitting exercise and usewear analysis were undertaken. The usewear analysis used standard methods (e.g. Odell and Odell-Vereecken 1980; Odell 1981; Mallouf 1982; Tringham *et al* 1974) and the flint was examined at x20 magnification. For the refitting exercise the material was laid out to enable the identification of refits or cross joins. Groups of related raw materials were also sought. The results are discussed below.

RAW MATERIALS AND CONDITION

The majority of the flint is in good condition with only a little later edge damage. The unstratified collection has much more extensive edge damage. The flint ranges in colour from brown through grey and orange, where cortex survives it is white or buff. Cortication is generally light. Only a single piece of burnt unworked flint was recovered and very little of the worked flint was burnt. Probable usewear was identified on several pieces, which is discussed in more detail below.

DESCRIPTION AND DISCUSSION

The flint is dominated by debitage (Table 12) and all elements of the reduction sequence were recovered, although chips are under-represented, which may simply reflect the method of recovery rather than being a real absence. The majority of the debitage is typical of a controlled method of reduction. The cores are dominated by opposed (Fig. 49, 1-2) and single

platform blade types. Platform preparation and maintenance is attested by crested flakes (Fig.49, 3), platform edge abrasion and core rejuvenation flakes (both tablet and face or edge types were recovered (Fig.49,.4). Also found was a possible truncated blade (SF 147). Blades and blade-like flakes were recovered (Table 12), and some flakes have previous blade scars on their dorsal faces. Both hard and soft hammers were used to remove flakes. This controlled method of flintworking is typical of the Mesolithic period.

A discoidal core and a couple of crudely worked core fragments suggest a later prehistoric presence, probably of Neolithic date. However, the lack of definite later retouched forms precludes a firm dating for this material.

A fairly extensive range of retouched forms was recovered (Table 12) all of which suggest a domestic aspect to the site (including scrapers, awl and pierces, retouched, serrated and utilised flakes (Figs 49, 5-8). The majority of the retouched forms are typical of Mesolithic flintworking both typologically and technologically. A microlith (Fig. 49, 8, SF 44) is a rod type; it is a relatively large example, which may suggest it is of earlier Mesolithic date. However, without other examples it is difficult to be precise about the dating of this material. Possible evidence for on site manufacture of microliths can be seen, a microlith or microburin fragment (SF 141) and another possible microlith came from the spoil heap, and it is likely that this piece was broken during manufacture. The retouched forms and the distinctive debitage all point to a Mesolithic date, possibly earlier Mesolithic, for the majority of the assemblage. A range of domestic activities were occurring including knapping, microlith manufacture, food and possibly hide preparation.

This assemblage seems to fit into a pattern of sporadic occupation and probably represents seasonally visited camps. In the locality two Mesolithic axes were found at Colney Heath Farm (Lightfoot 2001, 7) and scatters of flint was recovered from the evaluation (Percival and Richmond 1996). In the wider context lithic material has been found along the Colne Valley (e.g. Lacaille 1961; 1963; Lewis 191, 247, fig. 23.1, 254). An extensive late glacial and Mesolithic scatter has been found at Uxbridge (Lewis 1991). Mesolithic, Neolithic and Bronze Age flint has been recovered from excavations at The Grove, Watford (Bradley in prep a). Upper Palaeolithic through to Neolithic flintwork has recently been recovered from extensive excavations at Hatfield Aerodrome (Bradley in prep b). This pattern of seasonal occupation is mirrored nationally for example in the Kennet Valley (Healy *et al*. 1992), the Vale of Pickering (Schadla-Hall 1989) and the Upper Thames Valley (Bradley and Hey 1993).

USEWEAR AND REFITTING ANALYSES

Although much of the raw material is obviously from the same or similar flint source no refits were found.

It is possible that further close examination of the assemblage may reveal refitting material. Fifteen pieces of flint had usewear identified on one or more of their edges. The results are summarised in Table 13; it can be seen that cutting and whittling damage dominates the identifiable usewear. Only three pieces have scraping usewear and there were no identifiable instances of boring usewear. The cutting and whittling usewear is dominated by pieces with medium damage, which may perhaps be the result of use on materials such as green wood or more durable vegetable matter. One piece (55) may have been a very worn serrated flake. Another piece (57) has some additional retouch along the edge with the usewear, cortex along the opposite edge may have provided backing to enable the piece to be held more comfortably. Soft damage may have resulted from working substances like meat and plant materials. Hard damage may be the result of working seasoned wood, bone or antler. The results of the usewear analysis provide some insight into the use of the flint on the site.

Catalogue of illustrated pieces
1. Opposed platform blade core, neat removals, platform edge preparation. SF 51.
2. Small opposed platform blade core, some platform edge preparation, neatly worked. SF 100.
3. Crested flake. SF 136.
4. Core rejuvenation flake (tablet). SF 61.
5. Piercer with wear at tip. SF 80.
6. Multi-purpose tool, serrated flake with worn point, used also as a piercer. SF 28
7. End scraper, neatly worked. SF 32.
8. Rod microlith, broken at tip. SF 44.

ACKNOWLEDGEMENTS

The writer is grateful to Lafarge Aggregates and Andrew Richmond of Phoenix Consulting Archaeology Ltd, for commissioning the work. The author would also like to thank John Rowsell of Herts and Beds Excavations Ltd for carrying out the machining, and Claire Griffiths for post excavation assistance. The fieldwork was carried out by the author and Jonathan Hunn, the flints were analysed by Philippa Bradley.

Table 12: Summary of flint assemblage

Flakes	Blades, blade-like flakes	Chips	Cores, core fragments	Retouched forms	Total	Burnt unworked flint
150	43	5	29:- 6 multi-platform, 12 opposed platform, 5 single platform, 1 irregularly worked core, 1 discoidal, 4 core fragments	46:- 25 retouched flakes, 2 piercers, 2 misc. retouch, 4 end scrapers, 4 end and side scrapers, 1 rod, 1 microlith, 2 serrated flakes, 1 notch, 1 awl, 1 scraper fragment, 1 backed blade, 1 multi-tool	274	1

Table 13: Summary of identified usewear

Hardness of action	Scraping usewear	Cutting and whittling usewear
Hard	1	2
Medium		7
Soft	2	3

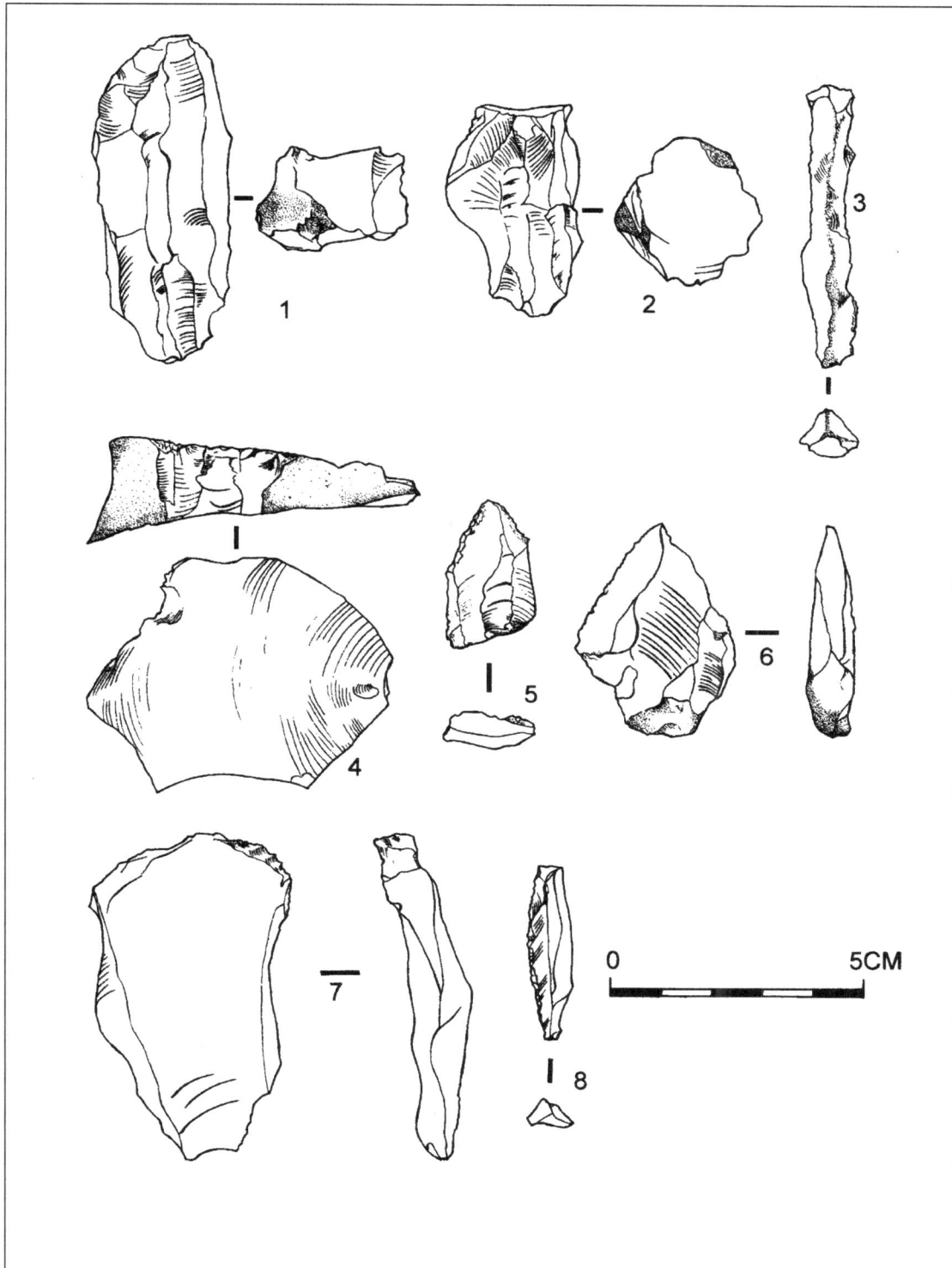

Fig. 49: Flint artefacts

PART 3

EXCAVATION OF A RING-DITCH TO THE SOUTH OF TYTTENHANGER PARK (COURSERS RD).

by Jonathan Hunn & Martin Lightfoot

SUMMARY

In September 2002 an archaeological excavation was carried out by ASC Ltd in the area of the new extension to Tyttenhanger Quarry, south of Coursers Road. A ring ditch that had been identified by aerial photograph and subsequent evaluation was fully excavated. Its preservation was very poor, with no internal features surviving. The only datable artefacts were some sherds of late Iron Age pottery the upper horizons of the circular ditch. Nevertheless, the ring ditch is believed to belong to the Bronze Age period.

INTRODUCTION

The excavation of a single ring ditch was the culmination of work that was begun in 1996 by Tempvs Reparatvm and a programme of field evaluation undertaken by *Archaeological Services and Consultancy Ltd* (ASC) between 1997 and 1999. The excavation took place on land adjacent to Coursers Road Tyttenhanger (NGR TL 204 041: Fig. 50).

The project was commissioned by Phoenix Consulting on behalf of Lafarge Aggregates Ltd, and was carried out according to a *Brief of Archaeological Works* issued by the County Archaeological Office, and a written scheme of investigation prepared by *Phoenix Consulting* (Richmond 1999).

SETTING

The gravel quarry to the south of Coursers Road comprises an area of 84 ha (208 acres) situated between the south side of the River Colne and the rising ground of the South Hertfordshire Plateau. The terrain varies from flat to gently sloping (lying between the 71 m and 82 m contours OD). The desk-top assessment report

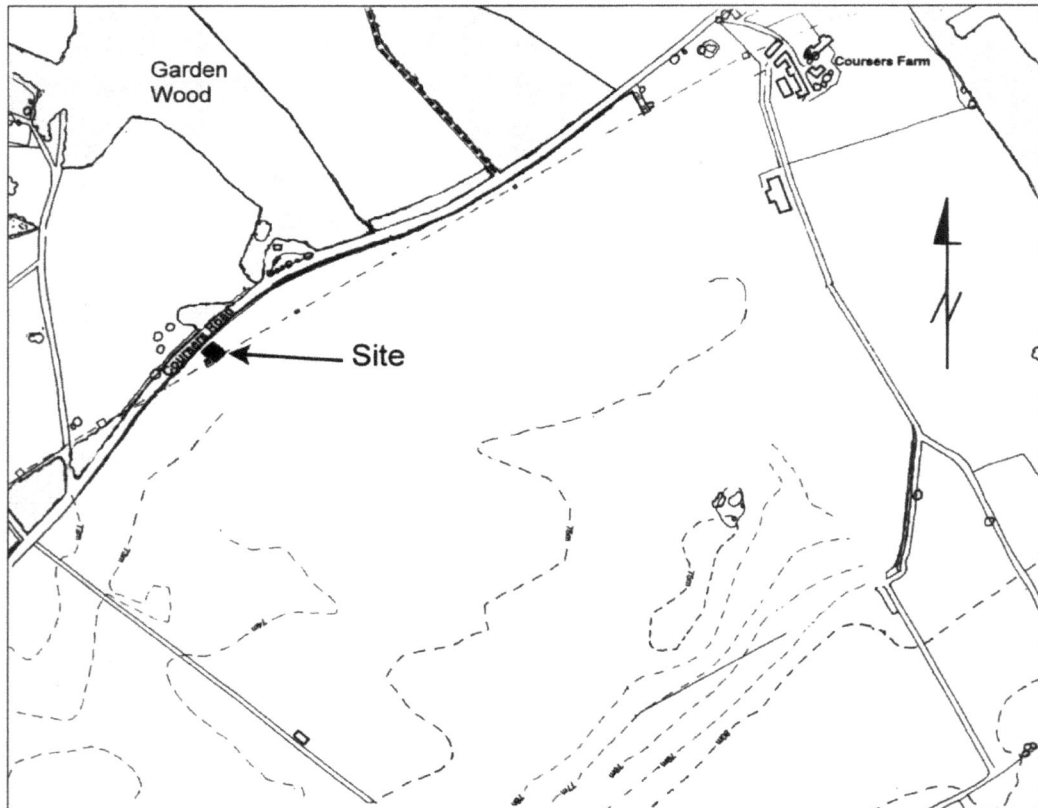

Fig. 50: Site location of former barrow (ring ditch)

illustrates a portion of sheet 239 derived from the British Geological Survey 1: 50,000 drift edition (Howlett and Lisboa 1996, fig 2). This shows that over 90% of the area being classified as 'glacial gravels'. However, the bore-hole data reported in the desk-top revealed the presence of an extensive area of brickearth amounting to some 50% of the proposed extraction zone (Howlett and Lisboa 1996, 8-9). A more recent soil map of the area distinguishes between the two deposits though at a scale of 1: 250,000 it is not easy to be sure where the soil changes actually occur (Soils of England and Wales sheet 6, D. Mackney et al 1983). It would appear that the area marked as 711v belonged to the Gresham Association (Aeolian drift and till) may relate to the area marked as boulder clay on the British Geological Survey map illustrated by Howlett and Lisboa (1996, fig 2). The remainder of the area to the east belongs to the Hamble 2 Association (571z), which is an Aeolian silty drift (Mackney *et al* 1983). These distinctions are important in terms of the physical characteristics of the soils and have been confirmed by the observations of McRae (1996). He states that the soils vary from 'deep, stonefree, silty soils developed in brickearth' (36.7%) in the middle, 'shallower, stonier and slightly sandier soils, developed in a mixture of brickearth and gravels' (47.5%) to 'soils with slightly impeded drainage overlying clay at depth' (24.8%) to the south east (McRae 1996). The application area is oversimplified as being classified as Grade 2 land (MAFF 1963, *Agricultural Land Classification of England and Wales*, Sheet 160). However, according to McRae, one third of the area (36.7%) consists of Grade 1 land (i.e. the brickearth terrain).

HISTORICAL BACKGROUND

The development area falls within a central portion of the northern end of the parish of Ridge. The parish itself was a comparatively late creation having been recorded as a 'capella' (chapel) of the church of St Peters (St Albans) in 1291 (Taxatio Ecclesiastica) and then in 1349 there is a mention of a presentment to the vicarage (VCH II, 391). Therefore, an early 14th date seems the most probable. This fact, by itself, is not remarkable. However, what is of interest is what the parish was actually based on. We know that it originally formed part of the parish of St Peters which was created in the early 11th century (VCH IV, 47). This parish comprised the townships of Thancton, Sleape, Harpesfield and what was later to become the parish of Rugg (Ridge).. The township of Tyttenhanger (villa) has been tentatively interpreted as being equated with Smallford

Ward, which was a detached portion of the parish of St Stephens (Hunn 1994, 84). The two should not necessarily be confused. Levett has suggested that the term soke reflects the survival of a grouping far earlier than the manor, which corresponded with the primitive halimote (Levett 1962, 136). The lesser halimotes or local courts may have became subsumed within the general term 'soke' (the soke was a private jurisdiction independent of the Hundred). What is important is the significance of the parochial unit of Ridge. It is almost certain that Ridge was based an a much earlier unit of administration and, most probably, on an estate or communal unit such as a township. Whether there was a coincidence between the soke and villa of Tyttenhanger is difficult to say. We do know that the manor of Ridge was identified with Tyttenhanger in the medieval period (VCH II, 387). Though this unit was not necessarily the same as either the soke or township. Certainly, by the mid 16th century the manor and park of Tyttenhanger lay partly in the parish of St Peters and Ridge (VCH II, 388). According to a court roll of 1657 the bounds of the west and south parts of the leet of Tyttenhanger were described. This extended from the 'Mounsditch' (Monks Ditch) of St Albans '*and along in the said ditch by Mr Robotham's wall to Cocklane; down the said lane to a house called Red Cross Croft, and along the lane called Cudmerwood and Mamfield to a close called Little Heath, and also between Pondfield and Churchfield and to a corner of Colney Heath, over the hedge in Lane End which leads from St Albans to North Mimms, and along the highway to High bank, and thence through the said Heath,......at a stile called the Hatfield stile*' (VCH II, 389).

There is now widespread acceptance that the boundaries of ancient parishes were themselves based on pre-existing estate or communal units (Bonney 1979, 41-51; Blair 1991, 12-34; Everson 1984, 123-27; Everitt 1986, 274-92; Hooke 1988, 123-152; Roffe 1984, 115-122; Taylor 1983, 125-150; Warner 1988, 9-34; Winchester 1990). Others would argue for an even earlier date, for example, from possibly even the late Iron Age (Bonney 1966). However, there is no evidence to support such an early date for the area to the south of St Albans.

It would be unwise to assume that all parochial units in southern England necessarily followed a similar pattern of formation. In southern Lincolnshire four elements of territorial organisation have been identified which could determine the extent and composition of parochial units (Roffe 1984, 117-18). These were described as 1) the holding (the basic unit of the manor); 2) the manor (the sum total of a group of holdings; 3) a group of manors (manors and settlements constituting and extended tenurial group and 4) communal and public institutions (e.g. a 12-carucate hundred). There is no reason to suppose that a similar range of diverse elements were absent from south Hertfordshire in the 11th century. In this area it' could be expected that the communal unit known as the 'vill' or township (see distinction in Winchester 1990, 19)

ARCHAEOLOGICAL BACKGROUND

The site has been subjected to several stages of archaeological evaluation. An archaeological desk-based assessment of the site considering the historical character of the landscape was undertaken in 1996 (Howlett and Lisboa 1996). This was followed by a fieldwalking exercise, which took place in the autumn of 1997 and covered an area of 72ha (Hunn and Coxah 1998). The results of the fieldwalking exercise demonstrated a level of artefact distribution in the plough soil to be in general low to almost non-existent. This indicated a very low level of archaeology across the site and where features existed beneath the topsoil then they were likely to be artefact poor.

An aerial photographic assessment of the site, also undertaken in the autumn of 1997 (Cox 1997) provided more positive results, with a series of crop marks both circular and linear concentrated in the north-western and south-eastern corners of the site. Those to the northwest appeared to represent the ploughed out remains of former circular burial mounds.

Subsequent to the programmes of fieldwalking and aerial photography a programme of trial trenching and test pitting was undertaken in the autumn of 1999 (Hunn 1999). Despite the cropmark evidence very few features of archaeological significance were encountered. Two trenches revealed archaeological features: the rest were devoid of any remains. One trench encountered the ploughed out remains of a prehistoric burial mound, the subsequent excavation of which is the subject of this report.

A shallow east – west running ditch was encountered in one of the other evaluation trenches, out of which was recovered a single struck flint. This ditch appears to represent an isolated feature, possibly relating to an episode of land division the date of which remains unknown.

During the autumn and winter of 1999 *Archaeological Services* carried out a programme of excavation to the north, and on the other side of the road from the current site (Turner and Hunn 2000). The findings were predominantly medieval and post medieval, though six flint tools were recovered.

In October 2001 *ASC* carried out a limited excavation on land again to the north of the current site (Lightfoot 2002). A large number of stratified and unstratified flints were recovered.

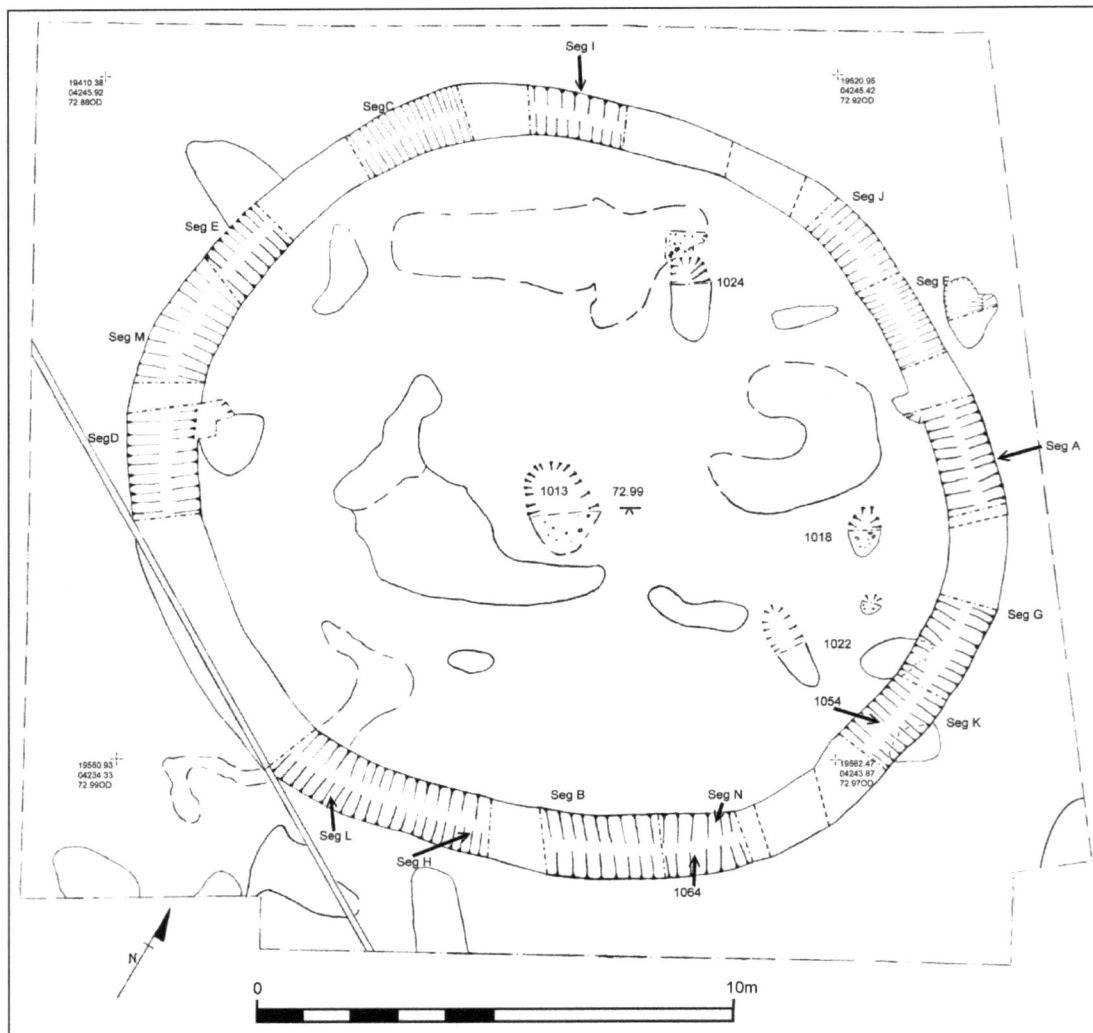

Fig. 51: Excavated plan of the ring-ditch

Typologically these were Mesolithic, though it is possible that some pieces represent later Neolithic or Bronze Age activity (Part 2).

AIMS & METHODS

The aim of the excavation was to excavate the previously identified remains of a possible Bronze Age round barrow, prior to topsoil removal and the construction of a bund on the site. The ring ditch was fully exposed using a JCB with a toothless ditching bucket. The area stripped was slightly less than that indicated by the Written Scheme of Investigation (Richmond 1999, 9) due to the proximity of overhead power cables and a busy road.

RESULTS

No trace of the mound was discerned during the excavation, nor were there any features consistent with inhumation or cremation discerned. In all 14 segments of the ditch between 2 and 2.5m in length were excavated. Including the sections excavated during the previous evaluation (Hunn 1999), over 70 per cent of this ring ditch was excavated.

RING DITCH

The ditch segments were generally very uniform, conforming to an open 'V' shaped profile in section and containing two or three discernable fills, though four fills were recorded in one segment (K). The lower fills of the ditch were predominantly reddish brown and contained a large amount of gravel and pebbles although there was some variation overall, and also an impression of possible slight variation between the east and west sides of the ditch, with the fills being more gravely on the west side. The darker fills were confined to the upper 0.10-0.25m and contained more clay and less gravel and pebbles than the lower fills. There was very little charcoal in general and the overall impression was that the ditch had gradually silted up.

FINDS

THE POTTERY

Every care was taken to maximise the amount of pottery recovered, each segment being excavated in 50mm spits, and the spoil carefully examined. Despite this, all but the upper fills of the ring ditch were almost totally devoid of any ceramics and even in the upper fills pottery was very rare, though a few sherds were recovered from the majority of segments excavated. Almost all the pottery came from the first spit (that is 50mm) in each segment with the next largest amount coming from the second spit (5-10cm). Only a small amount of pottery (calcite gritted ceramic), came from anywhere below this level at spits IV (150-200mm) (1008) and V (200-250mm) [1056].

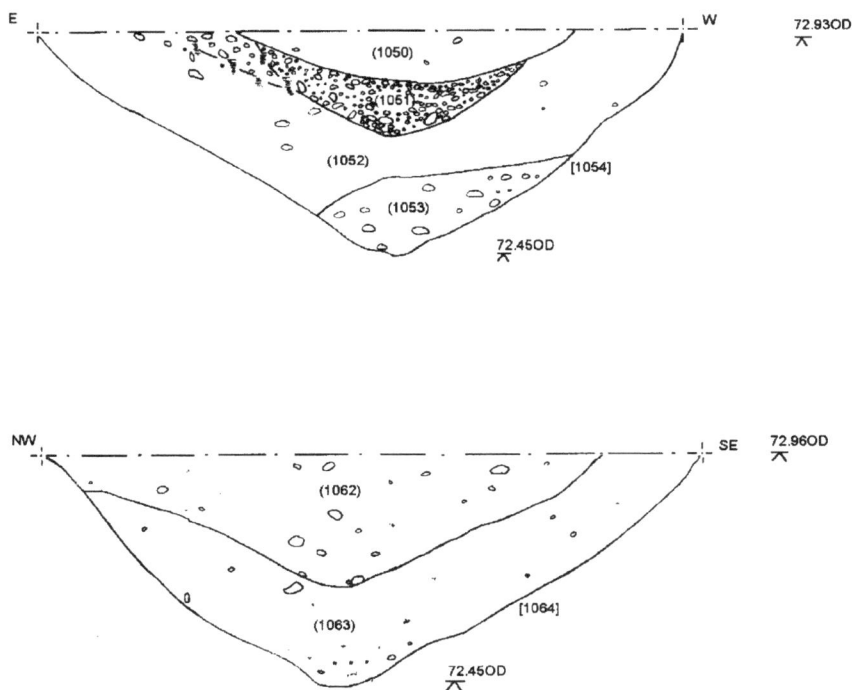

Fig. 52: Sections through ring ditch [1054] & [1064] segments K & N

Ceramic Identification

Table 14 includes the pottery recovered during the previous evaluation (Hunn 1999). The dates are AD.

Table 14: Ceramics

Context	No	Weight (grms)	Type	Date (AD)
9*	6	446	Grog tempered ware	Mid C 1st
1002	3	10	Miscellaneous grog tempered	C 1st
1008	7	5	Calcite gritted coarse ware	C 1st
1008	1	1	Miscellaneous grog tempered	C 1st
1029	1	1	Brown sandy ware	Late C 1st/2nd
1029	1	5	Grey ware	C1st-2nd
1033	1	5	Sandy local ware	Late C 1st/2nd
1050	2	4	Miscellaneous grog tempered	C 1st
1050	3	2	Flint tempered	LBA
1055	6	85	Sandy local ware	Late C 1st/2nd
1055	1	1	Fine grey ware	Early C 2nd
1056	4	10	Calcite gritted course ware	C 1st

* Hunn 1999, 17

Summary of the pottery

The ceramic assemblage from the ring-ditch is extremely modest, amounting to no more than 575 grammes. Most of the total weight is made up of the six sherds of a grog-tempered storage jar (446 grammes) belonging to the late Iron Age, and recovered during the evaluation (*qv*). There are only a few minute fragments of pottery likely to date earlier than the Late or Later Iron Age from the ring ditch [1050].

SUMMARY OF FLINTS

Only five worked flints were recovered from stratified contexts. No unstratified worked flints were found despite the surface being intensively cleaned and the spoil heaps examined for them. Of the five, two were crude scrapers of expedient character [1009/1033], the other three being waste flakes, probably from scraper or flake manufacture.

BONE

Only one small bone was recovered from the ring ditch [1002]. Though unidentifiable, it is likely to have come from a small animal, possibly dog or pig.

METAL

Despite the ring ditch, the surrounding area and the spoil heaps being gone over by metal detector, only one metal object was recovered, this being a small, broken, rounded lead object, measuring 10mm, with a hole in it; probably part of a larger cylindrical object or tube. Although this object is not identifiable and comes from the fill of the ring ditch [1002], there is a possibility that it is modern and may be a fishing weight.

The features excavated within the ring ditch were all likely to be of natural origin. Although some of them appeared quite regular on the surface they were all rather shallow and irregular in profile. These features, including that in the centre of the ring ditch are likely merely to be patches of brickearth or the result of floral or faunal activity.

ENVIRONMENTAL ARCHAEOLOGY ASSESSMENT
by James Rackham

Seven samples were taken from the ring ditch fills and other features for environmental analysis. These were submitted to the *Environmental Archaeology Consultancy* for processing and assessment (Table 15).

METHODS

The soil samples were processed in the following manner. Sample volume and weight was measured prior to processing. The samples were washed in a 'Siraf' tank (Williams 1973) using a flotation sieve with a 0.5mm mesh and an internal wet sieve of 1mm mesh for the residue. Both residue and flot were dried, and the residues subsequently refloated, to ensure the efficient recovery of charred material. The dry volume of the flots was measured and the volume and weight of the residue recorded.

The residue was sorted by eye, and environmental and archaeological finds picked out, noted on the assessment sheet and bagged independently. A magnet was run through each residue in order to recover magnetised material such as hammerscale and prill and a count made of the number of flakes or spheroids of hammerscale collected. The flot of each sample was studied using x10 magnifications and the presence of environmental finds (i.e. snails, charcoal, carbonised seeds, bones etc) was noted and their abundance and species diversity recorded on the assessment sheet. These, along with the finds from the sorted residue, constitute the material archive of the samples. The individual components of the samples were then preliminarily identified and the results are summarised below in Tables 15 and 16.

Table 15: Samples taken for environmental analysis

Sample no.	Context no.	Sample. vol.in l.	Sample weight (kg)	Feature
1	1042	30	36	Ring ditch fill
2	1046	29	36	Deposit
3	1047	30	42	Deposit
4	1048	30	42	Deposit
5	1055	33	36	Deposit
6	1059	30	30	Ring ditch fill
7	1060	29	35	Ring ditch fill

RESULTS

The most abundant finds in the samples were uncharred seeds, mainly *Chenopodium* spp. (goosefoots), *Galium* sp. (cleavers) and *Rubus* sp. (bramble) and numerous recent fibrous rootlets. This material, along with a few shells of the blind burrowing snail *Cecilioides acicula*, several larvae, millipede fragments, occasional beetle fragments, a few slivers of modern glass and very small fragments of coal and some cinder in the flots, is not considered to be contemporary with the deposits and is treated as a contaminant.

Table 16: Finds from the processed environmental samples

Context no.	Residue vol. (l)	Pot #/g	Flint #/g	Mg (g)	Hammer scale no.	Fired earth (g)	Glass no.	Coal	Bone (g)	
1042	2.5	2/35	51/121	<1	1	<1	2			Stone pebble
1046	2.7		8/75	<1	1	1		+		
1047	12		17/21	<1	1			+		
1048	17		51/18	<1		1		+		
1055	1.6		21/62	<1	3	<1				
1059	1.4		7/3	<1			1	+	<1	
1060	4.5		12/3	<1				+		

#/g = number/weight in grams
+ present

Table 17: Environmental finds from the processed samples

Context no.	Flot vol. (ml)	Char coal */<2*	Charred grain *	Charred seed *	Snails *	comment
1042	5	1/3			1	*Vallonia sp.*
1046	5	2/2				
1047	2	1/2		1		Indet.
1048	3	1/2	1	1		Cereal –indet, one pulse (pea?)
1055	15	3/3		1		Legume?, vole
1059	5	3/3		1	2	*Cecilioides acicula*, pulse?, indet burnt bone
1060	2	1/2				

* = abundance: 1=1-10, 2=11-50, 3=51-150, 4=151-250, 5=250+
/<2 = abundance >2mm/abundance < 2mm

The samples were extremely poor in respect of most archaeological and environmental finds (Table 16). The only context to produce any pottery was ring ditch fill 1042. Single flakes of hammerscale were recovered from three samples and one context, 1055, produced 3 flakes. At these densities the hammerscale could easily be intrusive. The only find in any abundance is fractured flint. Some of this may have been accidental fracture but several small flakes suggest that some flint working may be represented in the assemblage.

The environmental assemblages are even poorer. A few fragments of comminuted charcoal occur in all the samples, but none produced any quantity. One sample produced a single charred cereal grain, probably too poorly preserved for identification, and a single pulse, perhaps a pea, was recovered from the same sample. Three other samples produced single fragments of charred seed, two of which, although not identifiable to species, may be legumes. A tiny fragment of burnt bone was recovered from the fill, 1059, of the ring ditch, and a vole incisor, probably intrusive, was recorded in context 1055

CONCLUSION OF ENVIRNOMENTAL EVIDENCE

The extreme lack of environmental evidence, including charcoal, is consistent with an interpretation of the ring ditch as a barrow ditch. If this had been a house gully a much larger assemblage might have been expected. The deposits are fairly extensively contaminated with modern material and it is not possible to select material from the samples that could be used for radiocarbon analysis. The likelihood of contamination by more recent charcoal or charred seeds is too high to permit the use of this material for dating the feature.

The assemblages are so poor that no further work can be justified on the environmental evidence recovered from these samples.

CONCLUSION

The term barrow derives from the Old English *beorg* or *beorge* meaning mound of earth (Ashbee 1998). Round barrows were built to commemorate the dead, and are the commonest prehistoric monuments in the landscape (*op cit*). The survival of these barrows is poor in predominantly gravely or sandy areas, especially in fertile areas which have been heavily exploited. However, as ring ditches are a distinctive component of many round barrows they often survive when the funerary mound itself has long since disappeared.

Round barrows are typically associated with the Bronze Age, although the tradition of building circular funerary monuments goes back well into the Neolithic and continued into the early Iron Age, and some were constructed in Roman and Anglo-Saxon periods. Typologically, the more precise circles forming the ring ditch and accompanying mounds are generally thought to date to the early Bronze Age.

Despite the bulk of the pottery from the ring ditch dating from the Late Iron Age, it is almost certain that the barrow was constructed much earlier. The few sherds belonging to the 1st/2nd century AD could suggest that at this time the area was heavily ploughed. However, fieldwalking evidence does not suggest there is much evidence in the way of any discernible manuring activity. The relative lack of prehistoric pottery is probably attributable to its greater fragility when exposed to weathering.

Due to denudation and ploughing all that remained of this Bronze Age monument was the ditch that would have encircled the barrow. Not only has the mound itself and any cremation or inhumation associated with it long since disappeared, but the ditch may well have been significantly deeper than the 0.5m or so it is now.

It is often the case that round barrows were constructed in clusters, and it may be the case that there are more to be discovered in the area surrounding this one. An examination of the SMR data reveals three possible Bronze Age ring ditches running almost in a line to the east of the site, just to the south of Coursers Farm (SMR no's 2670, 2672 and 9648). Such monuments as round barrows are increasingly being studied as groups, in the context of other monuments and the topography of the area (e.g. Woodward & Woodward 1996). Although there may be little left of these barrows there is still potential for further study if they are considered in the context off the wider environment.

ACKNOWLEDGEMENTS

The writers are grateful to Andy Richmond of Phoenix Consulting for commissioning the work, Lafarge Aggregates Ltd who funded the project, and Jonathan Smith, County Archaeological Officer for Hertfordshire for monitoring the project. Thanks are also due to Alison Tinniswood for supplying SMR data. John Rowsell did the machining and the fieldwork was carried out by Martin Lightfoot, Jon Bolderson and Geoff Marshall, under the overall management of Dr Jonathan Hunn, who also commented on the pottery.

APPENDIX 3.1: CONTEXT SUMMARY
(RING DITCH EXCAVATION)

The levels cited are those for the base of cuts only

Table 18: Context summery & levels

Context	Type	Description and Interpretation	Level OD
1000	Deposit	Firm dark brown silty clay: ploughed topsoil	
1001	Deposit	Compact orangey brown pea-grit and gravel with inclusions of reddish brown clay: natural subsoil	
		Segment A	
1002	Fill	Firm, mid brown silty clay: secondary fill of [1004]	
1003	Fill	Compact, mixed brownish yellow silty clay: primary fill of [1004]	
1004	Cut	2.5m long segment of ring ditch	72.46m
		Segment B	
1005	Fill	Firm mid brown silty clay: secondary fill of segment B [1007]	
1006	Fill	Compact brownish yellow, silty clay: primary fill of segment B [1007]	
1007	Cut	2.5m segment of ring ditch	72.32
		Segment C	
1008	Fill	Friable dark blackish brown silty clay: tertiary fill of [1011]	
1009	Fill	Friable light orangey brown silty clay: secondary fill of {1011]	
1010	Fill	Friable mid greyish orangey brown silty clay with some sand and pebbles: primary fill of [1011]	
1011	Cut	2.5m segment of ring ditch	72.33
1012	Fill	Firm reddish brown clay with some gravel: fill of likely natural feature within ring ditch	
1013	Cut	Irregular feature roughly at the centre of the ring ditch.	72.76
		Segment D	
1014	Fill	Firm mid brown silty clay: secondary fill of [1016]	
1015	Fill	Compact brownish orange silty clay: primary fill of [1016]	
1016	Cut	2.5m segment of ring ditch	72.49
1017	Fill	Firm reddish brown silty clay: fill of likely natural feature [1018]	
1018	Cut	Irregular / rounded natural feature within the ring ditch	72.88
1019	Fill	Firm reddish brown silty clay: fill of likely natural feature [1020]	
1020	Cut	Irregular / roughly circular natural feature within the ring ditch	72.93
1021	Fill	Firm reddish brown silty clay: fill of likely natural feature [1022]	
1022	Cut	Cigar shaped probable natural feature within the ring ditch	72.84
1023	Fill	Firm reddish brown silty clay: fill of likely natural feature [1024]	
1024	Cut	Irregular / rounded, probable natural feature within the ring ditch	72.77
		Segment E	
1025	Fill	Firm mid brown silty clay: tertiary fill of [1028]	
1026	Fill	Compact brownish / yellowish orange: secondary fill of [1028]	
1027	Fill	Compacted orangey brown silty clay with some sand and pebbles: primary fill of [1028]	
1028	Cut	2m segment of ring ditch	72.39
		Segment F	
1029	Fill	Friable dark greyish brown silty clay: tertiary fill of [1032]	
1030	Fill	Friable, light orange/yellow/brown silty clay: secondary fill of [1032]	
1031	Fill	Light orangey brown silty clay with some sand and gravel: primary fill of [1032]	
1032	Cut	2m segment of ring ditch	72.40
		Segment G	
1033	Fill	Firm mid brown silty clay with some small rounded pebbles: secondary fill of [1035]	
1034	Fill	Friable reddish brown sandy silt with pebbles and gravel: primary fill of [1035]	
1035	Cut	2m segment of ring ditch	72.49
		Segment H	
1036	Full	Firm mid brown silty clay: tertiary fill of [1039]	
1037	Fill	Firm yellow orangey brown silty clay: secondary fill of [1039]	
1038	Fill	Compacted reddish brown silty clay with some sand and pebbles: primary fill of [1039]	
1039	Cut	2m segment of ring ditch	72.42
1040	Fill	Firm, mid orange brown silty clay: fill of [1041]	
1041	Cut	Irregular probable natural feature just outside the ring ditch	72.51
		Segment J	
1042	Fill	Friable dark greyish brown silty clay: tertiary fill of [1045]	
1043	Fill	Friable light yellowish brown silty clay: secondary fill of [1045]	
1044	Fill	Compact mid orangey brown silty clay with some sand, gravel and small pebbles: primary fill of [1045]	
1045	Cut	2m segment of ring ditch	72.37
		Segment I	
1046	Fill	Firm mid brown silty clay with some pebbles: tertiary fill of [1049]	
1047	Fill	Firm yellowish orangey brown silty clay with some sand and pebbles: secondary fill of [1049]	
1048	Fill	Compacted orangey brown silty clay with some sand and pebbles: primary fill of [1049]	

1049	Cut	2m segment of ring ditch	72.43
		Segment K	
	Fill	Firm mid to dark brown silty clay with some small rounded pebbles: fill of [1054]	
1051	Fill	Friable, dark brown gravel with some silty clay inclusions: fill of [1054]	
1052	Fill	Firm light reddish brown silt with some rounded pebbles: secondary fill of 1054]	
1053	Fill	Firm light greyish brown silt with some small rounded pebbles: primary fill of [1054]	
1054	Cut	2m segment of ring ditch	72.45
		Segment L	
1055	Fill	Firm mid brown silty clay with some rounded pebbles: tertiary fill of [1058]	
1056	Fill	Firm yellowish orangey brown silty clay with some sand and rounded pebbles: secondary fill of [1058]	
1057	Fill	Compact orangey reddish brown silty clay with some sand and rounded pebbles: primary fill of [1058]	
1058	Cut	2m segment of ring ditch	72.36
		Segment M	
1059	Fill	Friable dark brown silty clay with some pebbles: secondary fill of [1061]	
1060	Fill	Firm mid yellowish brown silty clay: primary fill of [1061]	
1061	Cut	2m segment of ring ditch	72.34
		Segment N	
1062	Fill	Firm mid brown silty clay with some small pebbles: secondary fill of [1064]	
1063	Fill	Firm reddish brown silt with some small rounded pebbles: primary fill of [1064]	
1064	Cut	2m segment of ring ditch	72.45

PHOTOGRAPHIC PLATES
(RING DITCH EXCAVATION)

Plate 25: Pre-excavation view of ring-ditch

Plate 26: View of excavated ring-ditch

PART 4

LANDSCAPE SURVEY OF LAND NEAR ARKLEY

By J.R. Hunn

SUMMARY

In Autumn 2000 a desk-based assessment and preliminary landscape survey was undertaken of land at Saffron Green (Arkley). The results of the project suggest that the area is part of an ancient landscape that has retained its pastoral character, despite changing patterns of land use. A rectilinear system of land division arranged on a co-axial basis has been tentatively identified. It may be of pre-Roman date, possibly even belonging to the Bronze Age period. Nevertheless, many of the existing field boundaries are of relatively recent (post-medieval) date, but have been imposed on an older, though more extensively arranged, pastoral system of land exploitation.

INTRODUCTION

In November 2000, *Archaeological Services & Consultancy Ltd* (ASC) undertook an archaeological desk-based assessment and landscape survey on pasture land at Saffron Green, Arkley Lane on the Hertfordshire/Middlesex border. The assessment was commissioned by Mr T. Hurley (Environment Dept) on behalf of *Hertfordshire County Council,* as part of the Council's strategic review of its land holdings and management policies.

SETTING

The study area comprises an irregular T-shaped conglomeration of fields within a pastoral setting. It forms a small part of a larger wedged shaped area of land defined by the A1 on the north, Rowley Lane to the west, Galley Lane to the east and the outer edges of Arkley and the A411 road to the south. Running through its centre from north to south is *Arkley Lane*, an overgrown and boggy morass, which is almost impassable in winter beyond Saffron Green cottage to Woodlands Farm to the south. The area is composed of no more than a dozen fields all down to grass, covering some 29.5 ha (73 acres). The land is classified as Grade 3 by MAFF (1970, sheet. No 160).

The natural unmodified soils of the area are derived from Tertiary clay belonging to the Windsor association. They are described as *'pelo-stagnogley soils...they have a grey and ocherous mottled clayey sub-surface....that become increasingly brown with depth. They are stoneless and usually well structured'.* A typical profile would be as follows: 0-200mm: dark grey, slightly stoneless clay loam or clay. 200-650mm: light brownish grey with many ocherous mottles, stoneless clay; moderate coarse prismatic structure. 650-1000mm: brown, slightly mottled structure; many fine manganiferous concretions (Hodge *et al* 1984, 358-9).

The terrain varies from flat to gently sloping. The highest ground lies at the southern end of the area at 105m AOD and slopes gently down to just above 91m AOD on the northern side, where a shallow brook runs from west to east. Beyond the brook the terrain begins to rise gently in height, almost imperceptibly. Thus the estate lies, more or less, in a shallow saucer-shaped valley.

The fields are divided by boundaries consisting almost exclusively of hedges and ditches. During the three visits that were made to the site most of the ditches contained running water. For a description of the field boundaries see Appendix 4.1.

ARCHAEOLOGICAL & HISTORICAL BACKGROUND

The individual land parcels and their boundaries are described in the next section. Here the Arkley estate is described in relation to the general context of its historical and archaeological landscape. For the archaeology of this particular County Council landholding, hereafter referred to as the 'Arkley estate', there is very little available evidence. The SMR lists only several manorial sites and one find-spot, adjacent to Saffron Green. Two possible palaeolithic 'struck flints' were found in a stream at Fold Farm (TQ 233 975; PRN 6436). There is no further information until the medieval period, which has probably more to do with the pastoral nature of the terrain and lack of fieldwork than anything else. There is a moated site at Fold Farm (TQ 2258 9751; PRN 2648) in South Mimms (formerly in Middlesex), and another site at Dyrham Park (TQ 2240 9850; PRN 6207). Neither of these sites has a direct bearing on the Arkley estate, though their locations are of interest in terms of the overall character of the composition of the landscape (below).

There is good aerial photographic coverage of the study area between 1947 and 1990. Although the 1947 photograph (AP Herts 51/29NW 86) is at a smaller scale (1:10,560) than later photos, sufficient detail is present to show that between that date and 1972 there was little change to the composition of the Arkley estate. There are slight variations in the state of the hedgerows shown between 1972 (HCC AP sheet TQ 2097/2197, 889) and 1990 (HCC AP sheet TQ 2097/2397, 889). Only on the photograph taken in May 1980 is there anything of archaeological interest. This shows a curvilinear, possibly circular, feature on the east side of Field 8 (TQ 22125 97175). If the latter were so, the feature would be *c.*115 m diameter and about 12m wide. It could be a geological phenomenon, such as an old palaeo-channel or, alternatively, a henge monument. The eastern side of Field 8 also contains a curvilinear boundary. However, it is clear from the photograph that this was once a separate field. Interestingly, this part of the field lies outside the present day County Council holding. The crop-mark and the curved part of the boundary do not appear to be related, but such a relationship is not impossible. The balance of probability suggests that the curvilinear feature is natural. There is certainly no evidence for an associated bank. However, this part of the estate is on slightly higher ground and may, conceivably, have been cultivated in the pre-medieval period, thus destroying the evidence. All that can be said is that an extant aerial photograph shows an unexplained feature which may or may not be of natural origin.

The Arkley area lay towards the southern end of the ancient parish of Ridge whose antecedents are most probably derived from a late Anglo-Saxon estate, and may be even older. However, the surviving historical evidence for the pre-Conquest (1066) period is negligible. The area formed part of the lands belonging to St Albans Abbey, whose principal manor was Tyttenhanger. It is not mentioned under this heading in the Domesday Survey (1086), but the *Victoria County History* for Hertfordshire (Page 1908, II, 387) suggests that it was entered under the abbot's holding for Shenley. If this were so, then the information gleaned from Domesday indicates the existence of a fully developed agrarian landscape. However, it does not give any information on what proportion of the holding was heathland or 'waste', still less the area of pasture (Morris 1976, section 10.2). The Arkley estate is and probably always was part of an extensive area of pasture. The evidence for the sub-division of this pastoral landscape is discussed below.

In order to discover the historical geography of an area, especially one as small as the study area, it is necessary to have sufficient place and/or field name data available to trace those elements back in time. The more information is available, the more confident we can be in reconstructing the historic landscape. This aspect will be discussed further on; here we are concerned with the information derived from manorial records.

The earliest place-name element occurs in 1331 when in an extent of Tyttenhanger a meadow called 'Erkefordemad' containing 4.5 acres was mentioned (B.Lib Add Mss 36237). In the same document an 'Arkeleyslond *et* Raisoneslond' was mentioned as containing 1 virgate (*ibid.*). The single most important source of historical information is contained within a book of extracts from manorial court rolls for the years 1238-1460 (HALS D/EB 2067B). The 13th and early 14th-century references mention the names of individual land-holders and the amount of land (virgate, ferlingate and their sub-divisions) held. Only in the 14th century is reference made to place and field names. There are references to lands abutting on Arkley Lane from the later

part of the 14th century (*Edw. III, 45th year*). Some are direct and some indirect references to holdings that may possibly be associated with the present Arkley estate. The link is suggested by those names whose elements may have survived from the 14th century to the Tithe Apportionment survey of Ridge in 1836. Several names may be given as examples of this (Appendix 4.2). However, they are no more than possibilities, and proving their longevity is another matter.

According to the *English Place-Name* volume for Hertfordshire the name 'Arkley' is of uncertain derivation (Gover *et al* 1970, 69). However, it is one of those names whose suffix suggests that it was derived from the old English word meaning a woodland clearing (Gardner 1967, 5). This would certainly accord with the historical record (below). Apart from Arkley the only other surviving name is 'Saffron Green'. Curiously, this is not mentioned by Gover (*ibid.*). However, it is shown on Dury and Andrew's survey of Hertfordshire of 1766 Fig.55, and Bryant's map of 1822. In a survey of the Tyttenhanger estate in *c.*1777 there is mention of a 'Shapham Green' which appears to be an alternative version of 'Saffron' (HALS D/Ecd E39). As yet, no earlier version of this name has been identified, but there is no reason to dismiss it as a purely post-medieval creation. There are some areas called *Saffron Field* in the adjacent parish of Shenley (TA 565, 566, 567, *in* HALS DSA4 94/1). It may be that the name derives from *Colchicum autumnale*, the poisonous meadow saffron, rather than *Crocus sativus*, the culinary herb (Field 1972, 189). The suffix 'green' and other similar names are discussed further on.

One interesting aspect of the landscape is the way that all the pre-modern roads, lanes and trackways follow a NNW-SSE alignment. This may be readily observed in the area from Watling Street in the west (west of Boreham Wood) to Stagg Lane in the east, north of Cockfosters (Middx). It may be no surprise that, since many of the parish boundaries follow these lines of communication, they also tend to have a similar orientation. This observation may also be applied to many of the field boundaries. There are four, possibly five such principal co-axial boundaries within and adjacent to the Arkley estate. To the east the estate abuts on the county boundary (Galley or Gallows Lane) dividing Hertfordshire (parish of Ridge) and Middlesex (parish of South Mimms, now part of Hertfordshire). The outer western edge of the estate has been cut short by the A1 road where it would have abutted onto a principal NNW-SSE field boundary. This ran parallel to the parish boundary between Shenley and Ridge, which bisects the estate Fig. 53. Despite its irregularity, Arkley Lane is also follows a similar alignment, and a further NNW-SSE boundary may be half hidden within the present landscape.

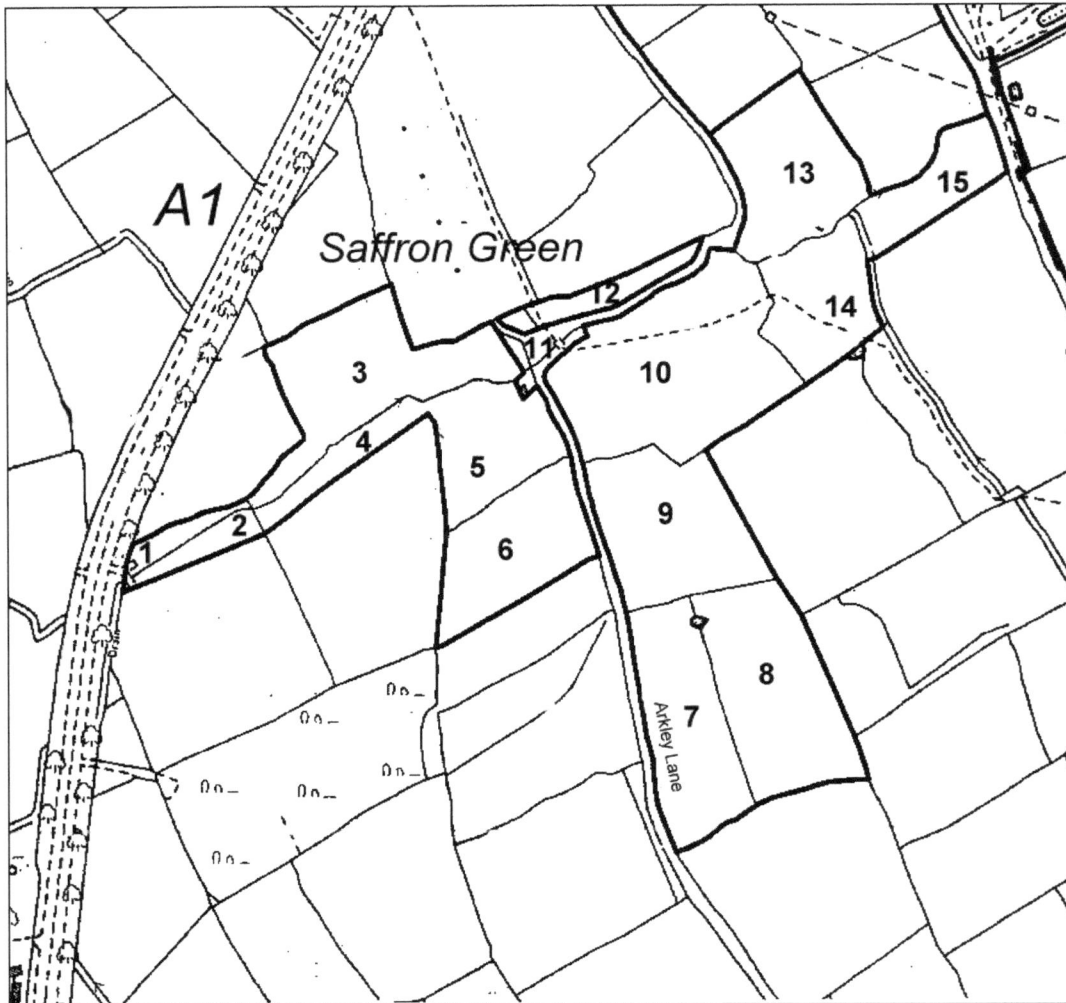

Fig. 53: Arkley estate numbered for field descriptions

RESULTS

Each land unit or parcel is individually described with reference to Fig. 53

Land parcel no:	1
Type:	Narrow pasture field
Dimensions:	210m x 35m
Area:	c. 0.252 ha (0.62 acre)
Location:	Parish of Shenley
Co-ords:	NGR TQ 21350-97350
TA no:	563
TA name:	Part of Fourteen Acres.
Land use:	Neglected pasture land, now waste.
Description:	Wedged shaped piece of ground lying adjacent on the north side of the Saffron Green brook. Its northern boundary is a discontinuous hedge.

Land parcel no:	2
Type:	Narrow portion of larger field
Dimensions:	210m x 35m
Area:	0.315 ha (0.77 acre)
Location:	Parish of Shenley
Co-ords:	NGR TQ 21352-97300
TA no:	563
TA name:	Part of Fourteen Acres
Land use:	Set aside
Description:	Wedged shaped piece of ground lying adjacent on the south side of the Saffron Green brook.

Land parcel no:	3
Type:	Irregular field
Dimensions:	365m x 195m max
Area:	3.058 ha (7.55 acres)
Location:	Partly in Shenley and partly in Ridge
Co-ords:	NGR TQ 21620-97647
TA no:	550 (Shenley) and 358 (Ridge)
TA name:	Brook Field
Land use:	Set aside
Description:	An inverted T-shaped field composed of two, possibly three smaller parcels lying adjacent on the north side to the Saffron Green Brook . No distinguishing features observed.

Land parcel no:	4
Type:	Long, thin rectangular field
Dimensions:	250m x 35m
Area:	0.875 ha (2.16 acres)
Location:	Lying in Shenley parish
Co-ords:	NGR TQ 21585-97430
TA no:	550 (Shenley)
TA name:	Part of Brook Field
Land use:	Set aside
Description:	Lies adjacent to the Saffron Green brook, which divides it from 'Brook Field' to the north. It has a hedged boundary to the south and overgrown vegetation at its western end.

Land parcel no: 5
Type: Short quadrilateral
Dimensions: 130m x 160m
Area: 1.81 ha (4.48 acres)
Location: Between the boundary separating Shenley from Ridge and Arkley Lane: abutting Saffron Green cottage, south of stream.
Co-ords: NGR TQ 21745-97466
TA no: 356 (Ridge)
TA name: Four Acres
Land use: Set aside
Description: Gently sloping featureless pasture field bounded by hedgerows.

Land parcel no: 6
Type: Short quadrilateral field
Dimensions: 185m x 120m
Area: 2.46 ha (6.1 acres)
Location: Lies between the open parish boundary and Arkley Lane south of Parcel 5.
Co-ords: NGR TQ 21743-97347
TA no: 355 (Ridge)
TA name: Part of Long Field
Land use: Set aside
Description: Lies to the west of Arkley Lane and abuts on no. 5 to the north. There are no distinguishing features.

Land parcel no: 7
Type: Long quadrilateral field
Dimensions: 275m x 100m
Area: 2.7 ha (6.72 acres)
Location: Lies on the east side of Arkley Lane in the parish of Ridge.
Co-ords: NGR TQ 21980-97150
TA no: 304 (Ridge)
TA name: Angers Mead
Land use: Unmown pasture
Description: This field is defined by hedgerows and ditches. There were no surface features observed within the field.

Land parcel no: 8
Type: Long quadrilateral field
Dimensions: 280m x 127m (belonging to HCC estate)
Area: 3.55 ha (8.77 acres)
Location: South eastern most field of Arkley estate lying adjacent and to the east of Parcel 7
Co-ords: NGR TQ 22100-97150
TA no: 303 (Ridge)
TA name: Great Lands
Land use: Unmown pasture
Description: There were no surface features noted in this field. According to its cartographic history it is part of a larger field whose ownership appears to have become sub-divided at some point in its history. To the east lies another portion, which would increase its size to 4.7ha (11.65 acres). The field has a crop mark anomaly (section 4.2, this report). The field is bounded by hedges and ditches.

Land parcel no: 9
Type: Irregular square quadrilateral
Dimensions: 170m x 150m
Area: 2.93ha (7.26 acres)
Location: Adjacent to Arkley Lane on its eastern side besides Saffron Green Field.
Co-ords: NGR TQ 21949-97400
TA no: 297 (Ridge)
TA name: Further Seven Acres
Land use: Rough grass
Description: Flat with no discernible features.

Land parcel no: 10
Type: Irregular quadrilateral field

Dimensions: 3262m x 186m
Area: 4.57ha (11.3 acres)
Location: At the corner of the change of direction of Arkley Lane on its southern and eastern side
Co-ords: NGR TQ 22000-97600
TA no: 296 (Ridge)
TA name: Saffron Green
Land use: Grass (recently cropped)
Description: Flat with no obvious surface features (discussed below)

Land parcel no: 11
Type: Truncated triangular plot.
Dimensions: c. 100m x 30m
Area: 0.030ha
Location: At the junction of Arkley land with the brook and the footpath from Galley Lane.
Co-ords: NGR TQ 21805-97600
TA no: Parcel of Arkley Lane
TA name: Unnamed
Land use: Partly waste and partly planted with willows
Description: This plot of ground is probably the surviving core of the ancient 'green'.

Land parcel no: 12
Type: narrow sinuous plot of ground
Dimensions: 254m x 26m
Area: 0.66ha (1.65 acres)
Location: On northern side of Saffron Green adjacent to Arkley Lane.
Co-ords: NGR TQ 21900-97700
TA no: 359 (Ridge)
TA name: Site of four cottages
Land use: Pasture
Description: Mostly flat and featureless; surrounded by trees and vegetation.

Land parcel no: 13
Type: An irregular short quadrilateral field
Dimensions: 177m x 127m
Area: 2.26 ha (5.6acres)
Location: East of Arkley Lane and north of Saffron Green brook
Co-ords: NGR TQ 22135-97810
TA no: 293 (Ridge)
TA name: Great Park Water
Land use: Pasture (recently cropped)
Description: Flat to gently sloping field fringed with hedges and trees; no distinguishing surface features.

Land parcel no: 14
Type: An irregular short quadrilateral field.
Dimensions: 144m x 126m
Area: 1.8ha (4.48 acres)
Location: South of Saffron Brook
Co-ords: NGR TQ 22150-97600
TA no: 295 (Ridge)
TA name: Long Field (part of)
Land use: Pasture (recently cut)
Description: Flat with few distinguishing surface features. Running water on four sides; on its eastern and western sides there are slight signs of former water courses.

Land parcel no: 15
Type: Irregular long quadrilateral field
Dimensions: 186m x 65m
Area: 1.27ha (3.15 acres)
Location: Abutting on Saffron Green on the north and on Galley Lane to the east.
Co-ords: NGR TQ 22300-97779
TA no: 294 (Ridge)
TA name: Little Park Water
Land use: Pasture
Description: Flat with no distinguishing surface features.

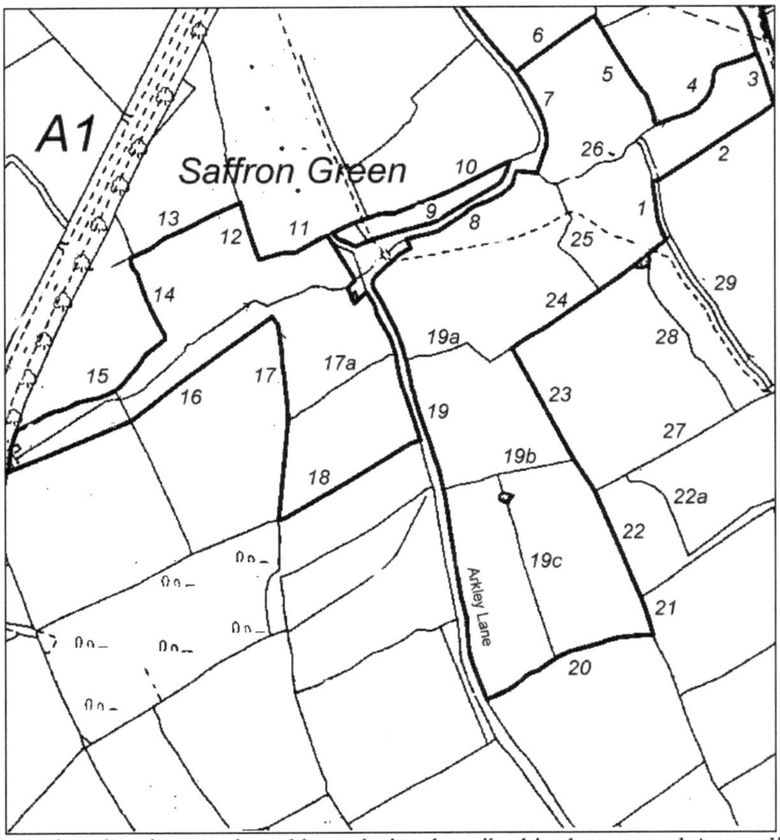

Fig. 54: Plan showing numbered boundaries described in the text and Appendix 4.1

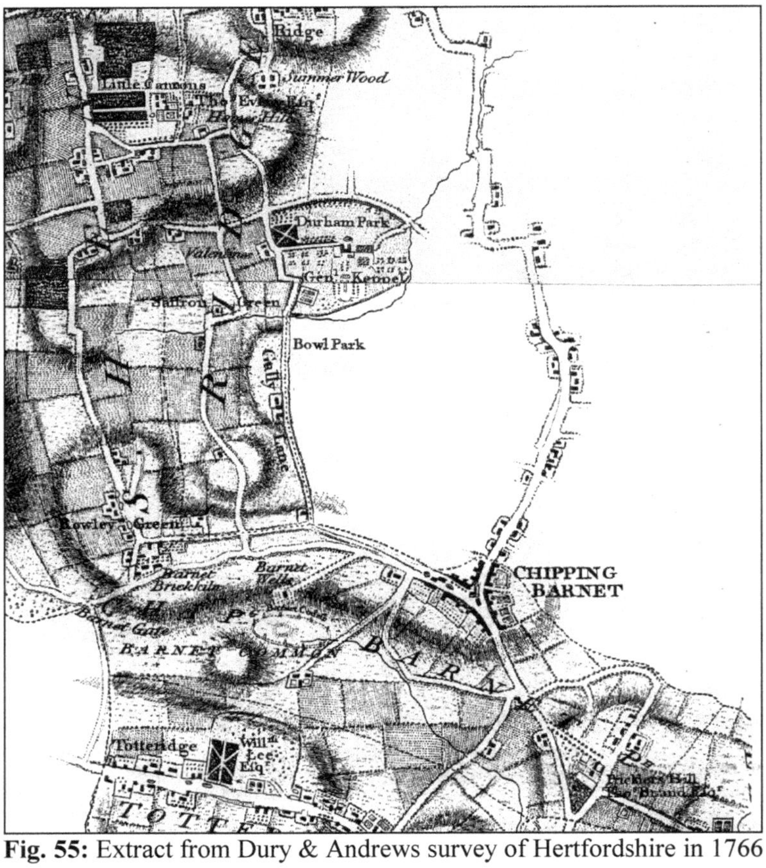

Fig. 55: Extract from Dury & Andrews survey of Hertfordshire in 1766

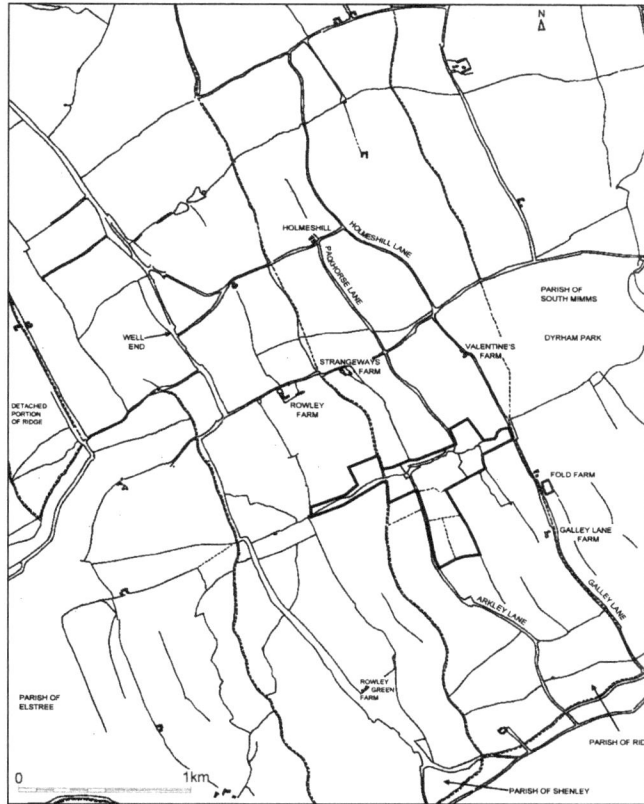

Fig. 56: Boundaries, communications & topography in the Arkley estate area

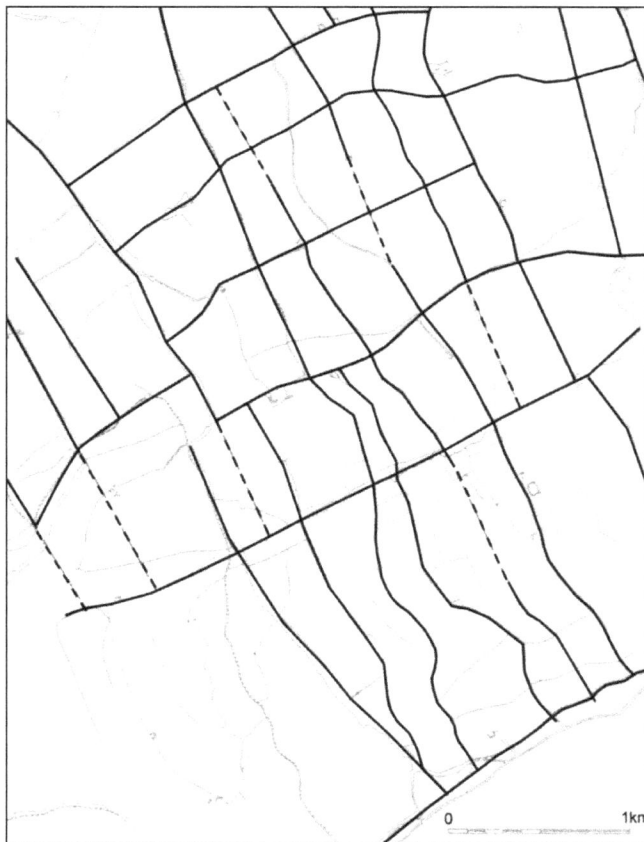

Fig. 57: Outline reconstruction of possible prehistoric land division in the Saffron Green area

DISCUSSION & CONCLUSION

The southern fringes of Hertfordshire, of which the Arkley estate forms a small part, may be classified as 'ancient landscape'. In other words, it is the product of slow evolutionary processes that have continued over a considerable period. Attempting to identify those processes and to understand their legacy on the landscape has been the principal aim of this study. The Arkley estate contains no obvious relict features or structures. Its principal focus of interest lies in the intersection of two topographical features, the eastward flowing 'Saffron Green' brook and Arkley Lane. This area is referred to as 'Saffron Green' on modern maps. We know that in the early Victorian period there was a small hamlet there, but very little else. A footpath from Galley Lane to Rowley Lane and beyond passes through this former hamlet. Whether this settlement was ever larger in the past is not known. At present, the only information we have is its name and the evidence that may be inferred from the topography.

The settlement pattern of the Arkley area consists of predominantly scattered farms and hamlets. The nearest villages were Chipping Barnet, 3km to the WSW, Elstree, 4.5km to the SW, Ridge, 3km to the north and Shenley, 4km to the NNW. With the exception of Barnet none of these settlements is of more than modest size. If these townships and their subsequent evolution into parishes were the focus of primary settlement then those lesser settlements, distinguished by the suffix 'green and 'end', are often interpreted as being secondary developments. However, such an interpretation is probably over-simplistic. It is now believed that between the 5th and 7th centuries in central and southern England there was a mainly dispersed form of settlement which was gradually replaced by a pattern of nucleated villages in the 8th and 11th centuries (Taylor 1995, 27). This model may well be applicable to south Hertfordshire. However, there is an alternative interpretation. This suggests that there was a gradual reclamation of woodland and moorland in the 12th and 13th centuries (*ibid.*). This model is supported by evidence in the St Albans area, where just such a process was demonstrably underway from the 11th century (Hunn 1994, 92, 172). There is mention of an assart lying on 'Arcleylonde' in the mid 15th century next to 'Newlonde' which is fairly intelligible (HALS D/EB 2067B F.1; Hen VI, 12 and 23). This almost certainly refers to an assart pre-dating the 15th century. The name *Newland* occurs at least by the 14th century and, to judge by medieval habit of using repetitive formulae, is most probably of an earlier date.

There are a number of place-names that carry the suffix 'green'. In an area from just north of Arkley and High Barnet to just south of St Albans, corresponding more or less with the ancient parishes of Shenley and Ridge, there are at least five references to greens and to a single surviving 'end'. These are Tyttenhanger Green, Bowmans Green, Creese Green (at the interesection of Packhorse Lane with Mimms Lane, Fig. 55), Rowley Green and Sapham or Saffron Green. There is a 16th-century reference to 'Gregories greene' which could be an earlier name for Saffron Green, but this is not certain (HALS D/EB 2067B M.25). Of the five greens mentioned above only one, Rowley Green, survives to any real extent (Fig. 55-57). Creese Green only appears on Dury and Andrews' survey of Hertfordshire in 1766, while Tyttenhanger and Bowmans Green survive to the present day in name. At Saffron Green, only a small vestige of settlement survives what must have been a much larger area. It seems more than just coincidence that that these 'greens' are to be found on the north-south tracks and roads. Whether or not this is due to a degree of formal planning is debatable. It may be that this arrangement is simply the product of a need for resting/watering places along local drove-ways for stock as they journeyed on their way to market, at either Chipping Barnet or St Albans. There is good circumstantial evidence to suggest that this may have been one of their functions, even if it was not a primary cause for their existence. Nevertheless, this aspect of landscape use can only be briefly mentioned here, since the topic is beyond the scope of this present study. It is relevant to ask here, to what extent was Saffron Green a product of primary or secondary settlement? The answer to this can only be qualified, since certainty is not possible in a study of this type. Nevertheless, there are several models that may be advanced in order to arrive at a probable hypothesis, though it is accepted that there are others which may be equally valid.

The landscape of the Arkley estate appears to have always been a product of the dual influences of topography and socio-economic stimuli. The first element to observe is the location of farmsteads in the area, all of which lie around the periphery of Saffron Green, on or above the 100m contour. Fold Farm, on the eastern side of Galley Lane, is fractionally below that contour, which passes through the now deserted moated site. Galley Lane Farm is the closest agrarian establishment to Saffron Green, about 850m to the south west, above the 100m contour. Valentine's Farm is about 800m to the NNE, on the 105m contour. Strangeways Farm is 750m to the NNW, on the 110m contour; Rowley Farm is 800m to the NW, on the 115m contour, and Rowley Green Farm lies 1400m to the SSE, on the 120m contour. In contrast, all the fields on the Arkley estate, with the exception of the southern portions of fields 7 and 8, lie below the 100m contour. The farmsteads of Valentines, Strangeways, Rowley Green and Fold Farm have medieval antecedents (Gover *et al* 1970, 68, 85) and Galley Lane Farm and Rowley Farm probably do. The fact that there is no farmstead on or close to Saffron Green does not imply that none ever existed. However, the lower-lying ground and the proximity of water courses were probably factors in influencing the choice of drier locations.

The location and juxtaposition of trackways and lanes passing through or adjacent to the Saffron Green area is important in understanding how they came to influence the landscape we see today. By examining the topographical information shown on the Ordnance Survey 1st Series 6" (1:10,560) maps of *c.*1868 it is possible to suggest, though not necessarily to prove, a possible sequence of events. The present day configuration of Arkley Lane appears to have come about by its merger with Packhorse Lane. Packhorse Lane exists today, proceeding from Holmeshill, a known medieval site (Gover *et al* 1970, 84), for about 1500m, where it turns abruptly 90° to the west. It is suggested that at one time it carried on, more or less, in the same direction. The same applies to Arkley Lane, proceeding from Saffron Green along the course of the present day footpath towards Strangeways Farm. Alternatively, it may have followed the parochial boundary between Shenley and Ridge to the north. Whichever is the correct interpretation, the lane that was formerly followed by the parish boundary went out of use. A similar situation may have occurred with Galley Lane, though in that case other influences may have been at work.

Galley Lane was formerly the boundary to a parish, hundred and county, proceeding from the A411 at Barnet to its junction and continuation with Holmeshill Lane. It could conceivably have proceeded further north beyond this point, but this is probably unprovable. What is interesting is the way the county boundary deviates from Galley Lane at its intersection with the boundary of Dyrham Park (TQ 22350-97920). The reason for this is unclear but it may be that the creation of the park pushed the original course of the lane westwards to its present position (Fig. 56). Alternatively, it may simply have fallen into disuse, as the Holmeshill/Galley Lane route assumed predominance over time. What is interesting, in terms of landscape development, is the way that communications and principal boundaries in the area have assumed a predominant NNW-SSE orientation.

Fig. 56 shows this configuration as far as the available data permits. Based on this information it is possible to propose a model of landscape development from the prehistoric period onwards. The area is dominated by soils derived from the Eocene deposits known as London Clay (Sherlock 1947, 35-39), of which the Arkley estate forms but a small part. These soils have a predisposition to support a pastoral farming culture (Chamberlain 1981, 47; Dony 1967, 48; Woolridge and Smetham 1931, 254). This predisposition is likely to have been even more marked in prehistoric times. What remains uncertain is whether the landscape ever collectively or individually farmed. Was there ever large scale apportionment on a collective basis, or a piecemeal approach to land division and usage? We know from the medieval evidence that this area was never dominated by large open sub-divided fields. The demesne lands of the manor of Tyttenhanger were arranged in a three-fold rotation of crops, but these were artificial, and made up of an assortment of different

sized fields (Levett 1938, 183). The normal pattern of land tenure was that of individual holdings, made up of an assortment of different units, some of which were described as 'hedged and ditched'. It is impossible to recover anything approaching a full picture of landholdings and land use in cartographic terms. However, this evidence is relatively late in terms of reconstructing the agrarian development of the landscape from its earliest discernible phases. Here there appears to be a persistent pattern of trackways and boundaries in a co-axial arrangement (Fig. 56). These divisions appear to have been organised on large scale, implying that at some time the land may have been apportioned on a collective basis. Whether this was by tribal agreement or imposition by seigniorial authority is not known. Fig. 57 illustrates this possible arrangement, the landscape being divided into units which ranging from anything between 200m to 600m wide and up to 1800m in length. This system may have extended across an area at least 5km wide (SSW-NNE) and 6km in length (SSE-NNW). The divisions appear to be drove-ways which passed through a pastoral landscape crossing the many tributaries that traverse the Thames catchment area. The genisis of this system is uncertain but, on the basis of analogous systems elsewhere, a pre-Roman date seems the most likely (Basset 1985; Bradley 1978; Caulfield 1983; Fleming 1987; Kissock 1993; Peterson 1990; Pryor 1980, 1984; Williamson 1987, 2000; Hunn and Rackham forthcoming).

The evidence from the hedgerow survey is not able to prove or disprove the above model. It is able to throw some light on the later developments of the system, which are of interest in their own right. Appendix 4.4 sets out in tabulated form the number of hedgerow species in relation to their date. It will be apparent that there is a relatively poor concordance between the number of species present and their suggested date. However, while this evidence does not invalidate the use of this methodology, there are some factors which need to be taken into consideration. Firstly, there is a discrepancy between the dates given in Appendix 4.1 and Appendix 4.4. This is because of the difference between the dates of the hedgerow and of the boundary. The most obvious example of this is where a hedgerow follows the line of a watercourse. The Saffron Green brook and its tributaries are post-glacial features, but the adjacent 'hedgerows' are probably as much a product of neglect as of deliberate construction. Secondly, there is the instance of a hedgerow with a low species count lying alongside the lane which marked the former boundary between the counties of Middlesex and Hertfordshire. There is no reason why the hedgerow should be as old as the shire boundary, particularly where it lies beside a public highway. There is a good reason for this. When adjoining land was enclosed, there was an assumption that the landowner was responsible for repairing the public highway. If the adjoining land was left unenclosed the public could pass over it when the road became impassable (Marshall 1899, 357-8). There are roadside 'wastes' along much of Galley Lane, though opposite Boundary 3 the width is greatly reduced. The implications are that this part of Galley Lane was enclosed at a relatively late date, the evidence suggests that individual fields become enclosed at different dates. Where the footpath between Fold Farm and Galley Lane Farm passes through the roadside boundary, consisting of a bank and ditch on its eastern side, the hedge appears to be older than Boundary 3. It is about 4m thick and 4-5m high, and contains Alderthorn, Hawthorn, Hazel, Willow and occasional oak. Being a former county boundary, Galley Lane must be at least of late Anglo-Saxon date, and in this study it is suggested that it is probably even older.

The richest hedgerow specie features on the Arkley estate are Boundaries 7 and 19 (Arkley Lane) and 19b (an E-W boundary). In the case of the former, we know this is an ancient trackway. It is certainly of medieval date and, if our model for the development of land division is correct, it could be of prehistoric date. The latter also had a high specie count. It may have formed the northern boundary of a field referred to as *Ankerscroft* in the early 16th century. Alternatively, the fact that it adjoins the botanically rich Arkley Lane boundary may also have been a factor. Howqever, not all the adjoining boundaries (eg. 17a, 10, 6 and 20) were similarly affected. The parish boundary between Shenley and Ridge represented by Boundaries 12 and 17 had above average species counts, but by no means wildly so. With between 5-6 species, including standing trees, they do not match their undoubted c.11th-century or possibly earlier date. The reason for this disparity is not known, but ithe aim of this study has been to attempt to create a relative chronology for the hedgerows on the Arkley estate. Establishing a precise chronological framework is another matter altogether.

From Appendix 4.3 it is apparent that there was a variation between the field names recorded in 1777 and those of 1838. In a space of sixty years most of the field units experienced some degree of change. Two exceptions to this were 'Seven Acres' and 'Great Field/Lands' (Fig. 53, Fields 8 and 9). Most fields appear to have undergone some reduction in size and, in one case, a change of land use. Whether this reflects a broader trend in the area is difficult to say, since the sample size is too small. It is only possible to note that not until 1838 did the landscape achieve, more or less, its present configuration. Even so, Field 8 appears to have been sub-divided in ownership but not in extent

and area. Other land units adjoining the estate have undergone a change of land use, reflecting the growing proximity of adjacent conurbation. The construction of the Barnet by-pass has effectively severed this area from its natural hinterland. The road (A1) has severed the continuation of Arkley Lane, that is, Packhorse Lane and an ancient footpath. The footpath is still marked, but the erection of obstacles and lack of stiles reflects the progressive isolation of this area in the modern era.

This study may be concluded by summarising the evidence. The Arkley estate is a small fragment of an ancient pastoral landscape, the development of which may be categorised as follows:

- The landscape was substantially cleared in the prehistoric period, possibly as early as the Bronze Age.

- A co-axial system was imposed in order to apportion land to meets the needs of a predominantly pastoral society.

- In the post-Roman period this arrangement was modified as a result of a combination of changing land use demands and encroachment by secondary woodland.

- In the medieval period much of the pastoral landscape remained predominantly open in character, though apportioned and managed through the offices of the manorial court of Tyttenhanger, part of the ecclesiastical of St Albans abbey.

- In the post-medieval period this open co-axially arranged landscape became progressively sub-divided into permanent pasture fields, ranging in size from 4 to 11 acres (1.6 to 4.5 ha). This process was completed only in the late 18th century and early 19th centuries.

- Since 1838 the sub-divisions of this landscape have remained largely unchanged, notwithstanding slight variations caused by changes in land ownership and a decline in the traditional methods of boundary maintenance.

ACKNOWLEDGEMENTS

The writer is grateful to Hertfordshire County Council for funding this desk-based assessment, and to Tony Hurley for commissioning it, and for his assistance. Thanks are also due to Alison Tinniswood HCC Sites & Monuments Officer, for her help, and to the staff at the Hertfordshire Archives and Local Studies, Hertford, for their customary help and advice.

Appendix 4.1: Summary of Hedgerows on the Arkley Estate

Table 19: Hedgerows (see Fig. 54)

Boundary No	Length described (m)	Average width (m)	Average height (m)	Wire fence	Wooden fence	Bank	Ditch	Bank & Ditch	Single hedge	Double hege	Hedge – well managed	Hedge – occasional gaps	Hedge – frequent gaps	Hedge – over grown	Hedge + Standard trees	Hedge – other	Buck thorn	Alder thorn	Buck/alder thorn	Hawthorn	Thorn	Wild rose	Dogwood	Hazel	Field maple	Elder	Crab apple	Elm suckers	Hornbeam	Crack willow	Willow	Holly	Oak	Ash	Sycamore	Hornbeam	Birch	No hedge species present	Probable date of hedge	Other Comments
1	90	4.0	3 – 4				✓		✓					✓	✓		✓	✓				✓												✓					4	Post-medieval	
2	200	1.3	1.5				✓		✓		✓				✓		✓			✓		✓		✓										✓	✓				6	Post-medieval	
3	70	1.6	1.6				✓		✓		✓							✓		✓																			2	Post-medieval	The ditch contains water. County boundary.
4	210	2.5	3.0				✓		✓					✓	✓				✓	✓	✓		✓									✓		✓					5	Post-medieval	Hedge on northern side, running stream on south.
5	210	1.7	2.0	✓			✓		✓		✓									✓		✓											✓						4	Post-medieval	Wet ditch on western side.
6	160	4.0	3 – 4				✓		✓					✓	✓				✓	✓				✓	✓								✓	✓				4	Post-medieval	The ditch on the south side was dry.
7	200	3.0	3 – 5				✓		✓					✓	✓		✓		✓	✓		✓		✓	✓	✓							✓	✓					8	Medieval	The ditch contains running water.
8	360	3.0	3 – 5				✓		✓					✓	✓				✓																				1	Post-medieval	Stream/brook c. 2m wide.
9	290	2 – 3	3 – 4				✓		✓					✓	✓		✓			✓							✓	✓	✓					✓					5	Medieval	The ditch contains running water.
10	320	2 – 3	3 – 5				✓		✓					✓	✓									✓										✓					2	Post-medieval	Willow trees growing in area of foot-bridge.
11	120	4 – 5	4.0	✓			✓		✓					✓	✓		✓							✓						✓				✓		✓	✓		5	Post-medieval	

Boundary No	Length described (m)	Average width (m)	Average height (m)	Type: Bank	Ditch	Bank & Ditch	Single hedge	Hedge – well managed	Hedge – frequent gaps	Hedge – over grown	Hedge + Standard trees	Species: Buck thorn	Alder thorn	Buck/alder thorn	Hawthorn	Wild rose	Dogwood	Hazel	Field maple	Elder	Willow	Holly	Std: Oak	Ash	No hedge species present	Probable date of hedge	Other Comments
12	100	4.0	3 – 4		✓		✓			✓	✓			✓	✓			✓	✓				✓		6	Post-medieval	Parish boundary.
13	200	1.7	1.9				✓	✓			✓			✓									✓		2	Post-medieval	
14	150	2.0	1.8		✓		✓	✓			✓			✓									✓		4	Post-medieval	
15	310	2 – 3	2.0		✓		✓		✓	✓	✓	✓											✓		3	Post-medieval	
16	240	3.0	2 – 3		✓		✓			✓	✓		✓	✓	✓	✓							✓		3	Post-medieval	The eastern half of this boundary exists but the western half does not exist.
17	150	4.0	3 – 4		✓		✓	✓			✓	✓	✓		✓	✓				✓			✓		5	Medieval	The ditch on east side. Parish boundary.
17a	190	2.0	3 – 4		✓		✓	✓			✓		✓	✓							✓		✓		2	Post-medieval	The ditch contains running water.
18	230	*	3 – 4	✓	✓		✓			✓	✓	✓	✓	✓	✓	✓							✓		6	Post-medieval	
19	600	3 – 4	4 – 5		✓		✓			✓	✓	✓			✓			✓	✓			✓	✓	✓	8	Medieval	**
19a	160	1.1	1.3		✓		✓	✓			✓				✓		✓						✓	✓	6	Medieval	The ditch on south containing running water.
19b	180	1.3	1.4		✓	✓	✓	✓			✓	✓	✓		✓		✓	✓	✓				✓	✓	8	Medieval	The ditch contains running water.
19c	280	1.2	1.6		✓	✓	✓	✓				✓	✓			✓		✓							4	Post-medieval	

Boundary No	Length described (m)	Average width (m)	Average height (m)	Wire fence	Wooden fence	Bank	Ditch	Bank & Ditch	Single hedge	Double hege	Hedge – well managed	Hedge – occasional gaps	Hedge – frequent gaps	Hedge – over grown	Hedge + Standard trees	Hedge – other	Buck thorn	Alder thorn	Buck/alder thorn	Hawthorn	Thorn	Wild rose	Dogwood	Hazel	Field maple	Elder	Crab apple	Elm suckers	Hornbeam	Crack willow	Willow	Holly	Oak	Ash	Sycamore	Hornbeam	Birch	No hedge species present	Probable date of hedge	Other Comments
20	260	1.3	1.5	✓	✓			✓	✓					✓	✓		✓			✓													✓	✓				4	Post-medieval	Beyond intersection with 19c there are Buckthorn, Hawthorn, Field maple, Wild rose and Oak (1.4 dia) present.
21	50	1.2	1.4						✓		✓				✓		✓			✓																		2	Post-medieval	
22/22a	175	1.3	1.5				✓		✓		✓				✓		✓			✓		✓																3	Post-medieval	The ditch contains running water. Adjacent to Arkley estate.
23	230	1.1	1.3				✓		✓			✓			✓		✓			✓		✓	✓	✓										✓			✓	6	Post-medieval	Ditch on east side.
24	260	1.1	1.3				✓		✓		✓				✓		✓					✓		✓										✓	✓				5	Post-medieval	Wet ditch on south side
																																								The ditch on west side containing running water. At eastern end the last 30m is composed of a double post and wire fence.
25	170	1.2	1.4				✓		✓		✓				✓			✓		✓		✓											✓					4	Post-medieval	

121

Boundary No	Length described (m)	Average width (m)	Average height (m)	Type													Hedgerow species present																Standard trees present					Dating		Other Comments
				Wire fence	Wooden fence	Bank	Ditch	Bank & Ditch	Single hedge	Double hedge	Hedge – well managed	Hedge – occasional gaps	Hedge – frequent gaps	Hedge – over grown	Hedge + Standard trees	Hedge – other	Buck thorn	Alder thorn	Buck/alder thorn	Hawthorn	Thorn	Wild rose	Dogwood	Hazel	Field maple	Elder	Crab apple	Elm suckers	Hornbeam	Crack willow	Willow	Holly	Oak	Ash	Sycamore	Hornbeam	Birch	No hedge species present	Probable date of hedge	
26	130	3 - 4	4.0				✓		✓			✓		✓	✓				✓	✓			✓							✓			✓					5	Post-medieval	This lies adjacent to the Saffron Green brook and is similar to no.4 except that it is more like a 'vegetation zone' than a hedgerow.
27	280	4.0	3 - 4				✓		✓		✓				✓		✓			✓						✓			✓				✓			✓		5	Post-medieval	Wet ditch. Lies outside the HCC estate.
28	250	3.0	1.5					✓	✓			✓		✓	✓	✓				✓		✓											✓					4	Post-medieval	Wet ditch. Lies outside the HCC estate.
29	235	3.0	4.0					✓						✓	✓		✓	✓				✓											✓					4	Post-medieval	The ditch contains running water. Lies outside the HCC estate.

* Backing onto wood

** This is Arkley Lane which is flanked by ditches; the eastern ditch is wider and contains running water. The hedgerows have so overgrown that they form a continuous band of trees. Same as no. 7

Appendix 4.2: Medieval to Victorian field & place names

Table 20: Possible continuity of field and place names from the medieval to the early Victorian period.

Medieval (see end column)	16th century (D/EB 2067 B T.9)	1777 (HALS D/ECd. E39)	1838 (DSA4 81/1)	Medieval Reference
	Ankerscroft		Angers Mead	
Arkeleyslond				B.Lib Mss 36237
ArkeleLane			Arkley Lane	D/EB 2067 B M.25 (1)
GaloweLane			Galley Lane	HALS 4732
Homefelde, le			Home Field	(1) 1447-8
Longefelde			Long Field	(1) 1400-1
Parkesfelde			Park Water	(1) 1433-4
		Shapham Green	Saffron Green	
Valentyneslond			Valentines	(1) 1423-4

Appendix 4.3: Land units in 1777 & 1838

Table 21: Comparison between land units in 1777 and 1838.

Field name in 1777	Acres	Farmstead	Field name in 1838	Acres
			Angers Mead	6.2.30
			Brook Field (R)	1.2.11
Brook Mead	7.3.28	Holmeshill	Brook Field (S)	8.0.27
Four Acres	4.2.8	Holmeshill	Four Acres ***	4.1.38
		(Shenley)	Fourteen Acres	15.0.5
Seven Acres	7.1.11	Holmeshill	Further Seven Acres ***	7.1.3
Great Field	11.0.14	Strangers Farm	Great Lands	11.1.26*
Great Park Water	7.3.29 (arable)	Gallow Lane Farm	Great Park Water	5.2.19 (grass)
Park Water Mead	4.1.32	Gallow Lane Farm	Little Park Water	3.0.29
Long Mead	9.0.37	Valentines Farm	Long Field	8.0.11**
			Part of Long Field	6.0.30
Great Saffron	8.1.35	Strangers Farm	Saffron Green	11.1.8
Little Saffron	4.2.31	Strangers Farm		
Shapham Green	2.2.25		Saffron Green	1.2.26

* this has been reduced by the loss of its eastern 'snout' shaped section.
** this has also been reduced since 1838.
***this is a common field name and could be applicable to several farms in the area.

Appendix 4.4: Hedgerow species & estimated date

Table 22: Botanical species count for each hedgerow and their suggested date (Fig. 54)

Boundary no.	Typology	Species count	Date
1	Slightly curved	4	Ancient ?
2	straight	6	Post-medieval
3	straight	2	Prehistoric/Anglo-Saxon ?
4	Sinuous	5	Ancient
5	Mostly straight	4	Post-medieval
6	Straight	4	Post-medieval
7	Curvilinear	8	Prehistoric ?
8	Mostly straight	1	Ancient
9	Curvilinear	5	Medieval
10	Mostly straight	2	Post-medieval
11	Mostly straight	5	Post-medieval
12	Straight	6	Prehistoric/Anglo-Saxon ?
13	Mostly straight	3	Post-medieval
14	Mostly straight	2	Post-medieval
15	Curvilinear	3	Post-medieval
16	Mostly straight	3	Post-medieval
17	Straight	5	Prehistoric/Anglo-Saxon ?
17A	Straight	2	Post-medieval
18	Straight	6	Post-medieval
19	Mostly straight	8	Prehistoric/Anglo-Saxon ?
19A	Irregular	6	Post-medieval
19B	Straight	8	Medieval

Boundary no.	Typology	Species count	Date
19C	Straight	4	Post-medieval
20	Curvilinear	5	Medieval
21	Straight	2	Post-medieval
22	Straight (AP)	0	Destroyed
23	Straight	6	Medieval ?
23a	cuvilinear	3	Post-medieval ?
24	Straight	5	Post-medieval
25	Irregular	4	Post-medieval
26	Sinuous	5	Ancient
27	Straight	5	Post-medieval
28	Slightly sinuous	4	Medieval ?
29	Slightly sinuous	4	Ancient ?

Appendix 4.5: List of sources used in this project

Table 23: Hertfordshire County Council Sites & Monuments Record

Type	Date	National Grid Ref.	SMR no.
Large struck flints	Palaeolithic	TQ 233-975	6436
Moat (Fold Farm)	Medieval	TQ 2258-9751	2648
Manor site (Fold Fm)	Medieval	TQ 2260-9750	1330
Manor site (Dyrham Park)	Medieval	TQ 2240-9850	6207
Dyrham Park	Late 15th/early 16th	TQ 225-985	9571

Table 24: List of Aerial photographs examined (HALS)

Reference	Scale	Date
51/29 NW no. 86	1:10,560	1947
TQ 2097/2197 no. 880	1:2,500	May 1972
TQ 2297/2397 no. 889	1:2,500	May 1980
TQ 2297/2397 no. 889	1:2,500	May 1990

Table 25: List of Cartographic sources consulted (HALS)

Source	Scale	Date	Notes
Dury & Andrews	2" to the mile	1766	Herts Publications 1980
Bryant's County Map	1.2" to the mile	1822	Herts Publications 1985
Tithe map and book	9" to 1 mile	1838	DSA4 81/1 & 81/2
Tithe map and book	26.7" to 1 mile	1840	DSA4 94/1 & 94/2
Ordnance Survey	25" to mile (1st ed)	1870	Sheet VI.2; XLV.2
Ordnance Survey	25" to mile (2nd ed)	1898	Sheet XLV.2
Ordnance Survey	6" (1st series)	1868	Sheet XLV
Ordnance Survey	6" (2nd series)	1898	Sheet XLV
Ordnance Survey	6" (3rd series)	1920	Sheet XLV
Ordnance Survey	6" (4th series)	1935	Sheet XLV
Ordnance Survey	1:10,000	1974	TQ 29 NW
Ordnance Survey	1:25,000	1999	Explorer 173
Ordnance Survey	1:25,000	1998	Explorer 182

Table 26: List of primary sources consulted in this project (all HALS except where shown)

Type	Reference	Date
Plan of estate in Ridge & Shenley	D/ECr/95	1803
Sale Particulars	D/ETr/T4	c.1800
Conveyance	D/EB 2067B/T9	1520
Extract from court rolls	D/EB 2067B M1	1238-1460
Survey & extent	D/EB 2067B M.25	1551
Extent	B.Lib. Add Mss 36237	1331
Survey	D/Ecd E.39	1777
Plan & particulars	27449	1774, 1887

Bibliography

Adkins, L. and R.A. 1983: *The Handbook of British Archaeology.* Papermac (London & Basingstoke).

Ashbee, P. 1998: 'Barrows, cairns and a few impostors' Simon Denison (ed) *Britist Archaeol.* **32**.

Astill, G. and Grant, A. 1988: *The Countryside of Medieval England.* Blackwell (Oxford).

Aston, M. (ed.) 1988: *Medieval Fish, Fisheries and Fishponds in England.* British Archaeol. Reps **182** (Oxford).

Avery, B. W. 1964: *The Soils and Land Use of the District around Aylesbury and Hemel Hempstead.*London. HMSO.

Bailey, M. 1988: 'The Rabbit and the Medieval East Anglian Economy', *Agricultural Hist. Rev.* **36**, 1-20.

Basset, S. 1985: 'Beyond the edge of excavation: the topographical context of Goltho' *in* Mayr-Harting, H. & Moore, R.I. (eds), *Studies in Medieval History presented to R.C.H Davis,* 21-39, Hambledon (London).

Birrell, J. 1992: 'Deer and Deer Farming in Medieval England', *Agricultural Hist. Rev.* **40**, 112-126.

Blair, J. 1991: *Early Medieval Surrey.* Alan Sutton (Stroud).

Bonney, D. J. 1966: Pagan Saxon burials and boundaries in Wiltshire. *Wiltshire Archaeol. & Nat. Hist. Magazine* **61**, 25-30.

Bonney, 1979: 'Early Boundaries and Estates in Southern England' *in* Sawyer, P. H. *English Medieval Settlement,* 41-51.

Bradley, R. 1978: 'Prehistoric field systems in Britain and north-west Europe - a review of recent work', *World Archaeol.* **9.3**, 265-80.

Branch Johnson, W. 1970: *The Industrial Archaeology of Hertfordshire.* Augustus M. Kelley (New York).

Campbell B., Galloway J., Keene D., Murphy M. 1993, *A Medieval Capital and its Grain Supply. Agrarian Production and Distribution in the London Region c. 1300.* Historical Geography Res. Series **30**.

Cantor, L. M. 1983: *The Medieval Parks of England: A Gazetter.* (Loughborough).

Chamberlain, P. 1981: 'Farming at the Crossroads', *in* Shirley, P (ed) *Hertfordshire – a guide to the countryside.* Egon Publishers Ltd (Baldock)

Caulfield, S. 1983: 'The neolithic settlement of North Connaught', *in* Reeves-Smyth T & Hammond F (eds). *Landscape archaeology in Ireland.* British Archaeol. Reps. **116**, 195-216.

Chauncy, H. 1824: *The Historical Antiquities of Hertfordshire.* 2 vols. 2nd edition. first published 1700. J. M. Mullinger. (London).

Clapham A.R., Tutin T.G. & Moore D.M. 1987, *Flora of the British Isles.* Third Edition. Cambridge University Press.

Cox, A. 1979: *Survey of Bedfordshire. Brickmaking: A history and gazetteer.* Bedfordshire County Council/RCHM (E).

Cox, C. 1997: Site south-west of Coursers Farm, near St Albans: Aerial Photographic Assessment. *Air Photo Services* Rep. ref. APSLtd/967/26

Chenevix-Trench, J. 1973: Coleshill and the Settlements of the Chilterns, in *Recs Buckinghamshire* **19**, 241-258.

Derricourt R. M. & Jacobi R. M., 1970:'Mesolithic Finds from Hampermill, Watford' in *Hertfordshire Archaeol.* **2**, 1-5.

Dony, J. G. 1967: *Flora of Hertfordshire.* Hitchin Urban District Council (Hitchin).

Drury, P.J. 1975: 'Post-Medieval Brick and Tile Kilns at Runsell Green, Danbury, Essex', *Post-Medieval Archaeol.* **9**, 203-11.

Drury, P.J. 1981 'The Production of Brick and Tile in Medieval England', *in* Crossley D.W. (ed) *Medieval Industry.* CBA Res. Rep. **40** (London).

Drury, P.J. & Pratt G. D. 1975: A late 13th and early 14th Tile Factory at Danbury, Essex. *Medieval Archaeol.* **19**, 92-164.

Dury, A. & Andrews, J. 1768: *A Topographical map of Hartford-shire.* Hertfordshire Publications 1980 (Stevenage).

Everson, P. 1984: 'The pre-conquest estate of Aet Bearuwe in Lindsey', *in* Faull, M. *Studies in late Anglo-Saxon Settlement.* Oxford Univ. Press (Oxford).

Everitt, A. 1986: *Continuity and Colonization: the evolution of Kentish settlement.* Leicester Univ. Press.

Field, J. 1972: *English Field Names: a Dictionary.* David and Charles (Newton Abbot).

Fleming, A. 1987: 'Co-axial field systems: some questions of time and space', *Antiquity* **61**, 188-202.

Fowler, Rev. H. 1893: 'Tyttenhanger', *St. Albans Architect. Archaeol. Soc,* 30-45.

Gaimster, D. R. M., Margeson, S. and Barry, T. 1989: 'Notes on Medieval Britain and Ireland', *Medieval Archaeol.* **33**, 214.

Gardner, H. W. 1967: *A Survey of the Agriculture of Hertfordshire.* Royal Agricultural Soc. of England (London).

Gould R.A. 1966: 'Archaeology of the Point St George and Tolowa prehistory'. *Publications in Anthropology* **4**. (Univ. California).

Gover, J.E.B., Mawer, A. and Stenton, F. M. 1970: *The Place-Names of Hertfordshire.* English Place-Name Soc **15**. Cambridge University Press. (Cambridge).

Greig J. 1991, 'The British Isles', *in* W. van Zeist, K. Wasylikowa, K-E. Behre (eds) *Progress in Old World Palaeoethnobotany*, 229-334. (Rotterdam).

Hare, J. N. 1991: 'The Growth of the Roof-Tile Industry in Later Medieval Wessex', *Medieval Archaeol.* **35**, 86-103.

Hayes, P. P. 1991: 'Models for the distribution of pottery around former agricultural settlements' *in* Schofield, A. J *Interpreting Artefact Scatters*, 81-92.

Hoare P. G., 1996: 'Tyttenhanger, St Albans, Hertfordshire: a preliminary report to Tempvs Reparatvm' *in* J. Percival and A. Richmond, *Report on an Archaeological Field Evaluation, in connection with a planning application to extract aggregates, Tyttenhanger Quarry, St Albans, Hertfordshire*. Tempvs Reparatvm, 15 October 1996.

Hodge, C. A. H., Burton, R. G. O., Corbett, W. M., Evans, R. and Seal, R. S. 1984: *Soils and their Use in Eastern England*. Soil Survey of England and Wales Bulletin **13** (Harpenden).

Hooke, D. 1985: *The Anglo-Saxon Landscape: The Kingdom of the Hwicce*. Manchester Univ. Press (Manchester).

Hooke, D (ed). 1988: *Anglo-Saxon Settlements*. Basil Blackwell (Oxford).

Hooke, D. 1988: 'Regional variation in Southern and Central England in the Anglo-Saxon period and its relationship to Land Units and settlement', *in* Hooke (ed) 1988, 123-52.

Howlett C. E. & Lisboa M. G., 1996: *Baseline Study Towards an Environmental Assessment: Archaeology and Historical Landscapes, Tyttenhanger (East), St Albans, Hertfordshire* Tempvs Reparatvm, 31150DCA.

Hunn, J. R. 1994: *Reconstruction and Measurement of Change: A study of six parishes in the St Albans area*. Brit. Archaeol. Reps **236** (Oxford).

Hunn J. R. & Coxah M. 1997: *Interim Report on Field Walking Survey at Coursers Farm, Tyttenhanger (East), Hertfordshire*, ASC Report ref. ASAC/CFR97/2.

Hunn, J.R. 1999: *An Archaeological Evaluation on Land to the South of Coursers Road, Tyttenhanger (East), Hertfordshire*. ASC Report ref. ASC/B:CFR/H99/1).

Hunn, J. R. & Rackham J. forthcoming: *Excavations on a multi-period landscape at Rectory Farm, West Deeping*. Brit. Archaeol. Reps.

Hurst, J. G. 1988: 'Rural Building in England and Wales', in Thirsk, J. (ed.) *Agrarian Hist. England & Wales vol. 2, 1042-1350*, 882-5.

Johnson, A. E. 1997: *Coursers Farm, Hertfordshire: Magnetic Feasibility Study*. Oxford Archaeotechnics Ltd, ref: 129097/COH/RED.

Keen, L. 2002: 'Windsor Castle and the Penn tile industry', in *Windsor: Medieval archaeology, art and architecture of the Thames Valley*. Brit. Archaeol. Assoc. Conference Trans. **25**, 219-237.

Kissock, J.A. 1993: 'Some examples of co-axial field systems in Pembrokeshire', *Bull. Board Celtic Studies* **40**, 190-97.

Koughnet, J.V. 1895: *A History of Tyttenhanger*. Marcus Ward (London).

Lacaille A. D., 1961: 'Mesolithic Facies in Middlesex and London', *Trans London Middlesex Archaeol. Soc.* **20.8**.

Lasdun, S. 1991: *The English Park: Royal, Private & Public*. Deutsch (London).

Levett, A. E. 1962: *Studies in Manorial History*. (reprinted from original Oxford University 1938 edition). Merlin Press (London).

Lewis J. S. C., Wiltshire P.E. J. & Macphail R., 1992: 'A Late Devensian/Early Flandrian site at Three Ways Wharf, Uxbridge: environmental implications' *in* S. Needham and M. G. Macklin, *Alluvial Archaeology in Britain*. Proceedings of a conference sponsored by the RMC Group plc, British Museum, 3-5 January 1991.

Lightfoot M. 2002: *A Report on an Evaluation and Excavation at Tyttenhanger Quarry West* ASC Rep, ref. ASC: TQW02/02

Mackney, D., J. M. Hodgson, Hollis, J.M. and Staines, S. J. 1986: *Legend for the 1:250,000 Soil Map of England and Wales. Harpenden*. Soil Survey of England and Wales. Lawes Agricultural Trust.

MAFF 1963: *Agricultural Land Classification of England and Wales*, Sheet 160.

Marshall, T.W. 1899: 'Boundaries and Fences in their Legal Aspect' *in* Vernon A, *Estate Fences: their choice, construction and cost*, 355-394. E. & F.N. Spon (London).

McCarthy, M. R. 1976 'The Medieval Kilns on Nash Hill, Lacock, Wiltshire', *Wiltshire Archaeol. Nat. Hist. Mag.* **69**, 97-160.

Morris, J. 1976: *Domesday Book: vol. 12, Hertfordshire*. Phillimore (Chichester).

McRae, S. G: 1996 Land at Tyttenhanger, London Colney, Hertfordshire: Soils and Agricultural Land Classification.

Mynard, D.C. 1975: 'The Little Brickhill Tile Kilns and their Products', *J. British Archaeological Association, third series,* **38**.

Nenk B., Margeson and Hurley, M. 1993: 'Notes on Medieval Britain and Ireland', *Medieval Archaeology* **37**, 223.

Nenk B., Margeson and Hurley, M. 1995: 'Notes on Medieval Britain and Ireland', *Medieval Archaeology* **39**, 264.

Page, W. 1908: *The Victoria History of the County of Hertfordshire, 4 vols.* Dawsons of Pall Mall. (London).

Pattison, P. 1998: *There by Design: Field Archaeology in Parks and Gardens.* Brit. Archaeol. Reps **267** (Oxford).

Percival, J. and Richmond, A. 1996: *Report on an Archaeological Field Evaluation of Tyttenhanger Quarry, St Albans, Hertfordshire.* Tempvs Reparatvm (Oxford).

Peterson J. W. M. 1990: Why did the idea of co-axial field systems last so long? *Antiquity* **64**, 584-91.

Pryor, F.M.M. 1980: *Excavation at Fengate, Peterborough, England: The Third Report.* Northamptonshire Archaeol. Soc. Monog. **1** & Royal Ontario Museum Archaeol. Monog. **6**.

Pryor, F.M.M. 1984: *Excavation at Fengate, Peterborough, England: The Fourth Report.* Northamptonshire Archaeol. Soc. Monog. **2** & Royal Ontario Museum Archaeol. Monog. **7**.

Petit-Dutaillis, C. 1911: *Studies and Notes supplementary to Stubbs' Constitutional History.* Manchester University Press (Manchester).

Platt, C. 1988: *Medieval England - A Social History and Archaeology from the Conquest to 1600 AD.* Routledge (London & New York).

Pyke, A. 1995: *A Gazetteer of Buckinghamshire Brickyards.* County Museum (Aylesbury).

Rackham, O. 1986: *The History of the Countryside.* Dent (London & Melbourne). Riley, H. T. 1867 *Gesta Abbatum Monasterii Sancti Albani A Thoma Walsingham.* Rolls Series. Longmans (London).

RCHME 1910: *An Inventory of the Historical Monuments in Hertfordshire.* HMSO, London.

Richmond, A. 1999: *Written Scheme of Investigation for Archaeological Works:* Tyttenhanger Quarry (East of Coursers Road), St Albans, Hertfordshire. Phoenix Consulting P/108/D.

Richmond A. & Percival, J. 1997: A scheme for an archaeological mitigation at Tyttenhanger *Phoenix Consulting* (P108A 2nd July)

Riley, H.T. 1869: *Gesta Abbatum Monasterii Sancti Albani A Thoma Walsingham.* Rolls Series. Longmans (London).

Riley, H.T. 1870: *Annales Monasterii S. Albani A Johanne Amundesham.* Rolls Series. Longmans (London).

Roffe, D. 1984: 'Pre-Conquest Estates and Parish Boundaries: a discussion with examples from Lincolnshire' *in* Hooke 1985, 115-22.

Roden, D. 1969: 'Fragmentation of Farms and Fields in the Chiltern Hills: 13th century and later', *Medieval Studies* **31**, 225-38.

Roden, D. 1973: 'Field Systems of the Chiltern Hills and their Environs' *in* Baker, A.R.H. & Butlin, R. A. (eds) *Studies of Field Systems in the British Isles,* Cambridge University Press (Cambridge).

Rowley, T. 1978: *Villages in the Landscape.* J.M. Dent. (London).

Ryan, P. 1996: *Brick in Essex: from the Conquest to the Reformation.* privately published (Danbury).

Salzman, L. F. 1952: *Building in England down to 1540: A documentary history.* Clarendon Press (Oxford).

Sawyer, P. H. 1968: *Anglo-Saxon Charters, an annotated list and bibliography.* Royal Hist. Soc. (London).

Sawyer, P. H. (ed) 1979: *English Medieval Settlement.* Edward Arnold (London).

Schofield A. J. 1991: *Interpreting Artefact Scatters: contributions to ploughzone archaeology.* Oxbow Books (Oxford).

Sheail, J. 1971: *Rabbits and theirHistory.* David & Charles (Newton Abbot).

Sherlock, R. L. 1947: *British Regional Geography: London and Thames Valley.* HMSO (London).

Shirley, D. (ed) 1981: *Hertfordshire – a guide to the countryside.* Egon Publishers Ltd (Baldock)

Smith, J.T. 1996: *Hertfordshire Houses.* RCHM(E) (London).

Soil Survey of England and Wales 1983a, *Soils of England and Wales, 1:250 000 sheet 4, Eastern England.*

Soil Survey of England and Wales 1983b, *Legend for the 1:250 000 Soil Map of England and Wales.*

Stamper, P. 1988: 'Woods and Parks', *in* Astill & Grant (eds) *The Countryside of Medieval England,* 128-148.

Strong, R. 1979: *The Renaissance Garden in England.* Thames & Hudson (London).

Taylor, C. 1995: Dispersed Settlement in Nucleated Areas. *Landscape Hist.* **17**, 27-34.

Thacker, C. 1989: *England's Historic Gardens.* Templar (Surrey).

Turner C. R. & Hunn J. R., 2000: *A Mitigation Report on Land at Tyttenhanger Park, Hertfordshire.* Archaeological Services & Consultancy Ltd.

Walker, J.S.F.,1997: *Tyttenhanger Quarry: Brief for an Archaeological Evaluation.* Univ. Manchester Archaeol. Unit

Warner, P. 1988: 'Pre-Conquest Territorial and Administrative Organisation in East Suffolk' *in* Hooke (ed) 1985, 9-34.

Webster, L. E. & Cherry, J. 1973: 'Notes on Medieval Britain and Ireland', *Medieval Archaeology* **17**, 154, 183.

Webster, L. E. & Cherry, J. 1974: 'Notes on Medieval Britain and Ireland', *Medieval Archaeology* **18**, 216-217.

Williams, D. 1973 Flotation at Siraf, *Antiquity,* 47, 198-202.

Williamson, T. 1987: 'Early co-axial field systems on the East Anglian boulder clays'. *Proc. Prehist. Soc.* **53**, 419-431.

Winchester, A. 1990: *Discovering Parish Boundaries.* Shire Publications (Princes Risborough).

Wood, E.S. 1968: *Collins Field Guide to Archaeology in Britain.* 2nd edition. Collins (London).

Woodward, A & Woodward, P 1996 'The Topography of Some Barrow Cemeteries in Bronze Age Wiltshire', *Proc. Prehist. Soc.* 275-292

Woolridge, S. W. & Smetham, D. J. 1931: 'The Glacial Drifts of Essex and Hertfordshire and their Bearing upon the Agricultural and Historical Geography of the Region'. *Geol. J.* **78**, 243-69.

Wright, J. A. 1972: *Brick Building in England: from the Middle Ages to 1550.* John Baker (London).

Youngs, F. A. 1979: *Guide to the Administrative units of England. Volume I: Southern England.* Offices Royal Hist. Soc. (London).

Youngs, S. M., Clark J. and Barry, T. 1986: 'Notes on Medieval Britain and Ireland', *Medieval Archaeology* **30**, 140.

Youngs, S. M., Clark J. and Barry, T. 1986: Notes on Medieval Britain and Ireland. *Medieval Archaeology* **30**, 164-6.

Youngs, S. M., Clark J. and Barry, T. 1987: Notes on Medieval Britain and Ireland. *Medieval Archaeology* **31**, 146.

Zeepvat, R. J. 1998: *Tyttenhanger Quarry, St Albans, Hertfordshire; Detailed Method Statement for Watching Brief and Related Archaeological Works,* ASC Ltd, doc. ref. TQ/SA/H98/1/r1.